RELIGION AND CULTUR

An Introduction to the Glossa Ordinaria *as Medieval Hypertext*

574

For John —

Thanks for the support
and encouragement —

'Tolle lege' (Take and read)

Best,

David

Series Editors
Denis Renevey (University of Lausanne)
Diane Watt (University of Surrey)

Editorial Board
Miri Rubin (Queen Mary, University of London)
Jean-Claude Schmitt (École des Hautes Études en Sciences Sociales, Paris)
Fiona Somerset (Duke University)
Christiania Whitehead (University of Warwick)

RELIGION AND CULTURE IN THE MIDDLE AGES

An Introduction to the Glossa Ordinaria *as Medieval Hypertext*

DAVID A. SALOMON

UNIVERSITY OF WALES PRESS
CARDIFF
2012

© David A. Salomon, 2012

All rights reserved. No part of this book may be reproduced in any material form (including photocopying or storing it in any medium by electronic means and whether or not transiently or incidentally to some other use of this publication) without the written permission of the copyright owner. Applications for the copyright owner's written permission to reproduce any part of this publication should be addressed to the University of Wales Press, 10 Columbus Walk, Brigantine Place, Cardiff CF10 4UP.

www.uwp.co.uk

British Library CIP Data
A catalogue record for this book is available from the British Library.

ISBN   978-0-7083-2493-6 (hardback)
       978-0-7083-2494-3 (paperback)
e-ISBN 978-0-7083-2495-0

The right of David A. Salomon to be identified as author of this work has been asserted in accordance with sections 77 and 79 of the Copyright, Designs and Patents Act 1988.

Typeset by Mark Heslington Ltd, Scarborough, North Yorkshire
Printed by CPI Antony Rowe, Chippenham, Wiltshire

Contents

	Series Editors' Preface	vii
	List of Illustrations	ix
	Acknowledgements	xi
	Introduction	1
1	The Glossing Tradition and the *Glossa Ordinaria*	6
2	History, the Text, and the History of the Text	33
3	Reading, Theory, and Reading Theory	63
4	Reading the *Glossa Ordinaria*: Genesis 1:1, 3:1 and John 1:1	82
5	The *Glossa Ordinaria* and Hypertext	93
	Notes	100
	Bibliography	115
	Index	127

Series Editors' Preface

Religion and Culture in the Middle Ages aims to explore the interface between medieval religion and culture, with as broad an understanding of those terms as possible. It puts to the forefront studies which engage with works that significantly contributed to the shaping of medieval culture. However, it also gives attention to studies dealing with works that reflect and highlight aspects of medieval culture that have been neglected in the past by scholars of the medieval disciplines. For example, devotional works and the practice they infer illuminate our understanding of the medieval subject and its culture in remarkable ways, while studies of the material space designed and inhabited by medieval subjects yield new evidence on the period and the people who shaped it and lived in it. In the larger field of religion and culture, we also want to explore further the roles played by women as authors, readers and owners of books, thereby defining them more precisely as actors in the cultural field. The series as a whole investigates the European Middle Ages, from *c.*500 to *c.*1500. Our aim is to explore medieval religion and culture with the tools belonging to such disciplines as, among others, art history, philosophy, theology, history, musicology, the history of medicine, and literature. In particular, we would like to promote interdisciplinary studies, as we believe strongly that our modern understanding of the term applies fascinatingly well to a cultural period marked by a less tight confinement and categorization of its disciplines than the modern period. However, our only criterion is academic excellence, with the belief that the use of a large diversity of critical tools and theoretical approaches enables a deeper understanding of medieval culture. We want the series to reflect this diversity, as we believe that, as a collection of outstanding contributions, it offers a more subtle representation of a period that is marked by paradoxes and contradictions and which necessarily reflects diversity and difference, however difficult it may sometimes have proved for medieval culture to accept these notions.

Illustrations

1 *Talmud Berakhot*, Venice, 1520–3, fols. 46v–47r. Courtesy of the Library of the Jewish Theological Seminary.
2 *Commentary on the Epistles of St Paul* by Gilbert of Poitiers. France, mid-twelfth century. Manuscript: France, mid-twelfth century. Photo © Victoria and Albert Museum, London.
3 Thomas Aquinas, *Catena Aurea, seu Continuum in Quattuor Evangelistas* (Venice, 1486). This work is part of the funds of the Biblioteca Valenciana and is digitized in the Biblioteca Valenciana Digital (BIVALDI) at *http://bv.gva.es*.
4 *Biblia Sacra cum Glossa Ordinaria . . . et Annotationibus de Nicolaus a Lyra*, 2A1v, published in Venice, 1588 edition. Reproduced by permission of the Huntington Library, San Marino, California.
5 *Biblia Latina cum Glossa Ordinaria: Facsimile Reprint of the Editio Princeps Adolph Rusch of Strassburg 1480/81*, Introduction by Karlfried Froehlich and Margaret T. Gibson (1992). Photo courtesy of Brepols Publishers, Turnhout, Belgium.

Acknowledgements

In *Letters to a Young Poet*, Rainer Maria Rilke writes, 'Everything is gestation and then bringing forth. To let each impression and each germ of a feeling come to completion quite in itself, in the dark, in the inexpressible, the unconscious, beyond the reach of one's own understanding, and await with deep humility and patience the birth-hour of a new clarity: that alone is living the artist's life – in understanding as in work.' Although its seeds were first planted in 1998, this book has had a long period of gestation. My interest in the margins of religious literature began with my doctoral dissertation on the Jesuit Robert Parsons's *Christian Directory* and its relationship to contemporary English Catholic spirituality in the late sixteenth century. While working on that book, and after reading her outstanding *The Voice of My Beloved: The Song of Songs in Western Medieval Christianity*, I invited the distinguished religious studies scholar, E. Ann Matter, to the University of Connecticut to give a lecture; she was, at the time, working on a study of the Church Fathers and the *Glossa Ordinaria*, and opened my eyes to this astonishingly rich work of the Middle Ages. I am grateful to her for her friendship, her guidance and her many insights. I also thank the editors of the University of Wales Press and the founders of its Religion, Culture and Society series for their patience as I switched positions, moved across country and started a family; I would especially like to thank Sarah Lewis and Dafydd Jones of the press for their guidance and shepherding of this study into print. I also acknowledge Susannah Chewning, who first made me aware of this exciting series.

I have been fortunate to have had a series of incomparable professors, beginning with the late Duane Edwards at Fairleigh Dickinson University, continuing with Angus Fletcher at the City University of New York and concluding with Thomas Jambeck at the University of Connecticut. I have received so much from each of these men, but I would like particularly to thank Tom Jambeck, from whom I have learnt the value of intellectual patience, academic and personal integrity and professional steadfastness. From all of my instructors I have gained insight into the life of the academic, a life I have embraced, loved and viewed as mine only to safeguard for a short time. As such, I have treated that life with the respect and honour it is due. My scholarly pursuits have always been grounded in intellectual curiosity, respect, and amazement, particularly as a Jew studying the history of Christianity and the Church.

A series of students has both informed my work and assisted on this project, including four research assistants through the years: Katie (Carr) Kiger, Tina (Beguin) Van Kley, Liz Romero and Cara (Baummer) Forrest. My students continue not only to enhance and enrich my work, they also enrich my life. No work such as this can be accomplished without generous library support. Particularly, I thank Linda Allbee for hours of interlibrary loan assistance (in South Dakota) and for her continuing friendship. Amy Pass, at the Sage Libraries, is a great friend and colleague. I would like to thank the library staffs at the University of Connecticut, Black Hills State University, and the Sage Colleges for their expertise, their help and their understanding. Numerous scholars have graciously corresponded with me throughout the course of this study, offering both insight and advice; they include John Contreni, Theresa Gross-Diaz, E. Ann Matter and John O'Donnell. My sincere thanks to the Harder-McClellan Chair in the Humanities at the Sage Colleges, which I held from 2007 to 2010 and which made some of this work's research and final publication possible.

I thank my colleagues at Russell Sage College, especially Jack Harris, Sybillyn Jennings, Deborah Lawrence and Sharon Robinson for their encouragement and collegiality. In addition, I acknowledge and appreciate the support of my colleagues in the Russell Sage College Department of English and Modern Languages. Thanks to Nancy Cumo, Natalie Farina, Amy Fuqua, Corey Jamison, Vincent King, Sally Lawrence, Henry Maas, Richard McCambly, Christine Mulford, Jeanne Neff and Terry Weiner.

My parents, Robert and Sheila, and my siblings, Steven and Lynda, have always been supportive. Finally, my life is made complete by my wife, Kelly O'Connor-Salomon, and my daughter, Phoebe. They are the central and guiding stars in my life, and it is to them that I dedicate this work.

Introduction

Today's readers take certain things for granted. Book titles are explanatory. Authors' names are clearly stated on title pages, as are publishers'. Books are arranged in a certain order, clearly noted by page numbers printed somewhere on a given page. Books are often arranged by chapter, thus dividing the larger body of text into smaller, more digestible sections. Footnotes or endnotes provide bibliographical references and, on occasion, further elaboration, but the difference between the footnotes or endnotes and what is called 'the main text' is rarely difficult to perceive.

However, some of the earliest printed texts defy these assumptions. Many have no titles or authors. Publishers' names are sometimes replaced with a printer's name, and not always. Page numbers are often absent, and the ideas of chapter headings and separation are non-existent. Even the use of punctuation and paragraphing is absent in many of the earliest printed works, making them almost unreadable by today's audience. And page layout in early printed works varies as much as the number of works themselves.

The majority of those first texts printed were Bibles. The importance of spreading the Gospel and the concurrent concerns with the Reformation were convenient coincidences. Many historians and theological scholars, particularly Elizabeth Eisenstein,[1] have remarked that without the printing press the Reformation could never have taken place. The printed word was so important to the forces of both the Reformation and the Counter-Reformation that the variety of translated Bibles printed between 1560 (the Geneva) and 1611 (the King James) are so many and so different that study of the printed texts of the period has recently received renewed interest.

One of the earliest and most important printed works was a glossed Bible that we now call the *Glossa Ordinaria*. Its full title, *Biblia latina cum glossa ordinaria*, reveals the text as a full Latin Bible (actually, Jerome's Vulgate), with what came to be referred to as 'the ordinary gloss', i.e., an accepted gloss – marginal and interlinear – on the Latin text. After several centuries of manuscripts, the entire glossed Bible was printed in 1480/1 and circulated throughout Europe. Its modest title belies its cachet and importance.

Any great piece of writing raises questions, and the art of questioning and debating with the text is especially evident in the medieval glossed Bible. The very layout of the text on the page encourages discussion and debate, and one can almost envisage the reader entering a debate already ongoing when he comes to the page. The cacophony of voices, coming at the text from the margins and between the lines, gives one the impression of coming into a discussion already in progress. One also realizes, quickly, that the discussion will not cease once the reader closes the book. One reason for this debate and discussion is the method of schooling used in the universities of the Middle Ages when most of the *Glossa Ordinaria* was constructed. *Disputatio, quaestio* and other forms of debate so popular in the medieval university find their way into this elaborate exegetical discussion.

In order best to understand the intellectual climate, it is important to understand the structure of everyday university life in the Middle Ages. Since most, if not all, students were in training to become clerics, teachers or theologians, it is only natural that we should find reading a central concern. My approach to understanding the *Glossa Ordinaria*, then, is as a textbook or as a supplement to the Bible. As Beryl Smalley has shown, the Bible text itself was displaced by the end of the thirteenth century, most often by Peter Lombard's *Sentences*.

My aim in this study is not to plough through the reams of studies and data on the myriad early *Glossa Ordinaria* manuscripts. The so-called 'authorship question' is also not my concern. Although it has become possible to attribute one or another *Glossa Ordinaria* book to a particular author or authors, understanding the overall authorship of the *Glossa Ordinaria* – 'who wrote the Glossa?' – is a problem that, I believe, is insoluble.

My overall aim here is to provide a primer on the *Glossa Ordinaria*, inviting the reader to consider the ideas of hypertext and hypertext reading that are held so dear in contemporary literary theory but are not new to computer-generated texts. In fact, if we look at a text such as the *Glossa Ordinaria*, we will find that the concept of hypertext is already in use in the fifteenth century in the earliest printed works. Instead of using a mouse to navigate text, the medieval reader used his cognitive process to navigate and 'link' sections both of the texts in front of him and of texts with which he was already familiar. How the *Glossa Ordinaria* may have been read is also reflected, analogically, in other early printed texts. In particular, religious texts of the sixteenth century, especially recusant texts printed in England, began to stress the importance of marginal notation to gloss the main text. The recent scholarly concern with footnotes and margins is, I think, quite significant in study of these early texts.

So what I offer here is a melding of seemingly disparate topics: the medieval glossed Bible and hypertext theory. I have always described my work as having one foot in the past and one in the future; in this study, I attempt to bring my two feet closer together. Beryl Smalley noted the relationship between the present and the past: the glossers rather 'see the glosses . . . as a pointer to their originals than as a substitute for them'.[2] The printed *Glossa Ordinaria* stands as a magisterial text, looming as a coda to the Middle Ages and as a harbinger of the past for the Renaissance. By the sixteenth century, it seems that every seminary-trained cleric in Europe was familiar with the *Glossa Ordinaria*, either through actual use or by reputation. Karlfried Froehlich has recently explained that the text was used throughout the sixteenth century in a variety of ways. In fact, the Council of Trent even noted the importance of the text as well as the importance of revising and correcting it – a feat never accomplished. In his important work, *Glossed Books of the Bible and the Origins of the Paris Book Trade*, Christopher de Hamel noted that 'there is no standard history of the Gloss and there is no modern printed edition of the text'.³ Froehlich and Gibson remedied the second problem; the present study is an attempt to remedy the first.

What I propose is to trace the development of attributed marginal references as the precursor of modern hypertext. My intention here is not to write a history of the *Glossa Ordinaria*, a feat most scholars of the gloss find daunting if not impossible. A complete history of the *Glossa Ordinaria* will require a team of scholars with access to hundreds of manuscripts housed in dozens of libraries and scriptoria throughout the world; that history would take years to complete and would probably fill five volumes. Instead, my intent here is to present scholars with an introduction to the *Glossa Ordinaria* and an understanding of how it developed from the first printed edition in 1480/1, through the last printed edition in 1634, to the *Patrologia Latina* edition in 1855, to a possible modern computerized edition. In this way, I hope to show that the *Glossa Ordinaria* acted as a hypertext even in twelfth-century manuscript.

I begin this work with many misgivings. A survey of available scholarship on the texts, dating to the early twentieth century, has been daunting. The mere number of manuscripts from the late eleventh and early twelfth centuries is enough to fill a small library. I come to the *Glossa Ordinaria* by way of looking back and not forward. What I mean by this is that I look to the *Glossa Ordinaria* as it influenced printed texts in the late sixteenth century and later and not from the point of view of a medieval scholar wanting to 'prove' authorship of the various books. This may trouble the reader – our graduate school professors always told us not to write about what we weren't going to do – but I think it is a necessary caveat. I have no delusions of grandeur; I do not plan to solve the authorship problem, a problem more than one *Glossa Ordinaria* scholar has argued is insoluble.

It is in the sixteenth and seventeenth centuries that the issues involved in understanding the *Glossa Ordinaria* become paramount: translation and use of the margins for commentary. Here, I believe, is the *Glossa Ordinaria*'s greatest influence and legacy: the ways in which printed texts eventually came to use the margins of the page in ways similar to the page layout of the early printed texts. This ultimately leads to issues regarding boundaries and borders, a topic William Slights notes is 'a deconstructionist's paradise in which writing regularly exceeds its own preset limits'.⁴ My study of the gloss began with a concern about intertextuality and marginal notation. A look at any *Glossa Ordinaria* manuscript or printed version evokes intertextual language: self-reference, intertext, hypertext, marginal symbols. I was originally concerned with the mystical nature of religious texts which subsume meaning in coded materials hidden in the margins of the text. The appropriate reader would understand the marginal remarks in the context of his faith and then be able to decode the material to reveal the 'correct reading' of the given text. What I discovered was that the *Glossa Ordinaria* was one of the earliest texts to employ such a strategy.

Rationale and Approach of this Book

The *Glossa Ordinaria* is an exceedingly difficult text. There are hundreds of manuscripts of different biblical books, and no single manuscript exists of what would become the first printed edition of 1481. Instead, that edition appears to be, as Froehlich calls it, the *editio princeps* – an edition that is an amalgam of many different manuscripts. Past studies have focused on individual manuscripts or individual books of the Bible, such as Theresa Gross-Diaz's masterly study of the Psalter. But no study has been done of the entire book, and it is not difficult to understand why. To do so would require a battery of scholars working for many years throughout the monastic and academic libraries of Europe. The publication of the facsimile of the 1481 edition advanced study of the *Glossa Ordinaria* immeasurably. Until that point, in 1993, the only universally available printed edition of the text was in Migne's *Patrologia Latina*, and that text was not only inaccurate: it was incomplete. Migne had chosen to exclude much of the interlinear notation with the argument that only the marginal notes were of importance. With the publication of the facsimile edition, scholars finally had access to the text as it had appeared in print.

But the questions of edition and manuscript history are not the only problematic issues the modern scholar confronts in studying the *Glossa Ordinaria*. One of the most important questions related to study of this text is exactly how the medieval student may have read it. Evidence for medieval theories of reading is sparse at best. Although we now have helpful studies, such as Brian Stock's *Augustine the Reader* and Harry Gamble's *Books and Readers in the Early Church*, there appears to be little evidence for what we now call reading theory in the Middle Ages. We can trace the development of reading as a practice, such as Augustine's silent reading, in Paul Saenger's work, but clear statements regarding systematic theories of reading seem absent. What Augustine tells us in *De Doctrina Christiana*, for example, deals more with semiotics than it does with reading, and although the two are certainly related, they are hardly the same.

As a result, the scholar is confronted with the problem of understanding exactly 'how' the medieval student read. Several texts deal with the 'why' question, but none I have found answers the 'how' question. One might expect perhaps to find some answers in illuminations depicting monks reading, but that search yields what we already know: monks read mostly sitting at great lecterns, since the volumes were too large and heavy to hold; they pored over the books and manuscripts but do not appear, when they are only reading, to be glossing or writing in texts.

So we are left to speculate just how the medieval student read, what the process was, and what the goal was. Using contemporary cognitive psychology and reading theory, we can develop a theory of reading for the Middle Ages, but, sadly, it will remain a theory without credible evidence. As a result, what I have tried to do in this book is to provide the reader with a primer on the *Glossa Ordinaria*, including its history, and then to discuss its relationship to modern hypertext theory. Because in-depth analysis of the entire text – four volumes in the facsimile edition – would be a lifelong project, I have left that to others, and have chosen to use the opening chapters of Genesis as my examples throughout the study.

I suggest a reformulation of our understanding of hypertext theory based on such texts as the *Glossa Ordinaria*, which encouraged the medieval reader to approach the work in an associative manner. Although organized first as a traditional Bible, moving from Genesis in the Old Testament to Revelation in the New Testament, the *Glossa Ordinaria*'s interlinear and marginal notation encourages the reader to make associations that will take him, virtually, off the physical page and into the space of the individual mind of that reader. In fact, as one of the earliest printed texts, the *Glossa*

Ordinaria violates many of the conventions of printed works. Although he is commenting about what he terms 'writing space', Jay David Bolter might be looking at the *Glossa Ordinaria* when he says, 'print will no longer define the organization and presentation of knowledge, as it has for the past five centuries.'[5] Bolter argues that this signals a 'shift from print to the computer', but I argue here that this shift occurred long before the computer age. The space of the *Glossa Ordinaria* page is as complex as any modern computer page, even more so in that it does not accommodate the reader with a tangible mechanism for making connections in the way that clicking on highlighted text to move from piece to piece might.

The very concept of reading in the ancient world remains unclear to us today. Ancient Greek has more than a dozen verbs meaning 'to read'. As Svenbro has noted, more often than not the Greek words used for 'read' imply instead an oral 'distribution' of the text. In other words, the act of reading was interpreted as the act of reading aloud. These are apparently not readers who are reading either for their own enjoyment or edification but only for the enjoyment or edification of others. In the equation 'reading = speaking', there is a great deal of space for interpretation by the reader and listener, and the listeners presumably do not know whether what they are being read is accurate or truthful, and their reception of the read text may indeed be quite different. How much space this allowed for faulty transmission we will never know, but we can assume that many a preacher altered a text for his own ends. This is what made the printing of the Bible so important: it allowed individuals to read and interpret for themselves, without the aid – or interference – of another. And, of course, this is what made that reading so threatening to those whose own interpretations were so politically, socially and theologically charged.

So we begin to understand that the act of reading (*legere*), through the early Middle Ages at least, was still viewed as a physical activity, the act of gathering texts and then distributing them, often through oral recitation. The significant shift, as we will see later, occurred with the development of silent reading and the encouragement then of reading for personal spiritual edification (*lectio*) and not exclusively (but inclusively) for the edification of the listening audience. Reading thus became a more personal and introspective activity, stripped of its physical connotations.

The reader will notice that, after years studying the *Glossa Ordinaria*, I have adopted many of the writers' ways. I quote directly, boosting myself up on the shoulders of the great scholars and theologians who have gone before me. I do not aim to reinvent the wheel; if Augustine said it best, you will read Augustine here. I have learnt much from these great thinkers, and I am greatly indebted to them for all they have taught me.

1

The Glossing Tradition and the *Glossa Ordinaria*

1.1 The Problem Stated

As Beryl Smalley writes, 'The "prehistory" of the Gloss presents many difficulties.'[1] In his *Histoire de la Vulgate*, Samuel Berger wrote in 1893 'L'histoire de cette volumineuse compilation ne peut être écrite aujourd'hui' ('The history of this great compilation has yet to be written').[2] And more than a century later, and some 800 years since its writing began, we still know precious little about how the text that came to be called the *Glossa Ordinaria* was compiled. What manuscripts contributed, ultimately, to the first printed edition of 1480/1? What person or persons were responsible for the compilation, if not the writing, of this landmark, magisterial work? We still await a complete history of the manuscript tradition that produced the *Glossa Ordinaria*, but such a project would require a cadre of dedicated and knowledgeable scholars with wide access to libraries and scriptoria throughout Europe. Because such a history is beyond my scope and limited resources, I have chosen to look at the 'prehistory' only cursorily and to focus this study on the first printed edition of the *Glossa Ordinaria*. Although most scholars agree that the 1480/1 edition may not be entirely faithful to the manuscript tradition it completes, it is this printed edition that gained the *Glossa Ordinaria*'s widest readership and reception throughout Europe in the late Middle Ages and well into the English Renaissance.

The development of a glossed Bible tradition has been well documented by Christopher De Hamel in his fine work, *Glossed Books of the Bible and the Origins of the Paris Booktrade*. What follows is largely a summary of De Hamel's research. Although there is no single source for the *Glossa Ordinaria*, by 1200 copies of the text were in almost every library in Europe. De Hamel calls the *Glossa Ordinaria* 'in effect, the twelfth-century bestseller'.[3] The development can be traced from the Laon school, through Gilbert of Poitiers and finally to the printed edition of 1481. In the present study, we will note Gilbert of Poitiers as perhaps the most significant contributor in that he introduced a new design in page layout: the *cum textu* format which changed the sizes of the text and commentary and assembled them in parallel columns, giving more space on the page to the commentary than to the text, thus stressing the importance of the commentary. A more detailed history of the *Glossa Ordinaria* itself will be presented in chapter 2.

1.2 'Gloss'

The act of glossing texts is as old as reading itself, but the English word 'gloss' is relatively new, the earliest *Oxford English Dictionary* citation for the noun *gloss* being in a 1548 edition of Erasmus' paraphrases on Matthew. The word's first appearance as 'a collection of such explanations, a glossary' is in Spenser's 1579 *Shepherde's Calendar*; the same text gives us the word's first use as a verb: 'to introduce a gloss, comment, or explanations upon a word or passage in a text'. In 1603, Florio's edition of Montaigne offers 'Some that studie, plod, and glose their Almanackes'. The English word derives from the Latin '*glossa*' and the Greek γλωσσα, meaning tongue or language. Note that any *Oxford English Dictionary* entry for the word postdates the Middle Ages and the publication of the *Glossa Ordinaria* in 1481. Lewis and Short note *glossa* as derived from the Greek and indicating 'an obsolete or foreign word that requires explanation'.[4] *Glossae* is 'a term applied to collections of such words with explanations'. They cite Ausonius as the earliest appearance: 'Eune, quod uxoris gravidae putria inguina lambis, festinas glossas non natis tradere natis' ('Eunus, to the extent that you lick the putrid groin of your pregnant wife, you hasten to bequeath your tongue to your children not (yet) born').[5] By the Middle Ages, the Middle English verb *glose* meant to comment or explain.[6] The practice of glossing texts dates to the earliest days of both writing and reading. The act of glossing permits the reader to accomplish two things: first, to respond to the text, and second, to engage with the text. In English the word 'gloss' does not appear until the mid-sixteenth century. The text is Erasmus' paraphrases on Matthew 23: 'Like as by a glosse ye subuerte the commaundement'.[7] The sense is certainly a negative one. The term 'glossator' appears much earlier in one of Wycliffe's 'controversial tracts'. Earlier still is the appearance of the noun 'gloze', meaning 'a comment, or marginal note; an exposition', and appearing in Richard Rolle's *Pricke of Conscience*: 'the glose of the book says always that . . .' But the word's Greek and Latin roots run through the Middle Ages back to ancient Greece and Rome. Hugh of St Victor notes that 'The word "gloss" is Greek, and it means tongue (*lingua*), because, in a way, it bespeaks (*loquitur*) the meaning of the word under it.'[8]

It is unclear when the *Glossa Ordinaria*, the 'ordinary gloss,' began to be called as such. The title is no doubt related to the legal glosses so popular throughout the early Middle Ages, 'Ordinary Gloss' being a title applied mostly to glosses on law, both secular and canon. Once Roman law was codified by Justinian in the sixth century, a history of glosses of that law followed.[9] Because the law being glossed was Church canon law,[10] it is no real leap to glossing of the Bible text, and we can generally assume that the writers of the *Glossa Ordinaria* had the legal glosses in mind. The structure of legal explanations of canon law could easily be applied to discussions and exegesis of 'the Law', i.e., the Bible itself. And no less an authority than Augustine himself seems to have encouraged a hermeneutical blending of legalistic strategies in explicating and understanding difficult texts, such as the Bible.[11]

The functions of the legal glosses, as described by Hermann Kantorowicz, were threefold: 'to serve as notes for the delivery of oral *lecturae*; as materials for the composition of systematic text-books (*summae*); as commentaries for the benefit of future readers of the text'.[12] Although all three functions are seen in the later *Glossa Ordinaria*, it is the third – commentary for future readers – which seems most applicable. As the biblical glossing tradition advanced, by the mid-twelfth century the biblical gloss served both the glossator and the reader – the intent was both edification and education, as I will discuss later.

What eventually came to be called the *glossa ordinaria*, or ordinary gloss, on canon law was the result of *apparatus* written in the twelfth century and first compiled in Bologna in the early thirteenth century by Johannes Teutonicus.[13] And, in fact, the layout of many of the glossed books of the Bible resembles the legal glosses in form. So, the concept of an 'ordinary gloss' is not new to the Bible text – it was actually used much earlier in legal texts – but the *Biblia Sacra cum glossa ordinaria* was unique in that it applied this glossing tradition, used almost exclusively until that point for secular texts, to the sacred text of the Bible. The effect of such glossing would be far-reaching, extending to Chaucer and even Shakespeare.

1.3 What is a Glossed Text?

The idea of glossing a text is so familiar to the modern reader that examining the nature of a glossed text seems almost absurd, so ingrained is it in our reading and scholarly psyche. What modern reader even thinks twice about underlining passages or writing in the margins of a personal copy of a text, whether a primary source such as a novel or a secondary source such as a scholarly work? The margins of contemporary personal Bibles are consistently littered with comments and notes of the owner, so much so that today many Bibles are printed with enough marginal space (and even notational apparatus, such as page tabulation and thumb indices), inviting the reader to make such marks. So-called 'reading copies' of books owned by authors are coveted for what they might tell the scholar about the writer's reading and, by extension, writing processes. H. J. Jackson's recent study, *Marginalia: Readers Writing in Books*, focuses on books annotated by writers, from Samuel Taylor Coleridge to Graham Greene, in an effort to help us better understand the writers themselves through study of the books they owned and glossed.[14] In *Managing Readers: Printed Marginalia in English Renaissance Books*, William W. E. Slights looks at marginal notation that was actually printed in texts, and includes an important chapter on the margins of Renaissance English Bibles.[15]

College instructors routinely implore students to annotate their own reading copies of books, and such annotations can be telling, reflecting as they may the student's intellectual development. Study of these annotations might 'expose basic patterns in readers' practice'.[16] Reflection on one's own annotations of texts read earlier in life reveals a type of unintended autobiography. In such ways, then, the study of marginal and interlinear notation can build not only the autobiography of a reader but the autobiography of a text – the history of a given copy of a book.

Because we have now come to understand reading as 'an intratextual process governed by an active reader',[17] we need a better framework within which to understand the interrelation of texts and, as I will argue later in the present work, the hypertextual nature of reading itself. Through annotation the reader talks back to the text, but some of the most important glossed texts of the Middle Ages do not necessarily concern the reader talking back to the text as much as they do the reader interacting with the text. In the former the reader engages with the text as either kindred spirit ('great sentiment here') or as disputer ('no! This cannot be right!'). In this guise, the text remains an organic entity, and the reader, also an organic entity, interacts with the text in order perhaps to produce a third, new, entity. Thus no two glossed texts are identical, dependent as they are on the inclinations, personality and education of the glossator/reader. That reader may return to the text years later and see an entirely new text in the glossed work (and his prior glosses themselves). Equally, it seems as important to read a work without glossing – by either the reader or another. Some students dislike purchasing used books for that reason. Others rely on their own prior glosses to inform subsequent readings.

With clear implications related to boundaries, it is no surprise to find glossed texts and margins chief concerns of such literary theorists as Jacques Derrida and the theologian/sociologist Michel de Certeau. De Certeau has noted that 'an act of reading is the space produced by the practice of a particular place: a written text, i.e., a place constituted by a system of signs.'[18] Henri Lefebvre as well notes that 'every society ... produces a space, its own space,' and it is certainly possible to suggest that a society of readers, one that was especially exclusionary, did operate until the sixteenth century when literacy (particularly reading) expanded to the wider society.[19]

In printed texts, particularly of the late sixteenth century when religious battles were being fought on paper, the margins of texts are most often taken up with material not felt to be appropriate or legally permissible for the main text. Such religious concerns as mysticism had been effectively forced from the medieval text into the margins of the Renaissance text as the result of political, social and theological conflict. Thus the margins of the text became the site of such conflict. The margins of a text are often the sites of battle, and the material in the margins is often lobbying for admittance to the main text. In some cases, it eventually triumphs; in others, it is pushed entirely off the page and, effectively, into or out of cultural memory. Michel de Certeau has written extensively on mystical literature as marginalized in the sixteenth and seventeenth centuries and notes that in such cases 'the content [i.e., the mystical writing] remained, but it underwent a new treatment [i.e., the presentation].'[20]

1.4 Why Gloss?

There is a tradition of glossing texts as early as the ancient Greeks and Romans. As the Christian era unfolded, this tradition gravitated towards Scripture, and 'from at least the Carolingian period it was common practice to make additions in the margins and between the lines of manuscript books of the Bible.'[21] There has been no comprehensive discussion of glossing, and what we do understand of ancient texts is largely suggestion and intuitive supposition. We know, for example, that early readers and writers glossed texts, particularly those related to Latin grammar, as tools to further the education of the reader. But in a survey of images in illuminated manuscripts of the early Middle Ages, I have been unable to find an illustration of a scribe or student glossing a text.

However, the concept of glossing a text is interwoven with the history of the Bible itself. Because an understanding of the Bible depends on interpretation of the Bible, glossing of the Bible is a practice as old as transmission of the biblical texts themselves. We assume, as modern readers, that the practice of footnoting a text is a given, that footnotes help to illuminate unclear words and passages or to elaborate on what might otherwise be superfluous material. As Anthony Grafton notes, 'In the eighteenth century, the historical footnote was a high form of literary art.'[22] Earlier commentaries, such as those found in the *Glossa Ordinaria*, 'eventually came to be seen as integral parts of the texts they explicated. These were regularly taught with their commentaries.'[23]

Before footnotes and endnotes, manuscripts were adorned with marginal and interlinear notation and, sometimes, marginal illumination. Scribes painstakingly ruled pages to accommodate such remarks, and in some texts the remarks grew in importance to overshadow the text they glossed. In some modern examples, the remarks are indispensable. Such is the case with the biblical texts. Without the glosses of the Church Fathers, much of the Bible would be unintelligible to the ordinary reader. Enter the ordinary gloss, or the *Glossa Ordinaria*.

The Latin Vulgate Bible has a long and involved history, but it is a history that should also include extensive mention of the glossed Bible tradition. Unfortunately, the *Glossa Ordinaria* merits only four short pages in Samuel Berger's *Histoire de la Vulgate*. The importance of glossed Bibles is more evident in study of the history of the printed Bible. Clearly, the glossing tradition influenced the development of such important Bibles as the Geneva Bible, the Rheims New Testament and, ultimately, the King James Bible. The idea behind a glossed Bible is to develop a text that includes the types of comments and, more importantly, exegetical remarks that the 'ordinary' reader would find helpful and enlightening. In one sense, we might regard the entire corpus of patristic exegesis as an extended gloss. This is certainly true of the *Glossa Ordinaria*'s most frequent referent: Augustine. Augustine's work on Genesis dominates the *Glossa Ordinaria*'s pages of Genesis and beyond. For Augustine, the Bible is essentially the 'writing of the mysteries', and it is these mysteries that a biblical gloss aims to uncover and interpret.[24] It is in this sense that glossing the Bible has its origins in the so-called 'mystical' or allegorical interpretation of Origen. Glossing uncovers the mystery, exposing the truth in what seems to often be an encoded text.

The margins of the text, much studied in the critical pages of today's scholars, were in a nascent stage in the *Glossa Ordinaria* manuscripts, although, as Michael Camille has demonstrated, the margins of medieval art had already gained great importance by the first printed edition of the *Glossa Ordinaria*:

> If these edges were dangerous, they were powerful places. In folklore, betwixt and between are important zones of transformation. The edge of the water was where wisdom revealed itself; spirits were banished to the spaceless places 'between the froth and the water' or 'betwixt the bark and the tree'.[25]

But we still have the question: why? Why gloss the text at all? What purpose and whose purpose does a glossed Bible serve? As M. B. Parkes has noted, it was 'the exercise of Christian hermeneutics ... to produce personal readings or exegesis of the text'.[26] The practice of engaging the text in dialogue was noted by Gregory the Great. Perhaps more than most patristic authors, Gregory mentions reading and the importance of reading in his work.

1.5 Glossing, Memory, and the Modern World

The glossing of modern texts is achieved for quite different ends than for the medieval reader. Much of this difference can easily be related to the shifting importance of memory in the scholarly enterprise. Whereas the medieval reader, by necessity, exercised his memory in order to organize and 're-collect' material in his mind, the modern reader easily marks his texts, making notes both marginally and interlinearly, in an effort to support an underused and withering memory, a memory in many cases cursed with more information than could be stored in the hard drives of the mind. The medieval reader could no doubt quote countless lines of poetry with little effort, while the modern reader often has trouble recalling even a single couplet. Even the late nineteenth- and early twentieth-century student could easily retrieve entire poems, including complete books of *Paradise Lost*, from memory.[27]

A relationship certainly exists between glossing and the rise of literacy in the eleventh and twelfth centuries.[28] In fact, the advent of literacy produced 'a profound interaction between language, texts and society'.[29] Brian Stock has noted the important role of canon law in the rise of literacy in the Middle Ages, and it is the principles of writing and reading canon law that spilled onto the pages of biblical exegesis such as that found in the *Glossa Ordinaria*. Canon law 'was made up of unusual elements: quotations from the Bible and the fathers, decrees of synods and councils, papal letters and decretals, borrowings from indigenous traditions, and generalizations based on the developing institutions of the church itself'.[30] It is not difficult to see that the hermeneutic approach of the *Glossa Ordinaria* borrowed heavily from canon law. At the centre was the use of texts as evidence, a move from reliance on the verbal argument to a focus on the written organization of evidence.

Developing textual communities conducted their interactions through the written word, using writing as an insurance policy for retaining cultural memory. Reliance on the spoken word was quickly replaced by reliance on the written text, a central concern throughout the hermeneutics of the Middle Ages, particularly in the work of Augustine, Anselm, and Abelard. How much could the written word be trusted to reflect the truth, or The Truth? For centuries, a man's word was as good as his bond. But with the rise in literacy, a new orientation had to be arranged whereby a man could signify that his *written* word was as good as his bond. This led to discussion regarding 'the relationship between language, texts, and reality, and, as a consequence, the potential uses of knowledge'.[31] New languages had to be developed to deal with what Stock calls 'the potential uses of knowledge'. On the page, language looked and acted quite differently from when it was primarily spoken. Sentences were longer, arguments more involved, and, with the introduction of the margins, the author had the ability to annotate those arguments, with both citations and elaboration. More importantly, the reader gained the right to invade the text and introduce his own locutions in the margins, thus breaking down the boundaries of the text. In effect, the rise of literacy opened the figural doors of the work, inviting the reader not only to enter and observe but to become an active participant. Once those doors were opened, they would never be closed.

Brian Stock notes that Anselm 'becomes one of the first authors to conceive of a reading public in the modern sense'.[32] It is with Anselm that texts first act as 'an intermediary for discussion within his own mind'.[33] This is vital to our understanding of the

Glossa Ordinaria and the idea that these texts served as hypertexts of the mind, encouraging the reader to make connections, indeed to discuss 'within his own mind'. This is, after all, the very foundation of contemplative reading and reflection themselves. The text, then, operates in a dialectical mode, affording the reader the opportunity to engage in dialogue with the self as he reads, reflects, debates, and develops arguments in his own mind. That argument spills from the reader's mind, sometimes, into the margins of the text as comment or reaction to the main text.

In some ways, the *Glossa Ordinaria* reflects just such a reading process. Although the margins here do not necessarily reflect a reader's argument with the text (though they can), they do reflect a hypertextual construct by which the reader can gain more information, thus developing a more complete understanding of what he is reading. Such a reading process is tied to the sustenance of a cultural memory because, as de Certeau has shown, the margins of the text often reflect what society feels does not belong properly in the 'main' text. Thus, we understand the Christian explanation for the Fall narrative in Genesis 3 as most indebted to Augustine's exegesis. This then becomes a part of the cultural narrative of the Fall. Robert Scholes calls 'centrifugal reading' that which 'sees the life of a text as occurring along its circumference [i.e., around the edges] which is constantly expanding, encompassing new possibilities of meaning'.[34] 'Reading', he continues, 'is dialectical.' The boundaries of the text constantly expand as that dialectic grows. In Scholes's hermeneutic, this brings us to a very clear – and ever-widening – intertextuality, in which reading is the act 'of bringing texts together'.[35] Reading is then the connecting of signs that originate in a wide variety of locations – in the text, in the margins and off the page into other texts, both actual and cultural.

Thus a text like the *Glossa Ordinaria* involves certain revolutionary aspects of the rising literacy of the eleventh and twelfth centuries. First, it is a shift from the verbal to the written word. Second, it reflects the hypertextual mode of thinking that is human cognition and human being. Third, it pushes the boundaries of the text/page as it (fourth) engages in a dialectic. Finally, it invites the reader to reflect and contemplate its content as he helps to build a cultural memory that, in many ways, grows to replace the oral tradition.

1.6 What is the Glossa Ordinaria?

The *Glossa Ordinaria* is, simply, Jerome's Latin Vulgate Bible with marginal and interlinear glosses culled from the Church Fathers.[36] Rudimentary as that may sound, the *Glossa Ordinaria* grew to become the most important exegetical tool of the Middle Ages and beyond. It was common practice, beginning as early as Augustine, to gloss particular books of the Bible, commenting on and amending the text. The goals were understanding, edification – of both writer and reader – and, of course, a heightened closeness to God. The most popular books to gloss were the Song of Songs, the Psalter, and the Pauline Epistles, as is evident from the number of extant manuscripts of those books glossed between the sixth and twelfth centuries.

But it was not until the early twelfth century, at the Cathedral school at Laon in France, that the various glossed books were collected with the goal of a complete glossed Bible. The task was onerous, almost impossible, as gathering the various glossed manuscripts meant not only acquisition but some type of selection process: which version would be used, and why? For the wealthy, such a compilation was a mark of prestige. As Christopher De Hamel notes, 'One of the most celebrated groups of glossed manuscripts of this period are those presented by Prince Henry of France, son of Louis VI, to the Abbey of Clairvaux.'[37] Thomas Becket apparently owned twenty-one glossed books of the Bible, undoubtedly something to boast about.[38] De Hamel catalogues other extant collections in chapter 5 of his work, but one thing remains clear: ownership of any of the glossed books of the Bible was a sign of success, wealth and superior station. It reflected a certain currency and cachet, not unlike that of a modern person collecting first editions or owning a particularly rare map or document. We need to recall that at this point these various glossed books were all in manuscript form only – uncollated and disordered.

1.7 Modern Study

We are fortunate to have a facsimile edition of the *Glossa Ordinaria* with brilliantly insightful introductions by Karlfried Froehlich and the late Margaret Gibson. Because all later editions of the *Glossa Ordinaria*, at least until the Antwerp edition of 1634, are based on the 1480/1 edition, Froehlich and other scholars refer to the facsimile as the *editio princeps*. This four-volume facsimile is monumental in both size and scope. Over 1,200 leaves in 155 quires, the bound volumes occupy almost two feet of shelf space. Froehlich notes 180 extant copies of the 1480 edition worldwide;[39] another count suggests 250 copies. Such a relatively high number encourages us to appreciate the importance of this work over an extended period of time. We may compare this with the precious few copies of early editions of Chaucer that survive.[40]

However, there are several curious printing aspects of the work: it is anonymous, contains no title, no preface, no dedication and no printer's name. Scholars have established the printer as Adolph Rusch, a Strassburg printer, whose accomplishment was honoured in a panegyric poem published in 1486 where he is noted as a

> hero of book-making ... who, prompted by God and exercising the greatness of his mind, put his hand to the immense labour of [setting] the Bible with the *glossa ordinaria* in threefold type, printed it with the help of his extraordinary genius, not so much in the most elegant but the most correct form possible, and dispatched such a divine gift to the entire Christian world.[41]

Rusch's accomplishment, as noted in the poem, not only 'dispatched' a 'divine gift' to the world; Rusch effectively liberated the Bible from its monastic chains. Prior to the age of print, books remained chained to their library shelves, chiefly as a means of security. With the advent of print, multiple copies of a work permitted its extensive use and, most importantly, use beyond the chained shelves of the library. This probably is not the case with Rusch's edition of the *Glossa Ordinaria* – it was much too expensive for common use or widespread ownership, but the mere availability of such a work is an indication of wider readership and ownership to come in the following years. Besides, the work's size made it unwieldy and required the use of a bookstand or reading shelf of the kind one finds in the medieval monastic library.

We see the influence of Rusch's edition in religious texts of the late sixteenth century, and, as I will argue later in this study, the *Glossa Ordinaria* is one of the earliest printed examples of what we now call 'hypertext'. Because, as Beryl Smalley noted in her landmark study, *The Study of the Bible in the Middle Ages*, 'Bible study represented the highest branch of learning,' it is only logical to assume that the study of the Bible as conducted using a glossed text would only augment that learning.[42] Certainly throughout the early Church and well into the Middle Ages the prime motivation for reading was a closer and deeper relationship with God. The chief motive for reading by what would be called the earliest general reading public was the salvation of one's soul.

1.8 Glossing and the Glossa Ordinaria

The tradition of glossing Bible texts is as old as the writing down of Scripture itself. As we turn the corner on the twelfth century, we find a rich cache of glossed books of the Bible. But the concept of glossing dates to the earliest centuries of the Christian Church when Cyril of Alexandria (d. 444), an important enough figure in the early Church to have been designated a Doctor of the Church, gives us one of the earliest mentions of reading the text by integrating past commentary: 'It seems that he [Cyril] consciously and purposely extended the long established practice of adducing "proofs from Scripture" to include the "proofs from the Fathers".'[43] Although Johannes Quasten does note that 'he [Cyril] did not invent this method', he goes on to argue that 'nobody so far had employed it with such technical skill and perfection.'[44] Cyril established scriptural commentary as a valid theological tool. In fact, Cyril almost places the word of Scripture and the writing of the Fathers on the same level: 'These are the views we have been taught to hold both by the holy apostles and evangelists and by inspired Scripture in its entirety and from the true confession of the blessed fathers.'[45] In another letter, Cyril writes of reviewing 'the declarations of the holy fathers' and 'taking them with full seriousness',[46] a foreshadowing of the Church's eventual endorsement of certain Fathers' writing as doctrine.

What role, then, did early Christian writers see for both previous and contemporary interpretation in biblical exegesis? As time passed, interpretation and its literature became more important to an understanding of Scripture, but writers were careful not to allow interpretation to overshadow the text itself. This was the real problem: how to retain the primacy of Scripture without letting the interpretation and interpretative texts dominate. Thus, early exegetes developed the practice of glossing the text by positioning commentary either in the margins or in a column parallel to the text, usually in a smaller font and/or different colour than the main text. This side-by-side placement is referred to as *cum textu* format.[47] The dominant place of Scripture was never subverted on the page by the commentary. To do so would have smelled of heresy. This was a safeguard against 'creating' Scripture where there was none: the Descent to Hell is a good example. Supposed to have taken place on Holy Saturday, the day after the Crucifixion, the Descent to, or Harrowing of, Hell refers to Jesus' domination of Death or Satan and his rescue of Old Testament patriarchs (such as Adam, Noah and Abraham) and, in some redactions, matriarchs (such as Eve, Sarah and Rachel). The story, however, was deemed apocryphal by early Church Fathers and is extant only in texts such as the Gospel of

Nicodemus. In effect, this is a type of meta-commentary on the Passion sequence in the canonical Gospels. As such, it was, in some circles, deemed, if not heretical, at least questionable and suspicious. Reference to the story itself in the canonical Scripture was relegated to marginal notation on Nicodemus' presence at the Crucifixion in the Gospels.

As a result, ultimately, the goal of the medieval exegete was to ensure the divine nature and veneration of Scripture while commenting in order better to understand that main text, and because the practice of looking to authority dates to the classical authors, this practice of looking to the Church Fathers for commentary can be traced to the medieval academic concern with authority or *auctoritas*.

1.9 Authority and Auctoritas

Much of the *raison d'être* for the *Glossa Ordinaria* is the establishment of authority. As A. J. Minnis and R. H. and M. A. Rouse have shown in a variety of scholarly articles and books, the question of authority in the Middle Ages was at the forefront of readers' minds. As Rouse notes, 'The major works of the twelfth century . . . represent efforts to assimilate and organize inherited written authority in systematic form.'[48] The establishment of authoritative interpretations and readings of the biblical texts continued to be an issue in printed Bible texts well into the seventeenth century. Although the 'canon' of Church Fathers had been well established by the twelfth century (the patristic era is usually said to end with the death of Bernard of Clairvaux in 1153), how to read the text of the Bible was an important issue for the medieval reader.

The search for 'authority' in the medieval text most often seemed to end with the note or remark of a Church Father. Minnis has argued that Peter Lombard and Gilbert of Poitiers 'had in their Bible-commentaries applied the conventions and categories of secular literary theory to sacred literature'.[49] In those commentaries, the author sets himself up as the authority, but in the *Glossa Ordinaria*, a type of compendium of Church commentary, there really is no single author, so how do we deal not only with the question of authorship (which I will address in the next chapter) but with authority? Perhaps the one site of authorial authority, if you will, for the *Glossa Ordinaria* commentaries appears in the prologues to each book, if they survive. It is there that the individual authors most often display their personal ideas, agenda and theories. However, we lack such prologues for most books in the 1480/1 edition and have them only for a few.

Throughout the Middle Ages we find the kind of maxim Minnis offers: 'To be old was to be good; the best writers were the more ancient.'[50] As a result, and perhaps as a cause, the *Glossa Ordinaria* relies on older writers in lieu of more recent patristic exegesis. Augustine is most often cited, but we note a surprising absence of Apostolic writers, though this may have been due only to lack of access to those writers until the late Middle Ages.

It is only natural, whether one is writing in the twelfth century or the twenty-first, to look to the work of predecessors for guidance and authority – many have made their careers by standing on the shoulders of a previous giant. In the Middle Ages it was the *auctores* or authoritative Latin writers to whom biblical exegetes, in particular, looked. A. J. Minnis goes so far as to argue that the *auctores* studied in the schools of the Middle

Ages cast their shadows well into the fifteenth century. The commentaries produced by these *auctores* present us with what Minnis calls a 'medieval theory of authorship, i.e., the literary theory centered on the concepts of *auctor* and *auctoritas*'.[51] For some authors, the nod to the ancients was obligatory.[52] This sentiment – that anything considered old is superior – dominates Renaissance England as well; think of Spenser's dependence on an invented archaic English for *The Faerie Queene* or the various English dramas taking place in, or borrowing heavily from, the Middle Ages.

The *auctor* was the author or authority, a title related, as Minnis shows, to the Latin verbs *agere*, *augeo* and *aueo*, all words related to growth or performance. The product of the *auctor* was *auctoritas*, a quotation or relic of the *auctor*. In many medieval commentaries on the Bible, texts such as the Apocrypha are indeed doubtful or dubious (the meanings of *apocrypha*) owing not to their content but to their anonymous nature, the lack of a clear *auctor*. Thus, Hugh of St Cher writes: 'They are called apocryphal because the author is unknown . . . if neither the author nor the truth were known, they could not be accepted.'[53] The *auctor*, therefore, is of paramount importance as the authority – if there is no *auctor*, there can be no *auctoritas*, no authority. The *auctor* is not merely the author in the modern sense: he is instead inventor or creator.[54]

Augustine clearly lays out the role of authority and *auctoritas* in De Doctrina Christiana, the central text on pedagogy until Hugh of St Victor's *Didascalicon* appeared in the twelfth century. Augustine writes that by reading Christian literature,

> etiam praeter canonem in auctoritatis arce salubriter collocatum, quas legendo homo capax, etsi id non agat sed tantummodo rebus quae ibi dicuntur intentus sit, etiam eloquio quo dicuntur, dum in his versatur, imbuitur, accendente vel maxime exercitatione sive scribendi sive dictandi, postremo etiam dicendi, quae secundum pietatis ac fidei regulam senit.

> (which has been raised to its position of authority for our benefit . . . even one not seeking to become eloquent but just concentrating on the matters being discussed, can become steeped in their eloquence, especially if this is combined with the practice of writing or dictating, and eventually speaking, what is felt to be in conformity with the rule of holiness and faith.)[55]

The focus is continually on the ancient: old is good. The authority of the Church is called for in many instances. And the word *auctoritas* appears no fewer than fourteen times in the *Glossa Ordinaria*, usually in the context of the authority of Scripture. So, the *auctoritas* most often appealed to in the *Glossa Ordinaria* is either the authority of Scripture, established over time and by the number of Churches subscribing to it, or the writings of Church Fathers, also appealed to for their age and pedigree. Then, within biblical exegesis and the authority of Scripture, we find a ranking of exegetical priorities, owing to the principles laid out by such early exegetes as Origen. In the commentary on the Psalter, for example, the spiritual sense is deemed superior to the historical or literal sense.[56]

It seems, on the surface, that the ancient texts, whether sacred or secular, were respected most often for their handling of rhetoric. Much of early biblical commentary relates in tenor and method to the ancient handbooks of rhetoric that make direct connections between the *Glossa Ordinaria* text and, say, Cicero seem logical. Augustine writes often of the importance and influence of Cicero on his own life and writing. However, attempts at such connections invariably fail because the glossators were adept at stripping sacred work of any secular relationship. The sacred was, of course, better and more authoritative than the secular; therefore the secular was to be subsumed in the sacred. Nevertheless, a rhetorical approach lurks beneath the exegetical in many of the *Glossa Ordinaria*'s comments, appearing explicitly most often in the prologues.

The central concern in *Glossa Ordinaria* prologues is the intention of the glossed book: either edification or education. In some, glimpses of the *imitatio Christi* are even evident, as in this from Gilbert of Poitiers's preface to the Psalter gloss: 'For the prophet has in mind not only to teach those things which he propounds regarding Christ, but indeed in teaching to draw the affections of carnal men to the same end of praise.'[57] This is further reinforced in Gilbert's preface where 'The whole Christ, head and members, is the material of this work.'[58] This also reinforces our sense of the work as the *corpus mysticum* (the mystical body), i.e., the body of Christ. We are approaching a period in the Middle Ages when *imitatio* held the highest place, and the conflation of text and body became clearer in the writings of the medieval mystics. Thus the body of the text more easily related to the body of Christ, and both were venerated on almost equal levels. Illustrative of this principle is Richard Salomon's *Opicinus de Canistris*, an early fourteenth-century collection of maps, figures, astrological drawings and human figures. Several of the drawings of the human figure offer almost a palimpsest of text with the body of Christ.[59] A similar ethos permeates Henri de Lubac's work on the *corpus mysticum*, the Eucharist as mystical body in the Middle Ages.[60]

Glossa Ordinaria prefaces printed after the 1481 edition address the reader directly and provide what we might consider an academic outline of the work. In the 1588 edition, for example, *Ad Christianum Lectorem*, the preface briefly outlines the history of the work but is concerned more with indicating the marginal apparatus and its meaning. No names are mentioned with the exception of Jerome, whose *auctoritas* it is assumed carries enough weight on its own, given Jerome's authorship of the Vulgate itself.

In the Middle Ages a more complete understanding of the liberal arts was certainly an aid to study of the sacred page, with its complexities and intricacies. Nevertheless, many of the biblical exegetical techniques of the Middle Ages were clearly adapted and adopted from critical and explicatory techniques used on classical and ancient texts where the concept of *auctoritas* was founded. In the *Confessiones*, Augustine sets up *auctoritas* against *ratio* where parental authority is something to rely on beyond reason, but the appeal to authority is not that dissimilar to the exegete's reliance on *auctoritas* based solely on the supposed age of the authority: 'Authority is said to precede reason in time.'[61] He also notes that we must place our trust in authorities other than ourselves.[62] A. J. Minnis argues that the scriptural prologue, which we see so frequently in glossed books of the Bible, is the author's attempt to establish *auctoritas* for his commentary; those prologues also often act as apologies by the compiler. The authorship of the *Glossa Ordinaria* prologues has always been in question, and the argument that Anselm of Laon is responsible for developing the form remains unproven and dubious. Regardless of the authorship of the prologues, the intention is the same: to establish a type of authority for the commentary that follows. Later glossators accepted the prologue: 'Good prologue material was appreciated, and paid the ultimate compliment of being copied and incorporated.'[63] Minnis has noted that the prologue form was popular enough to merit their collection in anthologies.[64] And indeed the prologues to the glossed books of the Bible establish their authors' authority, based mostly on an appeal to previous, well-established authorities. 'The prologue provided a scholar with the occasion to reiterate those received interpretations of the text which seemed most appropriate to him, and to amplify such traditional doctrine with some ideas of his own.'[65]

1.10 The Genesis Preface

The *Glossa Ordinaria* preface to Genesis appears to be taken almost verbatim from Jerome, and so it is not actually a preface to the *Glossa Ordinaria* proper. In it Jerome discounts the myth of the Septuagint: 'I do not know whose false imagination led him to invent the story of the seventy cells at Alexandria, in which, though separated from each other, the translators were said to have written the same words . . . For it is one thing to be a prophet, another to be a translator.' But in the 1480/1 edition, there is another *incipit* inserted after Jerome's preface but before Genesis 1:1, and it is this 'preface' that intentionally introduces the *Glossa Ordinaria*. Its author is unknown, though it is possibly the product of Adolph Rusch, the printer, or another writer he commissioned. Its content is both instructive for the reader and informative for the scholar. A primer on what is to come, the preface is littered with patristic references or actual quotations. The Church Fathers' commentary, the preface tells us, 'noted which books of Scripture' ('*Notandum qi hæc scriptura*') were of utmost importance. But the intention of compiling the *Glossa Ordinaria* is the 'health of the catholic faithful' ('*sanitate catholicae fidei*'). In addition to these invectives, the preface is taken largely from the work of Augustine, specifically his works on Genesis.[66] Without naming him, the preface alludes to an Origenist hermeneutic, as biblical exegesis is clearly separated into the allegorical, anagogical, historical and tropological.

The opening of the prologue, taken verbatim from book 1, chapter 21, of Augustine's *The Literal Meaning of Genesis*, sets the tone if not the intention of the *Glossa Ordinaria* as a whole:

> Et cum divinos libros legimus in tanta multitudine verorum intellectuum, qui de paucis verbis eruuntur, et sanitate catholicae fidei muniuntur, id potissimum deligamus, quod certum apparuerit eum sensisse quem legimus; si autem hoc latet, id certe quod circumstantia Scripturae non impedit, et cum sana fide concordat: si autem et Scripturae circumstantia pertractari ac discuti non potest, saltem id solum quod fides sana praescribit. Aliud est enim quid potissimum scriptor senserit non dignoscere, aliud autem a regula pietatis errare. Si utrumque vitetur, perfecte se habet fructus legentis: si vero utrumque vitari non potest, etiam si voluntas scriptoris incerta sit sanae fidei congruam non inutile est eruisse.

> (When we read the inspired books in the light of this wide variety of true doctrines which are drawn from a few words and founded on the firm basis of Catholic belief, let us choose that one which appears as certainly the meaning intended by the author. But if this is not clear, then at least we should choose an interpretation in keeping with the context of Scripture and in harmony with our faith. But if the meaning cannot be studied and judged by the context of Scripture, at least we should choose only that which our faith demands. For it is one thing to fail to recognize the primary meaning of the writer, and another to depart from the norms of religious belief. If both these difficulties are avoided, the reader gets full profit from his reading. Failing that, even if the writer's intention is uncertain, one will find it useful to extract an interpretation in harmony with our faith.)[67]

This passage has great import as a defence of reading – and interpreting – Scripture when the meaning is not immediately clear or accessible. Augustine suggests that there are myriad interpretations of Scripture, but when meaning is not immediately clear, the reader should move through a series of decision-making stages. First, it is important to choose that 'which appears as certainly the meaning intended by the author'. But how? How does the novice reader, or even the experienced reader, make such a decision/ distinction? If this fails – or the process fails – he should choose the interpretation 'in keeping with the context of Scripture and in harmony with our faith'. This refers to the earlier phrase 'the firm basis of Catholic belief', and one assumes that this is the 'firm basis' upon which the *Glossa Ordinaria* text is built. Yet, if neither of the first two steps is successful, the reader should 'choose only that which our faith demands'. If the text is not clear, and the reader cannot discern the author's intentions, it is his duty as a Christian to look to his faith, to compare the interpretation with the 'norms of religious belief'. The focus throughout the passage is the repeated phrase 'our faith'. Cassiodorus echoes this sentiment in his *Introduction to Divine and Human Readings*: 'Let us consider as divine beyond doubt that which is found to be said rationally in the most excellent commentators; if anything happens to be found out of harmony and inconsistent with the rules of the Fathers, let us decide that it should be avoided.'[68]

What place does this have (1) in the prologue to the *Glossa Ordinaria,* and (2) in Augustine's work on Genesis? Let me address the second question first. Because the Book of Genesis, particularly the Fall narrative, is essentially an anti-narrative, a story with countless inconsistencies (several Creation versions) and surreal situations (a talking snake?), early Church and medieval exegetes aimed to make the story more understandable and palatable to their often unschooled audience. The fall of the angels and the serpent as the fallen angel Lucifer/Satan are just two aspects that were added by exegetes in order to make the canonical story sensible. Nevertheless, if one were to read just the Genesis narrative itself, and could find no reasonable interpretation, Augustine asks the reader to appeal to faith and interpret the story in keeping with the tenets of religious belief. Of course, here we encounter a major inconsistency between text (the Bible) and theology (Christian faith). If one were to read the text on a literal level, one would not understand the snake as Satan; in order to accomplish that reading, one must appeal to theological interpretation. This is exactly where the Church Fathers enter the discussion, in order to provide that theological interpretation – and gloss – on the text, leading to understanding and stronger faith.

This particular passage's placement at the opening of the *Glossa Ordinaria* is paramount because it establishes for the reader the tone, tenor and goal of the work as a whole. In some ways, this is an apology for what is to come – that is, in case the reader finds these interpretations unacceptable, he should appeal to his faith for understanding. The *Glossa Ordinaria* prologue is then followed by another passage from Augustine's text where he writes that it is possible to have 'different interpretations' of the text 'without prejudice to the faith we have received'.[69] This is repeated in Augustine's *De Doctrina Christiana*: 'Sometimes not just one meaning but two or more meanings are perceived in the same words of scripture.'[70] For the modern reader, this may seem revolutionary, but it is also surprisingly postmodern. It is, in essence, anti-fundamentalist and anti-literalist in that Augustine allows for multiple readings of a text and, thus, multiple interpretations, although no interpretation can possibly contradict the tenets of the faith.

Augustine's importance for the Middle Ages is, of course, unsurpassed, and the author of the *Glossa Ordinaria* prologue relies on Augustine for the majority of his material. And, although much of it is uncredited, more of this *Glossa*'s prologue is taken from Augustine than from any other authority. A survey of Augustine's importance to Christian theology in general and medieval theology in particular is unnecessary here.[71] Suffice it to say that, other than Jerome (whose authority was waning by the time of the 1480/1 publication of the *Glossa Ordinaria*), Augustine is *the* central authority for medieval biblical exegesis, and that authority is clearly reflected in the *Glossa Ordinaria*. In some sense, the *Glossa Ordinaria* is the product of a twelfth-century mind only in form; in content, it is a reflection of much earlier medieval biblical exegetical theories and concerns.

Of course, the study of authoritative texts forms the fundamental structure of education to this day. Without texts, university courses would be composed of nothing but a lecturer and students diligently transcribing lectures on paper, as before Aquinas. And it is certainly clear that knowledge and scholarship of the Bible were the chief impulses behind the development of Carolingian education.[72] Building on Augustine, Hugh of St Victor perhaps founded pedagogical theory in the early twelfth century. Medieval education became little more than explication of *auctores* and emendation with contemporary commentary. In a sense, all education is an endless cycle of reading, commentary, re-reading, re-commentary. The commentary of the next generation builds on the reading, commentary and authority of the past. In that way, the commentary of the next generation, ultimately, becomes authority itself. But in the case of texts such as the *Glossa Ordinaria*, the authority is culled from ancient sources – old is good, and the older is better. Thus we have marginal reference to the authority of the Septuagint writers as in this passage from the commentary on Genesis 50:1–3: 'et Septuaginta auctoritas, quae tanto divinitus facto miraculo commendatur, tanta in Ecclesiis vetustate firmetur.' In countless other places we find the phrase *Scripturae auctoritas*. Discerning the source of this *auctoritas* is not as important as recognizing that when *auctoritas* is appealed to, that is enough to make the case.

1.11 *From* Legere to Lectio

The movement from *legere* to *lectio*, from monastic reading to reading by a non-clerical audience, is one of the most significant shifts in the history of reading. In general, Lewis and Short note that the word for *reading* is *legere* pre-Augustine and *lectio* post-Augustine. It is important for us to understand this shift, because I believe it also reflects a different motivation and goal for reading. *Lectio*, with which most are familiar through *lectio divina*, indicates a more silent and personal reading, a process which follows *legere* or the collection of material. With the development of silent reading, we witness a visible shift in reading aloud for the edification of others to a more contemplative type of *lectio* intended to edify the reader; one of the indicators of this shift is a movement from use of *legere* to *lectio* to indicate the act of reading. Augustine most often uses *legere* to denote the act of reading.

Reading had been at the heart of the monastic life since St Benedict ordered that the activity be a part of the Rule. The type of reading Benedict ordered eventually developed into what contemporary monastics call *lectio divina*, and the reading of both Scripture and Church Fathers is ordained early in the Rule: 'Both the Old and New Testaments are read at Matins along with commentaries by famous and orthodox Catholic Fathers.'[73] Later he writes that reading 'the works of the Holy Fathers' will lead one 'to heights of perfection. For what page or word of the Bible is not a perfect rule of temporal life? What book of the Fathers does not proclaim that by a straight path we shall find God?'[74] The very act of reading Scripture and the Church Fathers is edifying, 'holy and sanctifying in itself'.[75] Ultimately, for Benedict, reading is a dialectical activity involving both eyes and ears and, eventually, the monk's own voice: 'Let us open our eyes to the Divine light and attentively hear the Divine voice, calling and exhorting us daily.'[76] As Roose has noted, the type of 'listening' (*ausculta*) Benedict prescribes 'develops into a true dialogue between the monk and the Lord through the employment of scriptural texts'.[77] This is most likely due to the sense that *ausculta* denotes not only listening but also obeying. As Jean Leclerq notes, 'the word "read" in this context can also mean "comment": the *Rule* will be read to him, and at the same time explained.'[78] Although Leclerq notes that the *Rule* does not state that the novitiate will learn to read: 'since children are offered to the monastery and destined to remain there as monks who will therefore eventually have to know how to read and write, there must be for them – and for them only – a school and also books.'[79] Leclerq later argues that *legere* means at the same time *audire*, so that a reader was also a listener. Indeed, this is a physical, sensual activity: 'when *legere* and *lectio* are used without further explanation, they mean an activity which, like chant and writing, requires the participation of the whole body and the whole mind.'[80]

This type of *lectio* is so ingrained in the monastic Rule that the scriptorium and/or library were central to the medieval monastery, and it is the monastic library that is the precursor for the cathedral school and its library, the university and its library, and, ultimately, the type of public libraries one finds today. The encouragement of reading as a holy act in itself lays the foundation for intellectual and spiritual development. I will discuss reading and reading theory in chapter 3, but it is important to note here the role of *legere* and the shift to *lectio* in relation to the development of the *Glossa Ordinaria*, a shift characterized not only by silent reading but also by a movement from reading solely as an act of edification to reading as *both* edification and intellectual development.

As silent reading took hold, the shift to a more intellectual type of *lectio* also took hold. By the seventh century Isidore of Seville explained that those who held the office of Lector in the Church were required to be 'deeply versed in doctrine and books'.[81] Elsewhere Isidore expressed his preference for 'silent writing which ensured better comprehension of the text, since [he said] the understanding of the reader is instructed more fully when the voice is silent'.[82] This is certainly contemplation, as in Augustine's reading, but it is both reflection and expression. By this, I mean that this type of *lectio* was not conducted only for contemplative reasons but now also for the purpose of sharing what one reads, developing a body of intellectual prowess and, ultimately, helping others to do the same. In this way, this activity contributes to the mission of the Church – to spread the Gospel and convert the masses through deeper understanding of that Gospel.

This shift, really a shift not only in writing and reading but a shift in thinking, is perhaps best reflected in twelfth- and thirteenth-century texts. It is here that we witness a shift from texts, as Ivan Illich explains, dictated to a scribe to texts actually written down by their authors, thus operating as a door into the world of scholarly and academic writing. As I here suggest, this shift also signals the development of the self in terms of a reflective, contemplative and thoughtful reader/scholar.[83] Illich explains a distinction between *sibi legere,* 'which means "reading to oneself"', and *clara lectio,* 'for the ears of others'.[84] As I have noted, this move from *legere* to *lectio* also indicates a closer and more personal relationship with the text, a relationship cultivated, silently, in the reader's mind, as opposed to exteriorized, by virtue of the spoken word. Illich goes on to note that *legere* denotes a physical activity as the word relates to picking, bundling, harvesting or collecting.[85] *Lectio,* however, is clearly more contemplative, silent, interior.

1.12 The Glossa Ordinaria *and Medieval Biblical Exegesis*

The use of the Bible in monastic settings is the chief catalyst in production of the glossed Bible and, probably, in production of the printed edition. Because 'Bible study meant the study of the sacred text together with the Fathers,' the glossed Bible became the chief teaching tool in the medieval classroom.[86] The task of glossing the various biblical books with the Fathers' remarks and exegetical concerns fell to a vast array of medieval scholars. But, I believe, it is their sources that are more important than their identity. In other words, scholarly attempts to answer the 'who wrote the gloss' question are not nearly as significant to understanding the *Glossa Ordinaria* as is the question: on what is the text based?

For hundreds of years, Church Fathers had written volume upon volume of exegesis in efforts to understand the Bible. For many of the Fathers, this meant a figural approach to biblical exegesis in which one section or book of the Bible (usually the New Testament) was read in light of its figural connections to another section or book (usually the Old Testament). Because no system of indexing had yet developed, this type of interpretation took place most often in the margins of the manuscript page. Over time, this type of marginal notation or glossing grew more integral to understanding the text at the centre of the page. With a highly sophisticated system of referents and marks, the glossator constructed a page that referred not only to itself but to materials and texts outside both the page and the book being glossed. The result is what we now term 'hypertext', as I will discuss in depth in chapter 5.

There appears to be little direct evidence in patristic literature guiding readers to gloss or annotate texts themselves, which is not surprising, since most readers in the Middle Ages, although they may have been able to read, could not write. Besides, the idea of a common reader glossing a text, particularly a sacred text such as the Bible, was considered blasphemous well into the age of print. The Bible was revered, elevated during the mass; the Church never went so far as to require a 'yad' or pointer, as was necessary when reading the Torah scrolls in the synagogue to avoid direct physical contact with the sacred text. As Mary Carruthers has noted, 'it is significant . . . that the manuscript illuminations [of the twelfth century] typically show [students] without pens.'[87] Instead, as she brilliantly shows, 'They would have mentally marked the important passages,' as memory was the chief 'tool' of education. The mind itself was developed as a type of hypertext, as the reader used memory as a text on which to inscribe information, experiences and data. Such memory use began to change in the thirteenth century, as has been demonstrated in the work of Richard and Mary Rouse, when works organized by index began to appear, in some sense replacing the need for memory to do the equivalent job of cataloguing. Many of those early indexed works were collections of biblical *distinctiones*, works 'designed to be used, rather than read'.[88] Whereas the *Glossa Ordinaria* was designed to disseminate scriptural commentary, the *distinctiones* of the thirteenth century 'represent efforts to search written authority afresh, to get at, to locate, to retrieve information'.[89] Although this represents a shift from the *Glossa Ordinaria* tradition, as we have it in the twelfth century, this shift actually feeds into the need for a printed edition of the *Glossa* by the late fifteenth century.

With the rise of the modern university in the late twelfth century, the importance of having reliable and consultable texts in front of the student arose. Earlier, it was sufficient to have the text in any form, and many texts were available in unreliable versions, in manuscript, original or copied. The majority of texts, however, were inscribed on individual memory. As the dawn of modern education and the university approached, the ability to search and retrieve an ever-growing amount of information from those texts grew in importance. The Rouses rarely argue that the *distinctiones* were important in the classroom. Instead, these volumes seem to have been more important to the preacher as a reference guide for sermons.[90] Thus, indexes begin to appear in collections of *distinctiones* and not in texts that might have been found on the classroom desk or the shelves of the monastic library.

The organization of information, then, became as vital as the information itself. Thus page layout grew more utilitarian; this is not just an aesthetic choice; it is a practical one that helped students with what the Rouses have described as new finding aids. Theresa Gross-Diaz describes this as a new approach to 'information management'.[91] Gross-Diaz continues, in the jargon of the computer age, saying that Gilbert of Poitiers aimed, for example, to make his commentary 'as "user-friendly" as possible'.[92]

In an imaginary dialogue between Augustine and Petrarch, published after the latter's death in 1374, Augustine tells Petrarch: 'This way of reading is become common now . . . But if you would imprint in their own places secure notes you would then gather the fruit of your reading.'[93] Speaking for Petrarch, 'Francesco' responds, 'What notes?' – to which Augustine says, 'Whenever you read a book and meet with any wholesome maxims by which you feel your soul stirred or enthralled, do not trust merely to the powers of your native abilities.' Instead, one should 'impress secure marks against them, which may serve as hooks in your memory, lest otherwise they might fly away.'[94] Carruthers concludes that the margins of Petrarch's books, which are 'full of such marks', are related directly to the 'secure marks' noted in the quotation above. However, it is never clear that the 'secure marks' are indeed actual marks in the text or instead marks, if you will, in the mind, intellectual holders.

1.13 Medieval Hermeneutics

Although Ivan Illich refers to Hugh of St Victor's *Didascalicon* as 'the first book written on the art of reading', perhaps the most important works on hermeneutics in the Middle

Ages are Augustine's *Confessiones* and *De Doctrina Christiana*.[95] From the opening page of the *Confessiones* Augustine is concerned with 'knowing' and 'understanding'. Nevertheless, if we look to Augustine for a holistic 'theory of reading', we are greatly disappointed. No detailed and structured method of reading is prescribed by Augustine. Nevertheless, discussions of reading and textual theory permeate the Augustinian canon, woven through the narrative of the *Confessiones* and underlying the centuries of commentary and discussion since. The lack of a theory of reading as such should not surprise us. 'Reading, though not an end in itself, is a means of gaining higher understanding; the contents of the mind can in turn be conceptualized through the sensory relations of reading – listening and seeing.'[96] As Brian Stock has argued in studies such as *Listening for the Text* and *Augustine the Reader*, reading in the Middle Ages was a complete sensory experience, involving not only reading itself but listening, seeing and even touching. 'The coming of literacy heralds a new style of reflection', a move from *legere* to *lectio* – a style of reflection characterized by a shift from the oral to the written, from the public to the private, and from the exterior to the interior.[97] This 'new style of reflection' demanded a new mode of reading and a new kind of text, something more conducive to the cognitive processes involved in reading (silently) and thinking, rather than primarily in listening. A type of hypertext of the mind thus developed, and the early attempts at interesting page layout suggest transfers of that hypertext to the printed page through the use of marginalia, interlinear notation, elaborate referencing systems and the development of the index. Perhaps the earliest printed precursor can be found in the complex page layout of the Babylonian Talmud, compiled around AD 500 (see illustration 1); the hermeneutic involved in reading the Talmud, however, differs in significant ways.[98]

Nevertheless, reading is perhaps more important in Augustine's philosophy and theology than it had been for any other early Christian thinker. The combination of autobiography and pedagogy found in the Augustinian canon presents reading as individual liberation. 'The person who knows how to read', Augustine writes in the preface to *De Doctrina Christiana*, 'does not require another reader to explain what is written in it.'[99] Such a person does not require 'another interpreter to reveal what is obscure', and he is able himself to 'arrive at the hidden meaning'.[100] In the *Confessiones*, he writes of certain books of the Bible, 'These books served to remind me to return to my own self.'[101] The very concept of the 'self' seems to have developed alongside the history of literacy as it is reading – that very solitary and very personal act – that catalyses the individual to withdraw and examine the self, thus leading the self to a closer understanding of, and relationship with, the divine.

Such liberation follows logically and directly from one of the intellectual revolutions of Augustine's time: the development of silent reading. Augustine notes, famously, in the *Confessiones* that he observed Ambrose reading silently: 'When he read, his eyes scanned the page and his heart explored the meaning, but his voice was silent and his tongue was still. All could approach him freely and it was not usual for visitors to be announced, so that often, when we came to see him, we found him reading like this in silence, for he never read aloud.'[102] In his study of the origins of silent reading, Paul Saenger connects 'the fragmentation of text' to the development of reading silently.[103] As the text fragments, it is the mind, through silent reading, that reassembles it in much the same way that hypertext arranges disparate textual fragments to connect and construct a whole. Reading silently – and internalizing that reading – actually promotes the fragmentation but also encourages the ability to rearrange the fragments into a new, and more personal, whole. This individual reading and interpretation are just what worried some, since it invited not only individual interpretation but also individual misinterpretation and, consequently, the possibility of heretical reading of a text. When one reads silently, as Paul Saenger has adeptly shown, one not only enters the world of the text, but also in some small way becomes a part of the text, engaging, disputing and contemplating the text. The reader becomes an active participant in the text in lieu of being a passive viewer or reader of words printed on a page.

The relationship between individual reading and the development of a deeper relationship with the divine certainly might lead to mysticism, literally a knowledge or glimpse of that which is hidden. For Augustine, as Brian Stock has shown us, reading was a 'prelude to mystical experience'.[104] It is through the act of reading, and the spiritual contemplation that followed, that Augustine gained entrance to the mystical meaning of the divine. Often this occurred through his reading of the Bible, but he did not limit such reading to Scripture. His reading of Cicero, particularly the *Hortensius*, which Augustine claims 'altered my outlook on life', is well noted in the *Confessiones*,[105] and that reading certainly influenced not only his own attitude to reading but his hermeneutics as a whole, including controversy, argument and rhetorical theory.[106] In *De inventione*, for example, Cicero suggests not only the importance of context but also intertexuality as important tools for interpretation. Cicero writes: 'So that if all the words, or most of them, were considered separately by themselves, they would appear of doubtful meaning. But as for those which can be made intelligible by a consideration of the whole document, these have no business to be thought obscure.'[107] Kathy Eden has remarked that Cicero encourages the student to 'consider both the *whole* text and the *whole* set of circumstances that inform its production'.[108] Eden later notes the presence of intertextuality in Augustine: 'To interpret Scripture, for Augustine, is in effect to weave its meaning.'[109]

This reading method built on Origen's allegorical/mystical reading of Scripture. Augustine quickly distinguishes between the literal and the allegorical meaning of the Bible, as in *The Literal Meaning of Genesis* where he writes: 'No Christian will dare say that the narrative must not be taken in a figurative sense.'[110] Augustine distinguishes between 'spiritual' and 'literal' meanings of the text. While the literal meaning is essential, the spiritual meaning often produces the most fruit. In the *Confessiones*, he tell us: 'when [God] lifted the veil of mystery and disclosed the spiritual meaning of texts which, taken literally, appeared to contain the most unlikely doctrines, I was not aggrieved by what he said, although I did not yet know whether it was true.'[111] This is Augustine's warning against taking the text too literally and not reading into it the figurative or spiritual meaning. As he writes in *De Doctrina Christiana*, 'all, or nearly all, of the deeds contained in the books of the Old Testament are to be interpreted not only literally but also figuratively.'[112] Certainly there are many places in Scripture where meaning is unclear and definitely not to be understood literally. Citing Geoffrey Chaucer, Jesse Gellrich writes: 'While these meanings are not "literally" present, neither are they hidden in the distant background: from the medieval point of view, they were written "with Goddes fynger".'[113] In Augustine's hands the text becomes a sacred tool used to further understanding and develop closer meaning of the divine. The text, Stock writes, is 'a direct, unprecedented, and decisive intervention in his life'.[114]

From the ancient world to Augustine, 'Learning to read meant going beyond texts and their seemingly grand theories and elaborate explanations, the obvious "dogmatic edifices" contained therein. One had to be able to "read" beyond this theory – check this more carefully.'[115] In fact, perhaps the most famous conversion after Paul, that of Augustine himself, began with reading. Nevertheless, in Augustine, 'the role of a book is clearer than the function of reading.'[116] The experience of illumination in Augustine's reading of Cicero does not include the Latin verb *legere*. Instead, 'what he describes is a change in "the heart".'[117] 'In sum, we have a conversion by means of a book in which there is a designated reader but no reading in the accepted sense. Reading is not a *cause* of conversion; it is a new *symbol* of conversion.'[118] It is ironic then that the *Hortensius* is a Ciceronian text largely lost. This would add to Stock's argument that it was not the reading of the text that compelled Augustine's conversion but the material book itself. Analogously, many contemporary Christians have been converted by the Bible, almost feeling a sense of kinship with the physical book, even when they may not understand what it is they have read. What then is the relationship between reading and understanding? This is at the very heart of the hermeneutic question Augustine fails to address. However, as we will see in chapter 3, reading is interpreting, a question of hermeneutics, and thus the 'correct' or 'proper' way (whether such a way is prescriptive or descriptive) to read a text is necessary to benefit in any way from its words.[119]

The very invention of the codex form led to a more active reader. Prior to the codex, most texts were read on rolls that required the reader to focus physically on rolling and unrolling the text.[120] Instead of concentrating solely on reading the words, such a reader is concerned with unrolling the text, co-ordinating his hands so that the rolls are even, struggling with the sheer heft of the rolls, and making sure not to drop either roll, which would cause it to unroll across the floor. With the invention of the codex form, the reader could now sit comfortably at a table or lectern with the codex placed in front of him – his hands are not needed other than to turn the page. This reader is free to focus on the words printed before him. The physical constraints of reading no longer exist. Of course, we may also posit that reading the text on a roll actually gives the reader more of a physical connection, a oneness with the text, but the freedom given to the reader by sitting in front of the text without having to use his hands actually to 'work' the text also gave him the ability to do something very important: to write in the text itself. H. J. Jackson points out that making marks in texts has been one of the more significant revolutions in reading. There is little stretch from making marks to glossing and then to footnoting.

The practice of footnoting is as old as writing itself, dating to the work of the Gnostics in Anthony Grafton's entertaining history. As peripheral materials meant to illuminate a 'main' text, footnotes both identify 'the primary evidence that guarantees the story's novelty in substance and the secondary works that do not undermine its novelty in form and thesis'.[121] From an old-school historian's point of view, 'the text persuades, the notes prove.'[122] One need only look at any contemporary work of scholarship to understand the importance of footnotes (or, for some publishers, endnotes). Without footnotes, the author's points are often questionable. Even when the foot- or endnotes are explanatory or tangential, their inclusion indicates importance – *auctoritas*. They promise validation, a sense of comfort in reliance on authority to support a claim.

The practice of footnoting a text is parodied in Nicholson Baker's wonderful 1988 novel *The Mezzanine* where the narrator glosses his own text in notes often longer on the printed page than the text itself.[123] Such a text prompts us to wonder which is the 'main' text, and it also raises the question of borders. Jacques Derrida exaggerated the deconstructionist attitude toward borders by printing his essay 'Tympan' in two columns (*cum textu*), with a running commentary alongside the 'main' text.[124] Michael Camille has noted the importance of the margins of the written text in the Middle Ages: 'Things written or drawn in the margins add an extra dimension, a supplement, that is able to gloss, parody, modernize and problematize the text's authority while never totally undermining it.'[125] 'The centre is', he continues, 'dependent upon the margins for its continued existence.'[126] As locations for debate, the edges of the medieval text were both powerful and dangerous.[127] The *Glossa Ordinaria* does not include any of the visual elements Michael Camille has so adeptly examined; its margins are filled with more text and not the sometimes scandalous drawings one finds so often in illuminated manuscripts.[128] Camille writes, 'The word margin – from the Latin *margoinis*, meaning edge, border, frontier – only became current with the wider availability of writing.'[129] This leads to the type of play in which Derrida engages in 'Tympan', where the margin is both border and edge; but if one stays within the borders, is one toeing a doctrinal line while the one who ventures beyond that edge and into the frontier is taking chances? Indeed, the margins of texts, from the Middle Ages on, often provide spaces for the voice of the oppressed or the disenfranchised. Much of what might be considered mystical in the sixteenth and seventeenth centuries appears in the margins – of texts and of society.[130] And, as argued in the final chapter of this study, hypertext theory, a concept delineated in the 1960s, actually intersects with texts such as the *Glossa Ordinaria* in its use of the margins, borders and the concept of notation. Of course, we need to make a distinction between authorial notation and reader notation, but this is a distinction that, largely, breaks down in a text such as the *Glossa Ordinaria* where the 'author' and the 'reader' often meld into one. If the reader becomes the author, as in Barthes's suggestion of the death of the author, then the *Glossa Ordinaria* and texts like it suggest an entirely new era of writing and reading.

But, of course, the most significant switch in reading theory in the Middle Ages was a shift that more importantly affected society at large. As a reading public began to grow, it was no longer necessary or imperative that texts be read aloud to others. This begins the practice of reading by the 'ordinary' person as a reflective and contemplative act, an essentially interior activity. Thus, the text came alive within a person's own mind, transmitted to the psyche and the soul by virtue of the individual's own powers, actions, and abilities, not merely relying on passive listening to the text preached from on high. Every individual experiences this for himself. It happens at the point when it is no longer necessary to have a book read aloud, one of the most significant advances in a person's intellectual development, usually completed today around the age of six or seven. It is at this point in a person's life that his interior development begins, and the life of the mind commences. We can see this especially in the memoirs of intellectuals (beginning with Augustine) where they note how the world opened to them with the onset of personal, especially silent, reading.

1.14 Implications

The scribal and textual tradition of the *Glossa Ordinaria* does not begin with the Christian West but was alive and flourishing in early Judaic and rabbinic literature.[131] In fact, it is clear that one of the predecessors of the *Glossa Ordinaria* glossing tradition is the system of glossing and notation of the Talmudic texts. Fishbane has also mentioned that 'One of the great and most characteristic features of the history of religions is the ongoing reinterpretation of sacred utterances which are believed to be foundational for each culture.'[132] As several Hebrew Bible scholars, including Daniel Boyarin, have noted, the Jewish commentators all but invented the concept of intertextuality.[133] The history of such commentaries as the Talmud attest to the earlier use of glosses and the *catena* or chain-link page layout. Whereas the margins of the text become a site for confrontation and dispute in the age of print, the manuscript tradition used the margins of the text more for edification and explanation. Naturally, these two purposes are integrated in the printed text, but once the text becomes fixed on the page by the printing press, the activity in the margins shifts from explanation to confrontation.

We will more clearly understand the role of glossing if we look at our own contemporary books and note the role of notation in them. Glossing is most often used today by the student who either underlines texts or uses a marker-highlighter pen. Less frequently, today, the student writes notes in the margins, and even less frequently than that, those notes actually 'respond' to the text. In 1907 Alfred Pollard noted that 'the practice of writing manuscript notes is dying out.'[134] 'There are', he continued, 'few Coleridges nowadays.' H. J. Jackson notes the importance of reader notation: 'they are valued *as a contemporary response.*'[135] Such notes also 'expose basic patterns in readers' practice'.[136] Most contemporary marginal remarks made by students are summaries of plots, much like the printed marginalia in novels of the late eighteenth and early nineteenth centuries. Ironically, reader marks made in those same novels often address the author or characters in the novels themselves. As Jackson writes, 'Writing marginalia is not so much akin to conversation or collaboration or correspondence as it is to talking back to the TV set.'[137] However, the notion that our glossators of the Bible were operating in the same way as contemporary readers today – with pen in hand, scribbling in the margins – is probably misguided. Pollard argued, incorrectly for the Middle Ages at least, that 'the chief object of margins is to give pleasure to the eye';[138] he may, however, have been thinking only of illumination. Although we know precious little of actual practice, we can tell from the manuscripts extant that the glossators worked meticulously, planned well, and undoubtedly concerned themselves greatly with every note and remark they left.[139]

The art of annotating a text is dying, even with the development of the electronic book and its much-heralded feature: 'take notes and save them in your own handwriting.'[140] Nevertheless, for the medieval writer glossing of the text was an aspect of his education: 'Annotation used to be taught as part of the routine of learning.'[141] Jean Leclercq tells us that glossing texts, biblical or classical, was 'a constant of medieval education'.[142]

1.15 Glossing and Glossaries

Glossaries apparently existed in the Laon cathedral school in France as early as the 900s, when we find evidence in Greek and Latin texts.[143] However, glossing a text as a tool for both edification and education does not appear to have been a concern in the Church Fathers. I have found no direct instruction on 'glossing' as a particular practice in any of the Fathers in the *Patrologia Latina*. Even Augustine, in *De Doctrina Christiana*, does not mention glossing texts to assist in understanding. Hugh of St Victor has much to say relating to reading scriptural texts in his *Didascalicon*, but he never actually touches on glossing. What Hugh does give us is justification for the *Glossa Ordinaria* when he writes that

> Haec vero non ideo dico ut quibuslibet ad voluntatem suam interpretandi scripturas occasionem praebeam, sed ut ostendam eum qui solam sequitur litteram diu sine errore non posse incedere. oportet ergo ut et sic sequamur litteram, ne nostrum sensum divinis auctoribus praeferamus, et sic non sequamur ut in ea non totum veritatis iudicium pendere credamus.
>
> (to interpret the letter safely, it is necessary that you not presume upon your own opinion, but that first you be educated and informed, and that you lay, so to speak, a certain foundation of unshaken truth upon which the entire superstructure may rest; and you should not presume to teach yourself ... This introduction must be sought from learned teachers and men who have wisdom ... the authorities of the holy fathers and the evidences of the Scriptures.)[144]

It would certainly seem that the construction of a Bible text glossed with the wisdom of the Church Fathers would provide both the authority and the evidence Hugh requires.

In fact, Hugh of St Victor provides us with much of the rationale behind the production of a glossed Bible. His *Didascalicon*, essentially a treatise on reading, was written in Paris in the 1120s and has been compared in importance and influence to Cassiodorus' *Institutiones*, Isidore's *Etymologiae* and Rhabanus Maurus' *De Institutione Clericorum*, and has been noted by none other than Beryl Smalley as a '*refonte complète*' or complete remodelling of Augustine's *De Doctrina Christiana*.[145] Hugh acknowledges Augustine's text as foundation: 'But Augustine, in mental ability or in self-knowledge, surpasses the studious efforts of all these men. He wrote so many things that no one finds enough days and nights in which to write or indeed even to read his books.'[146]

What I would like to do here is to survey the material on glossing and reading texts *c*.1480 when the printed *Glossa Ordinaria* first appeared. A popular question amongst recent scholars has been: how did the medievals read? The truth, of course, is that the larger portion of the medieval audience couldn't read. How most 'read' was through the reading of a preacher or teacher. Thus, any interpretative apparatus was effectively removed from the readers' hands and placed in the voice of the preacher or teacher who conducted the interpretation for the listener.

With the advent of a print culture, however, readers were forced to understand interpretative strategies for themselves, and they were helped by a variety of instructional texts. These included schoolbook-type manuals, early printed Bibles, and an array of short treatises and pamphlets, many not related directly to reading or education but taking the place of the hermeneutic type we see so frequently published today. Hugh of St Victor's *Didascalicon* is only one example. The idea that a knowledge of reading was necessary, particularly of books that contained Church doctrine, was perhaps first asserted by Isidore of Seville in the seventh century when he ordered that anyone holding the office of lector of the Church 'be deeply versed in doctrine and books'.[147]

Nevertheless, there appears to be little in the patristics regarding either the act of writing or of glossing a text. There is some focus on reading, mostly in Augustine, but the act of writing, either literally or metaphorically, is wholly ignored. This is disappointing when one is trying to reconstruct a history of glossing in the light of the *Glossa Ordinaria*, but it should not be particularly surprising. The early Church was not as concerned with writing as with interpreting, more concerned with hermeneutics than transcription, and that interpretation was primarily delivered orally. Later, during the English Reformation, Henry VIII made it illegal in England to gloss the Bible text, fearing that such apparatus would encourage doubt and the resulting disputation.

Once a glossed Bible tradition had grown throughout Europe, we find hundreds of manuscripts dotting the monastic and scholastic landscapes. Most gloss one book or a part of one book; some are more extensive, such as those on the Pauline Epistles or the Psalms, two of the most commonly glossed books we find. But how did this mass of manuscripts come to be termed the *Glossa Ordinaria* or the 'ordinary gloss' on the Bible? To answer this question, we must again return to definition. After centuries of use and expansion, the ordinary gloss became the accepted, i.e., the ordinary or common gloss or interpretation of the Bible text. The number of *Glossa Ordinaria* manuscripts attests to the common use of these glosses in libraries far and wide throughout the Middle Ages.

Whereas 'glossaries' did not come into fashion until the sixteenth century and the eventual development of English dictionaries, 'glosses' were used throughout the Middle Ages both for edification and for education. A gloss on a religious text not only helped its reader to realize a more full relationship with God; it also educated the reader in a variety of ways. First, a gloss was a language tool, assisting the reader in his understanding of the language at hand, most often Latin. Second, a gloss was a type of guide, standing *in absentia* for a physical teacher. As Guy Lobrichon has put it, 'une glose en était l'unité de base.'[148] Lobrichon goes on to draw a clear distinction between the gloss and the *sententia*: 'La *sententia*, c'était en effet le résultat de tout le travail d'interprétation effectué sur un texte, une belle phrase bien pesée, et sonnée, souvent l'œuvre d'un savant bénéficiant d'une autorité incontestée, en général un Père de l'Église' ('The *sententia*, indeed, was the result of all the work of interpretation performed on a text, a beautiful sentence well considered, and historical, often the work of an undisputed authority, in general a Father of the Church' (my translation)).[149] The term 'glossed books' begins to appear around 1100, when it was introduced by medieval librarians.

In some senses, the early *Glossa Ordinaria* texts served as commonplace books for the monks of medieval monasteries and, eventually, the students of the medieval classroom. The idea of a commonplace book, 'a book in which one records passages or matters to be especially remembered or referred to', dates to the ancient world but found its niche later in the Renaissance.[150] Nevertheless, we do find traces of it in early medieval texts. In his *Saturnalia*, dating from around AD 400, Macrobius arranges materials from a variety of sources. His chief role is 'author as compiler and transmitter'.[151] Unlike the *Glossa Ordinaria*, where, presumably, the Fathers are quoted verbatim, Macrobius tells his reader: 'You should not count it a fault if I shall often set out the borrowings from a miscellaneous reading in the authors' own words . . . but be content with information of things of ancient times sometimes set out plainly in my own words and sometimes faithfully recorded in the actual words of the old writers.'[152] We note the practice again in Boethius, whose commentaries on Cicero display 'no interest in the place as *auctoritas*'.[153]

The glossed Bible tradition fits into the history of the commonplace book in that early glossed Bibles served a similar purpose. They were compilations of important *sententiae* and even *distinctiones* on biblical verses and words. Their authors did not aim necessarily to 'write' a book of their own, but instead to create a volume for reference and consultation rather than one for direct study. Their authors picked the best flowers for a fresh arrangement – a *florilegium*, 'a collection of extracts taken by one person from the writings of others'.[154] *Florilegia* that collected patristic quotations were apparently used widely between the twelfth and fourteenth centuries. For example, the *Liber scintillarum*, a patristic *florilegium* compiled by the monk Defensor of Liguge, survives in some 360 manuscripts. *Florilegia*, then, may be seen as the parallel or perhaps the predecessor to the *Glossa Ordinaria* texts: a collection of important comments made, in this case, about a particular text.

The *Glossa Ordinaria* met several different needs: first, it was a Latin Vulgate Bible; second, it was a compilation of the best patristic commentary on the Vulgate. The problem for modern scholars is discerning just how this monumental text was read. E. Ann Matter has offered something of a prolegomenon in which she concludes that the *Glossa Ordinaria* 'is a particularly good example of medieval intertextuality', but her study is mostly suggestive.[155] Without truly understanding the reading habits of the Middle Ages, when a 'reading public' was in its nascent form, it will be difficult to address this question, which I will come to in chapter 3.

1.16 The Rusch Edition of the Glossa Ordinaria

By the fifteenth century, as both Smalley and De Hamel have shown, the practice of biblical glossing had largely ceased. With the development of a print culture, the *Glossa Ordinaria* tradition moved to the printing press. By the time Adolph Rusch published his edition of the *Glossa Ordinaria* in 1480/1, the tradition of biblical glossing had come to an end. Nevertheless, the printed edition became an important piece of early incunabula. For some thirty years, the misconception that fifteen editions of the *Glossa* were printed before the end of the fifteenth century had been advanced in the influential *Cambridge History of the Bible*.[156] Karlfried Froehlich, in his introduction to the facsimile edition, has sufficiently disproved this; he notes that 'The number would be more correct if it included everything that was printed with the word *gloss* or *glossa ordinaria* in the title.'[157] As Froehlich later notes, the Rusch edition, which he terms the *editio princeps*, is notable for 'its unique content, its typographical achievement, and the mystery which surrounds its origins'. Since the number of extant copies may reach 250, we can assume that many more existed in the late fifteenth and sixteenth centuries. If we compare this with the known extant copies of *The Canterbury Tales* printed before 1500, we find that the 250 copies of *The Glossa Ordinaria* reflect its importance in the culture – Chaucer's pre-1500 printed work survives in only two dozen or so copies. The

1634 reprint of the Rusch edition is extant in fewer than a dozen copies. We then come to a long break until the much-flawed *Patrologia Latina* edition of Migne was published in the 1860s. Migne's edition neglects to reprint the interlinear notes and so is an incomplete reprint of Rusch. We are glad to have the Froehlich/Gibson facsimile edition printed by Brepols in 1992.

The Rusch edition of 1480 is certainly a monument for early printing, but why Rusch and why the French border town of Strassburg?[158] In his overview of information technology and the eighteenth-century revolution, Manuel Castells notes 'the importance of local seedbeds of innovation', adding, 'technological innovation is not an isolated instance.'[159] The Rusch volumes contain over 1,200 leaves printed in folio format; the modern facsimile fills four volumes and almost two feet of shelf space. Although Rusch was celebrated in a panegyric poem as having freed the book from the chains of the monastic library shelf, it is difficult to fathom how the 'ordinary' reader could have handled such a bulky volume; in fact, it would seem that Rusch's edition is tailor-made for the chains of the monastic library, where the book would have been pulled from the shelf and opened on a lectern attached to the shelf, its chain connected it to a bar running the length of the bookcase itself. A towering 50 cm, the volume is larger than the 34 cm 1623 First Folio of Shakespeare.

It is virtually impossible to discern which manuscripts Rusch used for his edition.[160] Instead, the edition seems to be a type of recension or redaction of the *Glossa Ordinaria* manuscripts. While not necessarily painstakingly accurate to one or another manuscript tradition, modern scholars can confidently use the Rusch edition as an exemplar for the *Glossa Ordinaria* tradition.

Perhaps the most frustrating endeavour for a scholar of the *Glossa Ordinaria* is discerning how frequently the printed edition may have been consulted. I have found few if any references to the *Glossa Ordinaria* in literature or memoirs. Nevertheless scholars of history, literature and religion agree that the *Glossa Ordinaria* was one of the most important religious texts ever printed. On what do they base this argument? The number of extant copies combined with what appears to be 'borrowing' from the *Glossa Ordinaria* commentary and its glossing tradition in writers after 1500 would lead us to believe the text occupied an important spot on most libraries' shelves.

2

History, the Text, and the History of the Text

2.1 A Riddle Wrapped in an Enigma

The history of the *Glossa Ordinaria* is still masked in heavy smoke. Although some scholars have begun to clear the smoke over the last thirty years, what they have then encountered, more often than not, is only thick fog below the smoke. When the Froehlich- and Gibson-edited facsimile edition first appeared in 1992, it seemed that contemporary work on the *Glossa Ordinaria* could truly begin. However, precious little progress has actually been made. Apart from Beryl Smalley's work,[1] Theresa Gross-Diaz's fine work on Gilbert of Poitiers,[2] Mary Dove's edition of the *Glossa Ordinaria* Song of Songs,[3] and several helpful articles written by Karlfried Froehlich,[4] E. Ann Matter[5] and the late Margaret Gibson,[6] we seem to know little more about the origins and use of the *Glossa Ordinaria* now than we did fifty years ago. Froehlich and Gibson, who seemed to be pioneers in *Glossa* study, soon found the project too unwieldy – Gibson died in 1994, and Froehlich retired and never truly completed his intention to put together a comprehensive study.

Although volumes of individual articles have been written regarding particular manuscripts or manuscript trees, the central problem is one of cataloguing. The libraries, monastic, municipal, national and academic, of Europe are littered with manuscripts of one or another book of the *Glossa Ordinaria*, and cataloguing and collating all of them is a monumental task. In her article on 'The Place of the *Glossa Ordinaria* in Medieval Exegesis', Margaret Gibson recounts the erroneous history of the *Glossa*: 'Every schoolboy knows that the *Glossa ordinaria* is in two parts: the marginal gloss was written by Walafrid Strabo in the early ninth century, while the interlinear annotation is the work of Anselm of Laon in the later eleventh. Every schoolboy also knows that this is *wrong*.'[7] Until her death, Gibson worked to correct these erroneous assumptions. This chapter is a brief history of the *Glossa Ordinaria*, working towards and through the printed editions, in order to sort out the errors in the assumption Gibson noted and to move towards a more complete understanding of the history of this important and influential work.

In summary, Walafrid Strabo's authorship of the *Glossa Ordinaria* was largely discounted by J. de Blic,[8] whose research supported a claim made by Beryl Smalley: the *Glossa* was written not by Strabo but by Anselm of Laon and a great number of students in his school. Froehlich explains how Strabo's name became associated with the *Glossa* beginning with the 1590 printed edition. And Smalley has established that most of the *Glossa Ordinaria* and its tradition originate in the school of Laon. However, she and other scholars have also traced different strands of the *Glossa Ordinaria* to other sources. Let us begin, then, with the school of Laon.

2.2 The School of Laon

The town of Laon, approximately 150 km north-east of Paris, is home to one of the most important Gothic cathedrals of the Middle Ages. A centre of learning since the early ninth century, Laon produced some of the sharpest theological minds of the Middle Ages: Alberic of Rheims, Lutolph of Novara and, most notably, Peter Abelard, who harshly criticized Anselm of Laon's methods;[9] particularly, Abelard felt that nothing Anselm delivered in lectures could not be gleaned from books: 'Anyone who knocked at his door to seek an answer to some question went away more uncertain than he came. Anselm could win the admiration of an audience, but he was useless when put to the question.'[10] As G. R. Evans notes, 'A high proportion of the prominent Old Testament exegetes of the late eleventh and early twelfth centuries were associated, at least for a time, with the cathedral schools of Paris and Laon.'[11] The school of Laon is most associated with the brothers Anselm (d. 1117) and Ralph (d. 1131/3). Perhaps more noted as teachers than as theologians, the brothers conducted a school of learning at Laon that helped to make the Paris vicinity the educational centre of Europe. Beryl Smalley calls Laon 'the first concerted effort towards theological systematization'.[12] It would not be without merit to argue that the influence of Anselm's style spread well beyond the first half of the twelfth century.[13] Perhaps the cathedral school's concerns are best expressed in the allegorical figures of Grammar and Rhetoric represented on the façade of Laon cathedral.[14] In this way, the cathedral notes itself as a link between the old and the new, an attempt to bring two of the most important aspects of classical (profane) education into the setting of spiritual (sacred) study. Grammar and Rhetoric would also seem to allude to Cicero, whose writing on the subjects was still respected by the medieval mind, as is evident in literature from Augustine's *Confessiones* to Dante's poetry.

The school at Laon, often referred to as 'the cathedral school of Laon', was well established by the time Anselm and Ralph arrived in the late eleventh and early twelfth centuries. Prior to that, there is little documentary evidence that indicates for us what the school had been like. John Contreni has examined the period 850–930, and his study includes a survey of the cathedral and its attached monasteries, but little of what day-to-day activity, monastic or otherwise, may have been like.[15] Our knowledge of such activity throughout the Middle Ages is lacking; the medieval man rarely wrote about his own daily activity and practices, and we are left to sift through the scant evidence we have in order to construct what is, at best, suppositional. Nevertheless, cathedral schools such as Laon, which Evans has called 'The Axis of Paris',[16] were the focal point of intellectual development throughout the early Middle Ages. C. Stephen Jaeger has shown us that these schools were important not only for what we now call 'education' but also for social and ethical development throughout Europe.

Cathedral schools such as Laon were established particularly for the education of choirboys and often provided free education for poorer boys living in the cathedral's city. The goal of most cathedral schools was to train future priests. 'The cathedral schools practiced a pedagogy aimed at creating the balanced, restrained, decorous, "well-tempered" human being.'[17] Many cathedral schools developed after the decline of the monastic school in the late eleventh and early twelfth centuries.[18] Because this type of pedagogy is text-based, it is only natural then that we look to written work in order to understand early education in the Middle Ages. 'We do not have a model of learning and philosophy that is not oriented to the written word.'[19] Nevertheless, the history of the cathedral school is marked by an absence of written documentation. Jaeger calls this 'a charismatic culture' characterized more by oral teaching than written, so that it 'cannot be assessed by weighing and measuring its documentation'.[20] And, as we will see later in the present study, because Latin was the focus of so much study in the cathedral schools, and the connection between study of Latin and glossing is so clear in ancient and classical works, it is no surprise that the two foci of study in the cathedral school, Latin language study and biblical exegesis, would morph into glossing the Bible.

By the time we arrive at the Laon of Anselm, in the early twelfth century, we discover a manuscript culture already well established, having developed from the ninth-century obsession with and protection of the cathedral's manuscripts. As John Contreni has noted, the majority of the surviving manuscripts are patristic, mostly commentaries on the Bible. Studies show that the cathedral monks read Augustine, Jerome, John Chrysostom and Rhabanus Maurus.[21] The cathedral also housed copies of Origen's homilies on Numbers, Cassiodorus' commentary on the Psalms, and at least one collection of saints' *Lives*.[22] But the library was not restricted to Scripture and patristic work; work by Priscian (the sixth-century Latin grammarian), for example, validates a concern with classical works, particularly those related to grammar and rhetoric – recall the foci of study of Latin and study of the Bible as well as the allegorical figures poised on the front of the cathedral itself. The variety of volumes owned by the cathedral reflects the focus of study during the period – what Jean Leclercq has called 'monastic theology'.[23] 'The principal literary course of monastic culture may be reduced to three: Holy Scripture, the patristic tradition and classical literature,' and indeed all three are evident in the library at Laon.[24] Because what Leclercq calls 'monastic exegesis' was wholly dependent on 'reminiscence', the type of memory Hugh of St Victor recommends (and which will be discussed later), 'One becomes a sort of living concordance, a living library.'[25] The mind itself functions as a figurative *bibliothèque*, i.e., a 'book chest'.

Exegesis in the monastery was characterized, at this point, by extensive reading and memorization of that reading, the memory to be consulted later upon further and more extensive reading. Without printed work to consult on a regular basis, manuscript culture relied more heavily on memory to catalogue one's reading, compiling what I would term a curriculum vitae of the mind. The individual as 'living concordance' of a 'living library' is an accurate reflection of a culture for which memory was the most important faculty of the mind, a culture for which the printed text, as a tangible extension of that memory, would only serve to aid the further building of that concordance.

The assimilation and adoption of texts both sacred and profane is perhaps the chief characteristic of early medieval monastic reading. One is as likely to find classical authors, such as Cicero and Seneca, consulted and referred to in texts as John

Chrysostom or Augustine. John Ward has argued that the commentary and glossing of such ancient texts ensured their survival.[26] In his classic study of monastic culture, *The Love of Learning and the Desire for God*, Jean Leclercq explains: 'on the one hand, the medieval monks are acquainted with the classics and they use them: that is an undeniable fact. On the other, it often happens that they speak disparagingly of them and advise against reading them.'[27] Nevertheless, even if the monks had been cautioned against reading classical writers, it is obvious then that those writers were in fact being read, and their influence has been noted in scholarship on medieval theology, including Henri de Lubac's majestical *Exégèse médiévale*. John Contreni demonstrates that the cathedral library had at least one manuscript containing Virgil, Servius, Juvencus and Sedulius.[28] In the modern world we would not even consider the study of Latin without reading the 'classic Roman poets', but the concern of the Middle Ages was reconciling balanced study of the ancients with study of Scripture and the Fathers. So activity at Laon does not seem to have been confined to reading religious texts.

The cathedral apparently also manufactured books, though what is meant here by 'manufacturing' differs greatly from our contemporary sense of 'making books' and 'publishing'. Laon was a centre for scribal work and manuscript copying. As Contreni notes, 'Books that came to Laon from other sources attest to the contacts that Laon masters had with other Carolingian intellectual centers and belie the isolation of the school implied by the silence of narrative sources.'[29] Two hundred years before Anselm arrived, Laon clearly had men with the intelligence and the ability to maintain what Contreni calls 'an active scriptorium.'[30] Although he has been unable to point to original works being produced, Contreni provides us with clear evidence that copying, if not original composition, was rampant, presumably for sale to wealthy buyers in order to support the cathedral. Evidence of production at Laon is easily noted in the titles of works in monastic and academic libraries throughout Europe. The school even developed its own script, what W. M. Lindsay called the 'Laon *AZ*-type'.[31]

2.3 Anselm of Laon

Anselm of Laon, trained under St Anslem of Canterbury,[32] is one of the more important figures in medieval biblical exegesis. Anselm taught at Laon before he was made dean in 1110, and he became archdeacon in 1115. Although he never completed the task, Anselm had wanted to gloss the entire Bible; Peter the Chanter tells us that Anselm was prevented from carrying out the task by his administrative duties, something with which the modern academic can certainly identify:[33] 'the canons whose dean he was, and many others, used often to hinder him in his work, by drawing him into their lawsuits, making much of him in adulation, oppressing the poor whom he was obliged to protect, or badgering him to take part in the business of his chapter.'[34] He did, nevertheless, complete glosses on the Epistles of Paul, on the first chapters of Genesis, on Matthew, and perhaps on the Song of Songs.[35]

J. Ghellinck has called Anselm 'an important link in the chain' of theological thought in the Middle Ages.[36] He goes on to argue that 'Anselm paid no attention to the canonical collections which constituted generally the Patristic *dossier* of contemporary theologians. The reason for this it [*sic*] that Anselm wished to use as the sources of his systematisation only the exegetical works of his predecessors.'[37] Thus Anselm's importance lay in compilation rather than composition, with such lack of originality not uncommon in medieval exegesis when, it might be argued, little new content was being added to the canon of commentary. The revolution, one which would be followed by an even greater one with the invention of the printing press, was in reorganization, compilation, concordance, indexing and conceptualization.

When Anselm died in 1117, his brother Ralph continued his work, glossing Matthew and perhaps the Minor Prophets, possibly using work Anselm had left behind. Based on the opinions of Peter Abelard, the school at Laon did little to advance doctrinal issues, the focus being instead on organization and method: Anselm and Ralph 'stimulated the systematic arrangement of theological sentence-collections which lay at the base of the theological movement of the twelfth, even of the thirteenth, centuries'.[38] In his study of Peter Abelard, Luscombe refers continually to the 'productive and organized tradition of Laon',[39] highlighting the importance of Laon in organizing a tradition that had already attained permanence and excellence.

2.4 Gilbert the Universal

Gilbert the Universal, also known as Gilbert of Auxerre or Gilbertus Universalis, bishop of London from 1128 to 1134, is another important link in the history of the *Glossa Ordinaria*. Although rarely mentioned in encyclopaedias or histories of the period, Gilbert's life and importance were noted well for us by Beryl Smalley.[40] It remains unclear whether Gilbert was a contemporary or a pupil of Anselm of Laon, but he appears in a defence of another of Anselm's pupils, Gilbert of Poitiers.[41] Gilbert the Universal's obituary remarks his contribution to the glossing tradition: 'Veteris et novi testamenti glosator eximius qui Universalis merito est appelatus.'[42] Gilbert leaves an important leaf in the book that is the *Glossa Ordinaria*: a commentary on Lamentations, prompting Beryl Smalley to write: 'His work cannot be considered apart from the *Gloss*.'[43] In early printed editions, in fact, the gloss on Lamentations is explicitly attributed to Gilbert. Gilbert, who died in 1134, 'boldly put his name to individual glosses . . . Even he, however, was anxious to stress that his work was gathered from the fathers. Gilbert glossed the Pentateuch and the Major Prophets, probably Joshua, Judges and Ruth, the four books of Kings and perhaps he, not Ralph, worked on the Minor Prophets.'[44]

Regardless of that question, Gilbert's and Anselm's activities at Laon are clearly significant. However, constructing a documentary history of the cathedral school of Laon has proved difficult, and the school still has an air of uncertainty and mystery about it. John Contreni notes: 'the bulk of surviving manuscripts . . . are jammed into an old, black safe in the Bibliothèque municipale of Laon.'[45] He has also remarked the need for 'a study of all ninth-century intellectual centers'.[46] That Laon was a centre of learning is undisputed. Along with Paris, Laon gives us more important biblical manuscripts from the period than any other single site in Europe. The library itself at Laon is easily reconstructed, but the everyday workings of the classroom and the library are more difficult to hypothesize. Volumes filled with biblical commentary lined the Laon library shelves, a testament to the importance of such criticism for the students and the teachers, and these books were undoubtedly used in the classroom.[47] For example, one codex, Wicbod's *Quaestiones in Octateuchum ex dictis sanctorum patrum Augustini, Gregorii, Hieronimi, Ambrosii, Hilarii, Isidori, Eucherii, et Iunilli*, offered the masters of Laon 'a handy and far-ranging repertoire of comments on the first eight books of the Old Testament', including the rich commentary of Church Fathers.[48] The commentary tradition was thriving at Laon. The library seems to have had a certain obsession with collecting all of Jerome's commentaries on the Bible; Contreni lists no fewer than a dozen such manuscripts in his contents list of the Laon library.[49]

Contreni has been able to trace the lineage of many of the manuscripts at the Laon library, and this kind of record is important in determining the provenance and origin of later commentary. Curiously, the standard works of patristic exegesis seem rarely to have been a concern at Laon, as far as the library tells us. More often, ancient authorities were used to establish history on a particular issue. 'Glossaries . . . are rarely evoked,'[50] further validating the Rouses' ideas that the glossary form developed later in the twelfth century. So what did this important library contain?

Glossaries, not indexes, were helpful complements to the library's other holdings. Used as study aids, these glossaries were undoubtedly consulted by the student. One such glossary, the *Liber glossarium*, would have been vital, and Contreni shows that at least one other manuscript, 445, contains the fragments of several other glossaries. Such manuscripts provide evidence of constant addition and emendation by later hands. But it is manuscript 444, a Greek–Latin glossary compiled by Martin Hiberniensis, that Contreni feels is 'the most impressive glossary' held at Laon. The fact that this manuscript includes a table of contents is 'proof that the manuscript was a working tool often consulted'.[51] Although the Latin Fathers are well represented in the Laon library, it comes as no surprise that the most important Greek patristic in the library is Origen, whose ideas on biblical exegesis formed the foundation for the development of the school of Laon. The strong presence of Origen at Laon, however, betrays the contents of most contemporary libraries, few of which included emphasis on Origen, while the Laon copies of Origen's works 'bear signs of serious use by Laon masters'.[52] A complete exploration of Origen's influence on the Laon School is yet to be conducted;[53] much of the relevant work has been concerned more with palaeography and manuscript study than biblical or historical exegesis.

Oddly, little of Augustine's work, not the *City of God*, the *Confessiones*, nor *De Doctrina Christiana*, can be located at Laon. 'If there is anything remarkable about Laon's collection of Latin Fathers, it is [a] penchant for abridgements.'[54] The Laon library contains several abridged volumes of the Latin Fathers, including various portions of Gregory's *Moralia in Job*. Ultimately, the library indicates a working faculty and student population engaged in serious study and teaching. As such, the list of so-called 'schoolbooks', such as Isidore of Seville's *Origines*, is long. And because this library was obviously what we would today call a 'working' library (as opposed to a collection of 'trophies'), it is only to be expected that the books include tables of contents, glossaries, and indexes providing for ease of use. One wonders how medieval scholars dealt with the reams of manuscript pages in libraries without the use of indexes or tables of contents. How did they find anything? As Michael Camille and others have shown, they left 'pointers' in the manuscripts, cluttering the margins of the texts with their own notes, illustrative markers and, in some cases, cross-references. The books in the Laon library, Contreni shows in an appendix, reflect a solid foundation in both patristics and classics.

Valerie Flint suggests a distinction between the school *of* Laon and the school *at* Laon, the former being an example of what she calls 'a much larger exegetical endeavour' throughout Europe, and the latter being the physical school located at Laon. Thus, we find an overwhelming concern throughout twelfth-century Europe with biblical exegesis, a concern we cannot ignore as a contributing factor to the compilation and organization of the *Glossa Ordinaria*. However, it is difficult to link the school of Laon or the school at Laon directly with any prevailing school of medieval biblical exegesis.[55] Instead, what we seem to have is an amalgamation of several exegetical strands assimilated in a particular place and at a particular time. Perhaps it is due to the growth of monastic learning and the eventual infusion of that ethos into the general culture of the time. Ultimately, Flint argues that there was no school of Laon at all:

> To understand the place of the cathedral schools in the twelfth century world of learning one must look to their capacity to transcend these limitations and to contain these reactions. We may not take the school at Laon as an archetype; it may in some ways [*sic*] been an unfortunate accident.[56]

Marcia Colish has responded to this claim, arguing instead that 'system-building is not synonymous with school theology in the period, and that the doctrinal continuities, and developments, within the Laon texts document the work of men who shared an openminded awareness of current ideas with a discernible group identity.'[57] Nevertheless, biblical exegesis does not seem to have been at the centre of Laon activity, but whether this exegesis was indeed 'original' or merely an important stage in the glossing tradition remains open for debate. Certainly Anselm of Laon contributed important original material to the *Glossa Ordinaria*, but one still wonders how much of his contribution is organization and theoretical and how much is substantive. Curiously Henri de Lubac, in his sweeping *Exégèse médiévale*, does not devote much space to Anselm of Laon or to the school at Laon considering their importance to biblical exegesis in the Middle Ages.

In the final analysis, the school at Laon is perhaps 'only one manifestation of a much larger exegetical endeavour'.[58] After all, the period of time between *c.*1100 and *c.*1300 witnessed the compilation, if not the codification, of some of the most important biblical exegesis in the history of the Christian Church.[59] The Laon school is perhaps the harbinger of all of that work yet to come in the late Middle Ages and early Renaissance. Valerie Flint notes the frustration with building an accurate history of the activities at Laon: 'it is difficult in the extreme to find among these collections any real unity . . . [T]he unity which can be found obstinately refuses to be linked firmly and finally with any recognisable body of biblical exegesis.'[60]

What, then, do we make of Anselm of Laon or of the school of Laon? Its importance has been debated variously by Marcia Colish, Valerie Flint, Beryl Smalley and other historians of the period. Because Peter Abelard dismissed his importance, Anselm had for a long time been regarded as a 'theological has-been'.[61] Anselm's direct contributions to what we now call the *Glossa Ordinaria* may be limited to a gloss on Paul, one on the Psalter and one on the Gospel of John.[62] As a result, Anselm is perhaps more important to the tradition of glossing than to the *Glossa Ordinaria* itself. Ultimately,

Beryl Smalley concluded that 'Peut-être Anselm eut-il d'autres aides.'[63] Thus, the mistake of attributing the interlinear gloss to Anselm of Laon, as had been traditionally assumed, might be revised: the school of Laon is responsible for this innovation, with Anselm of Laon at the helm.

Although we have no 'published' text from Laon, a specific text whose origin we can confidently trace to a Laon master, we do know through manuscript evidence that glossing texts was one of the central scholarly activities. As De Hamel has noted, 'There is absolutely no hint of a Laon "booktrade" of any kind. It is difficult to speak of the scholars of Laon "publishing" the *Glossa* when probably they simply lectured on the text and made the lecture script available for consultation.'[64] The influence of this school on the glossing tradition is indisputable. From Anselm, we can move directly to Gilbert of Poitiers, one of Anselm's students, without whose contributions to the glossing tradition the *Glossa Ordinaria* would probably not have surfaced as it did in the printed edition of 1481. But first we must examine Anselm's colleague in the traditional erroneous assumption about the origins of the *Glossa Ordinaria*: Walafrid Strabo.

2.5 Walafrid Strabo

For well over a century, students had been misled by J.-P. Migne's attribution of the *Glossa Ordinaria* to Walafrid Strabo. Strabo is listed as the sole author of the work in Migne's *Patrologia Latina*, published in the 1860s; but by the early decades of the twentieth century, scholars had already realized the attribution was specious, if not altogether erroneous. Research conducted and published by Beryl Smalley, Margaret Gibson and Karlfried Froehlich has clearly demonstrated what Froehlich has called 'the myth' and what Smalley called 'a bibliographical legend' that Strabo wrote the *Glossa Ordinaria*.[65]

Although the Strabo attribution is incorrect, Walafrid Strabo is most known to us as a gifted ninth-century poet whose *Visio Wettini* is 'one of the period's finest pieces of hagiography'.[66] Strabo's name[67] does not appear as explicitly connected to the printed *Glossa Ordinaria* until the publication in 1590 of the *Glossa* and the *Lyra* in Paris. So it is not until some 600 years after its composition, and more than ten reprints, that Strabo became associated with the text. It is in Johannes Trithemius' *De scriptoribus ecclesiasticis*, first printed in Basel in 1494, that we find the first mention:

> Finally, this Strabus is remembered as the one who first brought together from the sayings of the holy fathers the gloss on the entire Bible which is now called the 'ordinary' and which others amplified later by the addition of many further excerpts from the fathers.[68]

Froehlich argues that Trithemius himself created the myth, perhaps after noting the name 'Strabus' next to one of the marginal glosses in Genesis 1 in the 1481 printed edition.[69] Trithemius does indeed mention Anselm of Laon, who, he claims, 'explained the Scriptures of both testaments by a new kind of exposition through an interlinear and a marginal gloss taken from the writings of the fathers',[70] but Strabo, because he preceded Anselm by some three hundred years, is credited with creating the *Glossa Ordinaria*.

When Migne compiled his text of the *Glossa Ordinaria* for the *Patrologia Latina*, he expunged any material that could not be argued to be by Strabo: 'every gloss betraying its post-Carolingian origin by a later name attached to it had to go.'[71] This 'myth' of Strabo should not be unexpected. The romance associated with the magisterial *Glossa Ordinaria* having a sole author is difficult to undermine. The modern reflection that a single ninth-century monk meticulously compiled the text not only deepens the patina of the work; it also moves the work into an entirely new class of writing – a text inspired by God and penned by a solitary monk foreshadows the type of mystical writing found in the Middle Ages when the mystic acted as amanuensis for God's word. With the text remaining summarily 'anonymous', such a mythical story of its composition would be wholly lacking.

Nevertheless, modern scholarship has proved that Strabo had little to do with what became the *Glossa Ordinaria*. What then of the Strabo references in, at least, Genesis? One of two hypotheses is suggested by Smalley: (1) Strabo compiled the gloss on the Pentateuch himself; or (2) a later scholar compiled the gloss, extracting from a commentary by Strabo.[72] J. de Blic has proved the second hypothesis correct. In an article published posthumously, 'L'œuvre exégétique de Walafrid Strabon et la *Glossa ordinaria*', de Blic wrote: 'il n'est plus possible d'attribuer à Walafrid Strabon la *Glose ordinaire* de l'Écriture' ('It is not possible to attribute the writing of the *Glossa Ordinaria* to Strabo').[73] De Blic illustrates how later compilers of the *Glossa Ordinaria* extracted commentary from Strabo and inserted it into the text in particular places; he provides the scholar with charts of the Genesis and Exodus texts, keyed to Migne's edition, showing exact verses and phrases that are Strabo's. There is little, and, as Smalley writes, 'the genuine works ascribed to him are all written out continuously and not in the form of glosses; so it cannot even be held that he suggested, however indirectly, the lay-out of the *Gloss*. He simply had nothing to do with it.'[74]

2.6 Gilbert of Poitiers

Gilbert of Poitiers, who is responsible for introducing the *cum textu* page layout to *Glossa* texts, is perhaps the turning-point in our understanding of how the *Glossa Ordinaria* was read. Gilbert is responsible for 'the first major revision in the text part of the Gloss', what De Hamel calls 'the expanded version'.[75] Gilbert of Poitiers, appointed bishop of Poitiers in 1141 or 1142, died in 1154. De Hamel has argued that by 1130 the gloss on the entire Bible had been completed.[76] More than any other early writer, however, Gilbert was responsible for transforming the look of the page in the later *Glossa Ordinaria*. It is Gilbert who shifted page layout from the *catena* arrangement to the *cum textu* format. Although it is certainly true, as we shall later see, that Gilbert is responsible for some of the most important glossed books of the *Glossa Ordinaria*, his contribution to page layout is even more important for the present study because his page layout is a significant stage towards the printed *Glossa Ordinaria* that presents for the Middle Ages and Renaissance an early version of hypertext. Theresa Gross-Diaz notes that the commentary of Gilbert is of particular interest 'because the visual presentation of the contents plays such a vital role in them'.[77] Gross-Diaz's fine study of Gilbert's Psalms commentary offers the only modern scholarly discussion in English of

Gilbert's importance. In her work, she notes that Gilbert is usually overlooked 'because his commentary consistently has been dismissed as an unoriginal expansion of the *Glossa Ordinaria* on the Psalms'.[78]

As with so many names connected to the *Glossa Ordinaria,* Gilbert was a student of Anselm of Laon; however, Gilbert is rarely considered as representative of that school. Having been sufficiently introduced to the glosses used to teach grammar and rhetoric, Gilbert moved on to Laon where he studied *lectio divina* with Anselm. It is while he was at Laon that Gilbert produced a sophisticated commentary on the Psalms, a commentary that would subsequently be included in the *Glossa Ordinaria,* a work which combines marginal and interlinear glosses in a single longer text.[79] It is clear that Gilbert's glosses on the Bible, particularly his work on the Psalms and the Pauline Epistles, were written to meet a need, a need for texts in the classroom, a classroom in which students were being trained to become 'professional' theologians.[80] As study of the Bible moved from the *legere* of the monastic library to the *lectio* of the classroom, new tools were necessary. The twelfth century in particular saw the production of a bevy of these new tools, including glosses, concordances and indexes. Christopher De Hamel has argued that Gilbert was not directly involved in this new page design.[81] Gross-Diaz, however, argues that 'The parallel-column *cum textu* format is a unique contribution of Gilbert to biblical exegesis.'[82]

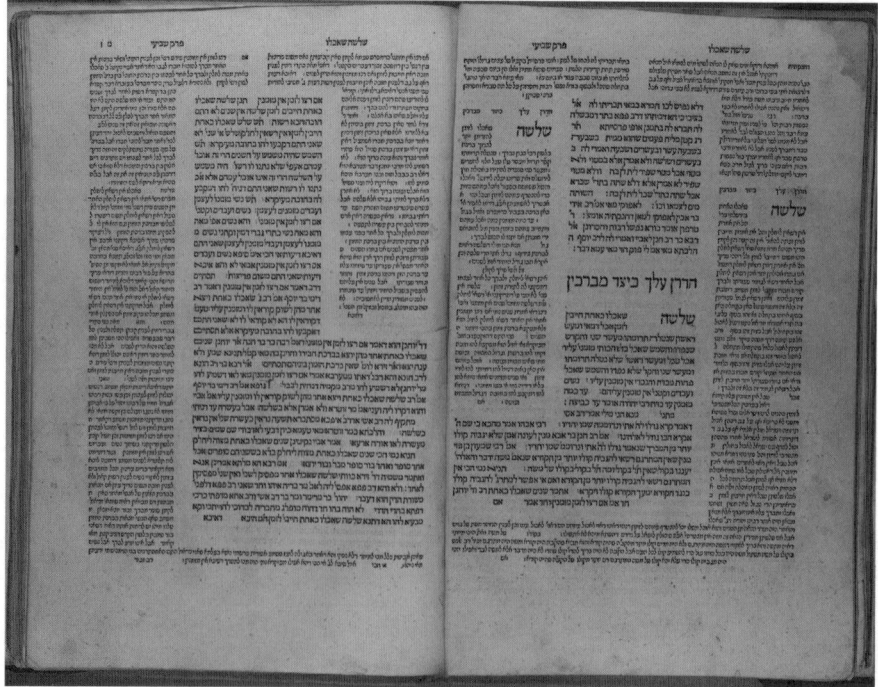

Illustration 1 Sample page from the *Talmud Berakhot*, Venice, 1520–3, fols. 46v–47r. Courtesy of the Library of the Jewish Theological Seminary.

2.7 Origins of the Glossa Layout

The *Glossa Ordinaria* format, as we see it in the printed edition of 1480/1, descends from the Hebrew Talmudic tradition as well as the manuscript tradition of the early Middle Ages. One look at the Babylonian Talmud and we imagine the *Glossa Ordinaria* scribe with a copy of that Talmud at hand for design guidance.

Gilbert of Poitiers seems largely responsible for introducing this format to the biblical commentary tradition. The majority of his Psalter manuscripts are in the *cum textu* format.[83] One of the central differences between the *cum textu* and the *catena* formats is that, in the *cum textu*, the complete primary text is sometimes sacrificed to keep the commentary text in parallel synchronization with the text it comments upon. This also means that the primary text is most often severely abbreviated. It is clear that in the *cum textu* format the focus is not on the primary text but on the commentary; thus the commentary makes the shift here to primary text (see illustrations 2 and 3).

The placement of the text in this way contributed to the shift to use of glossed texts as schoolbooks. As Gross-Diaz notes, 'the placement of the psalm text alongside the commentary [in Gilbert's case] guarantees the student immediate access to the work being glossed.'[84] In fact, it seems that it was in the 1160s that a change occurred in the layout of glossed books. It is here that the gloss and the text begin to intrude on each other's space, thus eventually giving us a page that looks like the old Babylonian Talmud, a primary text at the centre with marginal and interlinear notation littering the page around it. De Hamel believes this practice was introduced in the Peter Lombard manuscripts. Because the glosses were so closely paired with the texts they glossed, it became less difficult to discern the connection:

> The new form of layout largely solved the difficulty of knowing which gloss related to which part of the scriptural text because, now, as many glosses as were required could be inset into any given part of the central text. At the same time, however, there was no longer room for the reader to add his own personal glosses and an extra blank column was therefore ruled in the outer margins for the reader's notes.[85]

To be sure, as De Hamel has shown us, Peter Lombard's contribution to the *Glossa Ordinaria*, whether in actual substance or in tradition, is great. One of the greatest differences however, is the quantity of Peter Lombard's commentary in relationship to the text it glosses. His commentary often exceeds the text it glosses, and so the columns often do not match. Also, Lombard's glosses did not include an interlinear gloss. De Hamel concludes that the *cum textu* layout of the printed *Glossa Ordinaria* is attributable to Paris scribes working in the 1160s: 'It was, therefore, in Paris that the new layout of the rest of the Gloss was invented and, by the unusual method of tracing the "family tree" of a manuscript by examining its arrangement on the page, it is possible to claim Parisian ancestry for the glossed books written in all parts of Europe from the last quarter of the twelfth century.'[86]

The *cum textu* format is present throughout the work of Gilbert of Poitiers. His commentary on the Epistles, for example, presents the Epistles text in a narrow column on the left side of the page with the commentary in a wider space on the right side of the page. Gross-Diaz argues, however, that unlike the traditional concept of the *catena*, as a chain of compiled commentary with little that is original to the compiler, 'Gilbert's

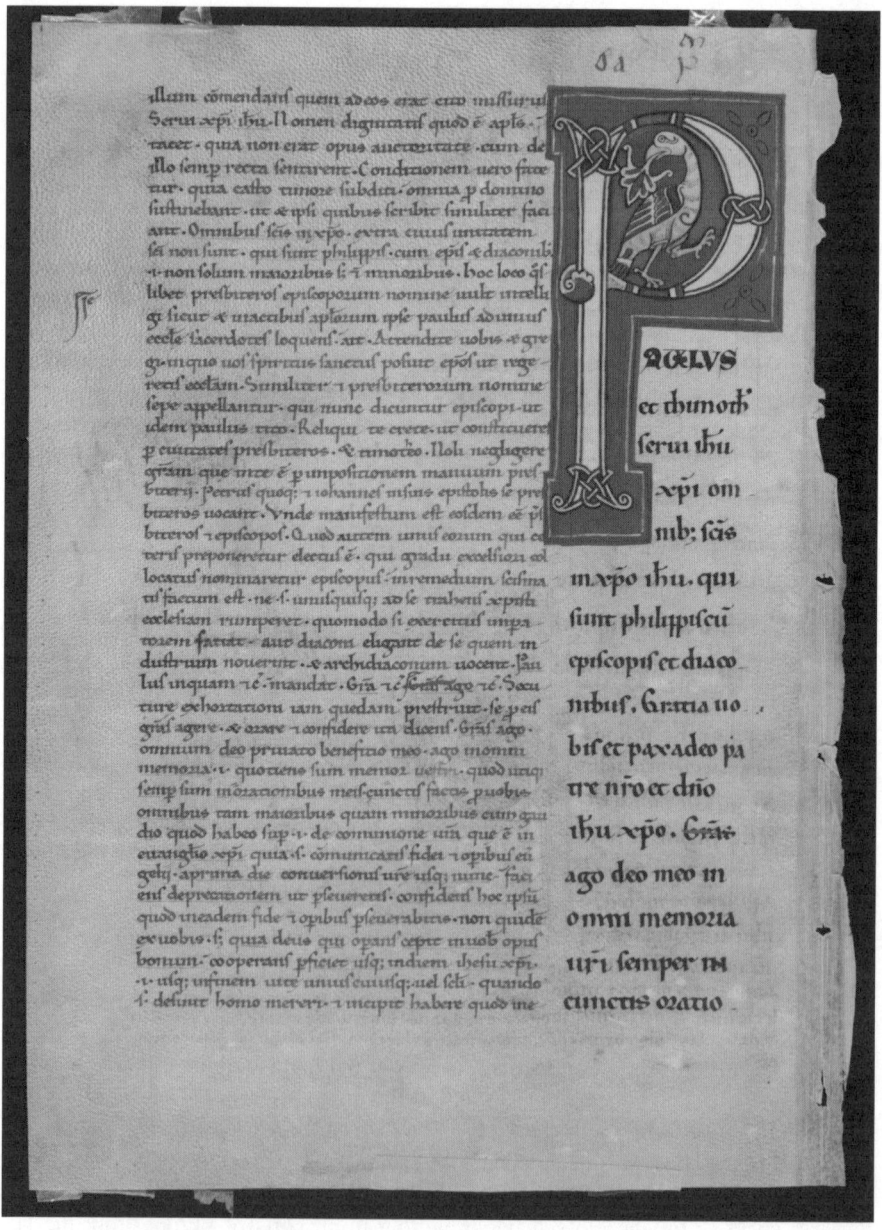

Illustration 2 Illuminated letter P from the commentary on the Epistles of St Paul, by Gilbert of Poitiers. France, mid-twelfth century. Manuscript: France, mid-twelfth century. The image is a good illustration of Gilbert's *cum textu* format in which the Bible text (in this case, verses from Paul in the right-hand column) are aligned with commentary which takes up the larger area on the page. Photo © Victoria and Albert Museum, London; museum number 9037B.

Illustration 3 Page from the *catena* commentary on St Matthew in Thomas Aquinas, *Catena Aurea, seu Continuum in Quattuor Evangelistas* (Venice, 1486). This work is part of the funds of the Biblioteca Valenciana and is digitized in the Biblioteca Valenciana Digital (BIVALDI) at *http://bv.gva.es*.

commentary is considerably more original than that.' She notes that Gilbert rarely cites his sources verbatim 'but prefers to paraphrase them to suit his argument'.[87]

In Gilbert's Epistles text, there are few if any referent symbols to link the text with its commentary. The chief indicator in the commentary of the text which it is glossing is an underlining of the word or phrase from the Epistles text. Font size for the Epistles text is larger than the commentary text, and it is indeed difficult to read the two texts side by side concurrently. The Epistles verses rarely line up accurately with the commentary. In order to get past this problem, in some cases, such as Gilbert's Psalter commentary, the text is abbreviated in, as Gross-Diaz notes, 'the interest of economy of space, time and parchment'.[88] She also remarks that, in Gilbert's example, what is left of the Psalms text is sometimes so abbreviated that 'one would be hard pressed to reconstruct each psalm from the lemmata provided, since the order of words and even of verses is often scrambled beyond recognition.'[89] Alternatively, in most of the *catena* formats, the sizes of the columns are fairly equal, with no priority given to either the primary text or the commentary. This is not the case with the *cum textu* format.

The *cum textu* format is ideal for the student. 'The placement of the psalm text alongside the commentary guarantees the student immediate access to the work being glossed.'[90] As the process and act of reading shifted from *legere* to *lectio divina* and *meditatio*, we note several other important changes. The nature and layout of the text are transformed, from a tool for contemplation and devotion, to a tool for scholarly learning and reflection. It is almost impossible to tell which came first: the dawn of the printed age, or the change in reading habits and goals. But perhaps the most important difference is a movement from study by memory and reminiscence to study by direct reading and reference. This is a movement also reflected in the increasing use of the gloss as an educational tool. Debate continues regarding the practical use of the *Glossa Ordinaria*. Whether or not it was actually developed with the classroom in mind may never be decided, but we do know it was used *in* the classroom from the cathedral school to the monastic library to the classroom of the earliest 'schools' of the Middle Ages, and its printing as late as 1634 reflects a continued use and continued respect for the work.

We might expect a text called the *Glossa Ordinaria* to have been continually glossed and updated, from printed edition to printed edition. This does not, however, seem to have been the case, as there is little addition by contemporaries in subsequent printed editions, the printer or compiler instead retaining a respect, perhaps even a kind of divine admiration, for the work of predecessors. Of course, as the Renaissance unfolded the rediscovery of ancient classical and even patristic work compelled the Renaissance mind to elevate such work in importance and cachet. And the late sixteenth-century obsession with Bible translations and Bible printings seems the likely reason that the *Glossa Ordinaria* saw a resurgence in the last twenty years of the sixteenth century. As the first English translation of the New Testament was printed in 1582 in Rheims, a new edition of the *Glossa Ordinaria* was being readied. By the time the Douai Old Testament was printed in 1609/10, fresh printings of the *Glossa Ordinaria* were also available. But, more importantly, we can see the influence of the *Glossa Ordinaria* in these English translations of the Bible. The profuse use of footnoting and marginal references points directly to the *Glossa Ordinaria* page layout and concerns. The Geneva Bible, printed in 1560, particularly reflects an understanding of the practical use of the marginal reference. And, indeed, the content of some marginal references can be traced to the *Glossa Ordinaria*.

2.8 *The* Catena *Format*

The *catena* label has traditionally been applied to a 'chain' of text 'in which the successive verses of the Scriptural text were elucidated by "chains" of passages derived from previous commentators'.[91] Borrowed from the Latin, the word was most often used to apply to Greek texts. Many *catena* texts are little more than continuous parallel-column commentary, often looking like a running glossary with words underlined (or in coloured ink) and their definition, gloss or explanation coming right after.[92] Such *catena* texts were sometimes 'one-offs', as John Ward calls them, 'monument[s] to private scholarship'.[93] The *Glossa Ordinaria* text is not arranged in true *catena* format. Indeed, the form seems to have been confined to use in the theological and philosophical commentary tradition itself, most often associated as it is with Thomas Aquinas.[94]

Gross-Diaz argues that the word was not used by contemporaries, either of Gilbert or of other *Glossa Ordinaria* contributors, to apply to the layout of the *Glossa* text. She notes that '*glosa, expositio, tractatus* and (less frequently) *commentum*' are preferred.[95] Instead, contemporaries more often referred to the work as 'continuous' (*continuum*) in order to distinguish it from the later marginal and interlinear notated works. In fact, Gross-Diaz argues that Gilbert's work should not be considered a *catena*, 'but as an exposition of the Psalter organized in the order of the psalms themselves'.[96] De Hamel rarely if ever refers to the *catena*, also choosing instead 'continuous'.

A true *catena* is a continuous chain of materials linked together by either common subject or logical chronology. Most common anthologies used in the modern-day classroom are *catenae* in a way – a chain of texts organized under a common issue, whether that issue be early medieval literature or the modern city. The *catena* text, presented as two columns, changes in minute ways in the work of Gilbert of Poitiers where the left column is used for the primary text, with the commentary text, running continuously, parallel to it. The nature of the commentary, as a continuous or 'running' commentary, is key to the *catena* layout. Dahan notes that only two texts from the Latin Middle Ages are true *catenae* – Aquinas' *Catena aurea*, a continuous chain of texts drawn from fifty-seven Greek and twenty-two Latin authors, and an anonymous compilation from the thirteenth century.[97] The *catena* is curiously both like and unlike the *Glossa Ordinaria*. In substance, the *catena* differs greatly: its author is merely a compiler and rarely adds his own commentary. He joins the links in the chain but does not necessarily have a hand in constructing those links themselves.

I suggest that we apply the *catena* as a metaphor to imply the linking together of texts to form a whole. The chaining together of texts to form links predates the type of linking we find in contemporary hypertext, which can easily and conveniently link texts, pieces of texts or just words to create a virtual *catena*. These virtual *catenae* constitute a modern hypertext, whether one constructed by the user or one pre-formatted by the author (such as Michael Joyce's *Afternoon: A Story*). This linking is so fundamental to human cognition that it should come as no surprise that early innovators employed it in the biblical glosses. To reiterate, I am not suggesting that the printed *Glossa Ordinaria* was a *catena* – it is not – but instead that we employ the metaphor of the *catena*, the text as a chain, to the *Glossa* text. With a growing number of commentators to draw on, the compiler/editor of a glossed text would naturally look to a way of linking the various comments on a given verse or word. By linking them together into a type of chain, the compiler offers the reader a technique of following a given thread. The *catena* form operates as a tool to organize and make interpretation comprehensible.

Where the *catena* format links texts together, the *cum textu* format may be viewed as the next generation in the commentary tradition, not merely linking texts but actually weaving the commentary into the text. No matter how important we may think the glosses to be, De Hamel argues, rightly, that the 'ruling of the pages shows that to the scribes the biblical text was more important than the gloss'.[98]

2.9 *The* Cum Textu *Layout*

Perhaps the feature of the *Glossa Ordinaria* most striking to the modern reader, and the one that connects it to modern theories of hypertext, is its page layout. With the *Glossa Ordinaria*, the reader seems to have several options in his approach to the text. He can use the work either as an index to patristic biblical commentary, or as a copy of the Latin Vulgate with explanations of the text available, 'without reaching for other volumes or even lifting his eye from the page'.[99] From the scribe's point of view, the construction of a page here is very complex.[100] However, the page layout of the first printed edition was probably not alien to the late fifteenth-century reader. Such a reader, familiar with layout of manuscripts and other early printed works, was probably better prepared to deal with the text than is the modern reader. The commentary tradition of the Middle Ages employed a vehicle in which primary text and commentary often appear together on the page. The *Glossa Ordinaria* page layout owes much to its predecessors, and a brief history of those predecessors will lead to a more complete understanding of the format. Reading theory and reading technique also play important roles in our understanding of page layout.

As many scholars have noted, the *cum textu* format is not new to texts in general, but it does seem that Gilbert of Poitiers was responsible for introducing it to the spiritual text of the Bible. Prior to this, the format had been employed in legal texts. In addition to his important commentary on the Psalms, this is Gilbert's most significant contribution to the history of the *Glossa Ordinaria*. Who exactly developed the *cum textu* format is not of concern here – it is as old as writing itself; it is Gilbert's use of it to comment on the Bible that is at issue. To weave human commentary into the word of God by placing that commentary in a column parallel to the Bible text was daring enough. The *Glossa Ordinaria* texts go one step further by wrapping the word of God in the human text, even going so far as to interject that human suggestion between the lines of God's word. Is this not exactly the objection that Protestants would later have to the Catholic approach to Scripture?

The palaeographic concerns inherent in the *Glossa Ordinaria* could fill several scholarly studies. And, in fact, more study of the *Glossa Ordinaria* has concerned itself not with the content of the *Glossa Ordinaria* but with how the texts were constructed by the medieval scribes, focusing on individual manuscripts. What we know about the medieval scribe's habits with the *cum textu* format is concisely described by Bernard Bischoff:

> Manuscripts which contain a text and, in a different writing area, a commentary, required a special layout of the page. The early medieval method was to write them in two columns

side-by-side; the column used for the commentary might have a different width and more lines for a different grade of script. Already in carolingian times manuscripts with one column each for text and commentary respectively are found, but there are also glossed psalters with columns of commentary to the left and right of the text and with double the number of commentary lines to text lines.[101]

Bischoff goes on to explain the changes during the twelfth century: 'From the twelfth century on the tendency is to unify text and commentary in one solid block of writing, but differentiated by scripts of different sizes. After various experiments, this goal was achieved to perfection in the two-column university manuscripts of Roman and canon law, in which the commentary encloses the text symmetrically.'[102] This parallel text, in which the full text appears in one column and a complete commentary on that text appears in a separate, parallel column, is noted by medieval writers themselves as *cum textu*. The *Glossa Ordinaria* takes that *cum textu* format a few steps further. Gone are the parallel columns, with commentary encircling/embracing the Bible text; gone as well is the complete commentary, replaced by excerpts and brief glosses on phrases or individual words. This is not a commentary that can stand on its own or be read independently of the Bible text.

The revolution here is, again, mingling the human word with the word of God. The visible result might (dangerously) be the swallowing up of God's word by the human commentary. The scribe's logistics must have been complex and complicated. Those interested in the palaeographic issues in the *Glossa Ordinaria* should consult De Hamel, who argues that 'The ruling of the pages shows that to the scribes the biblical text was more important than the gloss.'[103] Though this may be supported by the palaeographic evidence, I believe that as time progressed, particularly after the first printed edition, the gloss grew in importance. As the age of print dawned, and editions of the Bible were made more readily available, the unique component of the *Glossa Ordinaria* was the gloss and not the text of the Bible, which one could acquire through other, less expensive, means.

The *cum textu* format in biblical glosses is seen for the first time in Gilbert of Poitiers's reworking of the glosses on the Psalms and the Pauline Epistles where 'phrases of scripture, cited in explanation, are underlined in black or red but are written in the same script as the rest of the manuscript.'[104] Therefore, this manuscript is not explicitly a glossed text but is instead what Theresa Gross-Diaz calls a 'continuous' commentary. As time went by, the less academic or scholarly reader would require the full biblical text alongside the gloss, and so developed what we now see as the *cum textu* format. De Hamel feels that this addition did not occur during Gilbert's lifetime, and he has found evidence, in Magdalen College, Oxford 118, that scribes wrote out the full biblical text sometime after Gilbert's funeral.[105] However, Theresa Gross-Diaz continues to disagree with De Hamel's assessment.

We leave that debate in Gross-Diaz's very capable hands. Nevertheless, I argue that Gilbert of Poitiers introduced the *cum textu* format to the *Glossa Ordinaria*. The final printed page layout, in the Strassburg edition, is a further development of the *cum textu* design. Though glossing a text is as old as writing itself, the glossing of the sacred text of the Bible is a revolution in the process. Considering the primacy of the word (and the Word) in the Christian faith, a scribe who has the audacity to place his own words next to the Word might be deemed heretical.[106] That heresy never seems to have been an issue speaks to the need of early writers to explicate, commentate and interpret a complex text.

2.10 The Index

One of the most original components of Gilbert's work is his use of the cross-index, and this type of indexing is reflected, years later, in the printed editions of the *Glossa Ordinaria* where somewhat elaborate systems of referent signs are used. This cross-index, however, appears only in Gilbert's Psalms commentary (and not in the Epistles commentary). The cross-index is perhaps unique to Gilbert, and we do not really see anything like it until the elaborate system of Robert Grosseteste a full century later. The twelfth century, particularly, was the first age of compilation – a great effort to organize almost twelve centuries of Christian scholarship and commentary (the late nineteenth century, the age of the modern encyclopaedia, is the second age). Both Peter Lombard's *Sentences* and the *Glossa Ordinaria* circulated by the mid-1100s. Certainly the growth of formal education contributed greatly to the two works' appearance at that time, and the introduction of indexing enhanced the works' usefulness, both for private study and for classroom use.

Gross-Diaz writes that 'Gilbert devised his cross-index to facilitate study of the Psalms in an order other than that dictated by the Psalter itself,'[107] thus inviting study through a type of associative thinking, rather than the linear thinking encouraged by any numerical ordering of the Psalter.[108] Gilbert's cross-index appears to be a direct descendant of Cassiodorus' indexing in his work on the Psalms, *Expositio Cassiodori*, since Gilbert became acquainted with Cassiodorus' work at Laon in his study of *sacra pagina* under Anselm and Ralph. We see, then, a type of intellectual perfect storm at Laon. With the growth of formal education came a growing need for organized texts that could be used in the classroom. This, paired with the development of organized pastoral ministry in the Church, contributed to the development of such scholarly tools as the index and cross-index. Whether the reader be a student or a minister preparing for a sermon, indexes made consultation and compilation of biblical texts, references and commentaries more readily available. When we consider both that a scholarly work published today without an index is a rarity and that the lack of index makes consultation of such works more difficult, we can imagine what the eleventh-century reader had to deal with: a mass of manuscript texts, often bound carelessly and lacking logical order, that one had to mine to find a particular passage or reference. We need only image 'Pangur Ban', the Old Irish poem whose monk mined the Bible text as his cat, Pangur, searched for mice in the dark.[109]

Because texts such as Gilbert's Psalter commentary were school texts, the inclusion of an indexing system provides the student with the ability to cross reference and study in a more ordered and logical fashion. Such school texts were the 'focus of "ratiocinative scrutiny" and a source to be consulted for reference purposes, within the confines of a limited period of time'.[110] Prior to the 'invention' of the index, the reader's only tool for finding material was memory. As Leclercq writes, 'One becomes a sort of living concordance, a living library, in the sense that the latter term implies the Bible. The monastic Middle Ages made little use of the written concordance.'[111] The index then became an 'artificial finding device' for the student, although some evidence does point to monastic use.[112] In some ways, the page layout of texts such as the *Glossa Ordinaria* served as an enhancement to memory as a finding device. The layout of the *Glossa Ordinaria* page mirrors the process of cognitive recollection: the page layout reflects memory, especially given the associative nature of thinking and the somewhat tenuous connections the mind makes. Such connections are reflected on the *Glossa Ordinaria* page where connections between texts are not linear, and the reader is often led 'off the page' – virtually – to texts outside the one physically present before him.

That writing reflects memory and is a memory aid is not surprising – Socrates was first concerned with this in the *Phaedrus*, where he expresses dismay that writing will replace the exercising of one's memory.[113] Today's students often use written repetition and mnemonic techniques to remember vocabulary, scientific equations and mathematical formulae. After a student repeats verbally, the next logical step is to repeat in written form. The modern who collects books not only compiles a physical memory palace but uses his library's contents as substitute memory aids. When we cannot recall from our own memories, we use books as aids to rejuvenate that memory. In fact, libraries are in many ways compilations of cultural and intellectual memory, and an individual's library reflects not only that individual's lifetime of learning but his unique memory. No single person could possibly recall everything he or she has read over a lifetime with books becoming finding tools and memory aids, sometimes used as little more than the catalyst for accessing a part of memory that is, in what we would call in the computer age, in 'sleep mode'.

In the early Middle Ages, when the 'book' as we now know it was in its infancy, written texts were rarely used in similar ways for memory. Because personal copies were rare and often difficult to obtain, memory was still the primary mode of recall.[114] Individual copies of classical and ancient texts that survive the period reflect rigorous reading and glossing, proving that readers did gloss texts as aids to memory and for future consultation. As Mary Carruthers has noted,

> Observations by modern scholars that many full commentaries, such as that on Tully's *Ad Herennium*, sprang up virtually fully formed in the late eleventh and early twelfth centuries (as did so many other written scholarly tools) are best explained by their compilers having been able to draw upon a stock of glosses and comments, disseminated orally over a long time from one generation of masters to the next in monastery classrooms, and from one monastery to another via travelling scholars.[115]

Carruthers also notes, however, that 'the "authors" of most medieval commentaries of the twelfth century were in fact mainly compilers of a pre-existing store . . . After the eleventh century it was more usual for the glossator to sign his contribution.'[116]

It is possible to argue, then, that the glosses of the eleventh and twelfth centuries were little more than compilations of already existing glosses, and the *Glossa Ordinaria* text confirms this. The majority of what appears in the printed gloss of 1480/1 is not new: the glosses are transcriptions, paraphrases and direct quotations of material already available to the redactor/compiler. As such, there is little material in the *Glossa Ordinaria* that is truly 'original'; what remains original to the *Glossa Ordinaria* is the arrangement and the nature of the content, not the actual content itself. In other words, the fact that the Bible text was used is what is new, since previous glosses had dealt mostly with classical or legal texts. In this way, as Carruthers writes, 'every "ordinary gloss" was essentially a florilegium of Important Things To Remember, at least in the judgment of its compiler, arranged for easy storage and recollection.'[117] The development of a so-called 'ordinary gloss' speaks to the intellectual culture's adoption of a long exegetical tradition, so long and far-reaching that it became difficult to assign authorship – *auctor* – to the text, thus resulting in an 'ordinary gloss' that was developed 'from the mainly anonymous stock of glosses that existed before'.[118]

It does not, however, seem that once books had entered the classroom, students glossed texts or made notes in them as contemporary students do. No manuscript illumination I have found shows a student in the classroom with an open book and pen.[119] Instead, such students would 'mentally mark', in Carruthers's words, the text by memorizing passages or entire sections. Written texts worked in this way, as Hugh of St Victor observes, 'so that you learn outwardly what you ought to do inwardly'.[120] Reading continued to be spiritual practice through the Middle Ages, and the construction of memory was viewed as cultivation of the divine, the presence of God, within the reader. If one memorized the entire text of the Bible, one then literally had the word of God within him. Hugh refers to this as 'imprinting the form' on the heart of the reader.[121]

Texts then become artificial memory, both reflections and aids to the reader's natural memory. Hugh of St Victor's construction of Noah's ark as a visual aid to memory reminds one of the later use of hands as mnemonic devices and memory aids.[122] The Rouses have argued that 'Hugh of St Victor seems to be the last major figure to propose memory as the sole or principal means of retrieving information.'[123] With Hugh's death in 1141 we begin to see the seeds of what we now refer to as book culture. Memory for Hugh is achieved through 'orderly arrangement', because 'a classifying-system for material makes it manifest to the mind.'[124] It is through such arrangement and allegory that Hugh asks the reader to construct an individual *pictura* of the Ark, enabling the reader to accomplish 'the Spiritual Method of Reading'. This is, Carruthers and Ziolkowski note, 'the spiritual practice known in monasticism as *sacra pagina*, or meditation based upon contemplative reading of the Bible'.[125] This, I suggest, is what *legere* had become by the twelfth century – *lectio*.

2.11 'Education' and the Glossa Ordinaria

It would be well for us to understand better the state of education during the twelfth century, the most fertile period for the *Glossa Ordinaria*. Schoolrooms as we commonly know them today did not yet exist, but every monastery and every cathedral school did have a library of 'service books', with Bibles the most common.[126] This often but not always included commentaries on the Bible. Nevertheless, a library and learning itself lay at the centre of both monastic life and the cathedral school structure. Whether it is our concept of a library (a building housing books) or a scriptorium, every monastery had one. Until the early twelfth century, and the development of the school at Laon, 'real centres of learning were relatively few, and the best of these had their ups and downs, their periods of activity and of deep decline.'[127] At the oldest Benedictine learning centre, Monte Cassino, we find theological works as well as classical literature. Some extant work from Monte Cassino, such as Varro, the *Histories* of Tacitus and several texts of the Middle Ages survive in their only known copies from Monte Cassino.[128] 'That these books were read, as well as copies from a later age, we have abundant evidence.'[129] Of course every monk was, according to St Benedict's Rule, to read at least one book per year, so that the monastery library had to contain enough volumes, in both quantity and variety, to fulfil Benedict's order:

> In quadragesimae vero diebus, a mane usque tertia plena vacent lectionisbus suis, et usque decima hora plena operentur quod eis iniungitur. In quibus diebus quadragesimae accipiant omnes singulos codices de bibliotheca, quos per ordinem ex integro legant; qui codices in caput quadragesimae dandi sunt.
>
> (During Lent the brothers shall devote themselves to reading until the end of the third hour. Then they will work at their assigned tasks until the end of the tenth hour. Also, during this time, each monk shall receive a book from the library, which he should read carefully cover to cover. These books should be handed out at the beginning of Lent.)[130]

The active mind was integral to the Benedictine Rule, and the prime contributor to that activity was reading. Benedict indicated reading as a remedy for idleness.[131] However, he does go on to indicate the importance of reading as *lectio divina* and as a tool to assist meditation and contemplation. As Terrence Kardong writes, 'for the early monks, *lectio divina* was not a matter of scanning book after book for pious thoughts. Rather, it was the leisurely savoring of biblical texts that were mostly committed to memory. Some of this memorization was done for use in the Divine Office, but much of it was meant to equip the person for private rumination.'[132] As Jean Leclercq notes, 'There is no Benedictine life without literature.'[133] Bec Abbey, a Benedictine monastery in Normandy founded in 1039, was 'the most famous intellectual centre of the later eleventh century' and may have been the school of Anselm of Laon.[134] By the early twelfth century Bec had a library of 164 volumes, and it received 113 more from Bayeux in 1164.[135]

How did the instructors teach? What texts did they use? In what ways? Simply, we are just not sure. John Contreni writes, 'No Laon master stimulated a student to preserve a record of his teaching techniques, his interests, and his students.'[136] Library contents are easily verified through extant catalogues, but a student-written memoir or account of his years at the school seems never to have been written. As a result, we are left to speculate. 'Until problems of authorship [of works in the library] are resolved very little can safely be said about "thought" at the school of Laon.'[137]

What can we speculate? Certainly Bible study was at the centre of the curriculum, with much of the commentary written by the masters at the school itself. Whether or not the students added to that commentary, glossing glosses, is less certain. Certainly the cathedral and monastic libraries were ripe with patristic commentary, and Contreni believes the books could have been used in the school. Students also appear to have had access to classical authors such as Virgil. In fact, many of the major marginal sources in the *Glossa Ordinaria* appear in the library catalogues at Laon. Ultimately, such sources may have led both master and student at Laon to gloss a biblical text of his own, using the sources at hand.

We cannot overstate the importance of such a text. Its availability must have meant that the process of scriptural and patristic study would not only be easier, but such study would be available to a greater audience. There is little doubt about the impact of indexing on learning; however, I believe that the introduction of the parallel-column *cum textu* format was of equal importance as it presented the potential student with a contained course of biblical study, as well as the ability to conduct that study in solitude, without the aid of a reader or other instructor.

Theresa Gross-Diaz has noted that, at least for Gilbert's Psalms commentary, 'the visual presentation of the contents plays such a vital role in them.'[138] What Gross-Diaz terms the 'gilbertine' format is made up of two components: a set of marginal symbols, and the page layout itself 'in which commented text . . . runs in a column parallel to the commentary'.[139] The commentary, most often marginal references to patristic and Carolingian sources, offers the reader an entrée to the source material, often dramatically abbreviating and/or paraphrasing the material. As such, it is clear that the commentary was not meant to stand alone but was meant as an impetus for the reader to explore the cited work further. Whether Gilbert actually had a hand in the design of these pages is questionable, but it is a question not important to the present study.[140]

2.12 The Written Text as 'Artificial Memory'

When one wants information on the importance of memory in the Middle Ages, there is no finer source than Hugh of St Victor, and, because he predated the age of print by about 500 years, his discussions of memory are inherently related to a movement from psychological memory to the use of text as memory. The introduction of printed texts signals perhaps the most significant shift in the history of memory: a movement from memorization to the use of printed works as aids to memory. Mary Carruthers notes that the *catena* format uses texts such as the Bible and its commentaries and 'reproduces its memorial organization'.[141] The physical construction and layout of the printed text are inherently related to the use of those texts. Memory 'also signifies the process by which a work of literature becomes institutionalized'.[142]

In two works, particularly, Hugh outlines techniques for memorization and stresses the importance of memory: the individual who can remember history, for example, 'will find that he has built a good foundation for himself, onto which he can assemble afterward anything by reading and lecture without difficulty and rapidly take it in and retain it for a long time'.[143] In *The Three Best Memory Aids for Learning History* Hugh offers a technique for memorization through classification. Because 'Confusion is the mother of ignorance and forgetfulness', Hugh counsels the student to 'Dispose and separate each single thing into its own place.'[144] His other work on memory, *A Little Book about Constructing Noah's Ark*, was perhaps more widely read. In its fifteen brief chapters Hugh has the reader of the biblical text construct, either physically on paper or cognitively in the mind, Noah's ark as he reads through the physical description of the ark. 'The task of drawing Hugh describes is by no means easy, and Hugh sometimes anticipates or even contradicts himself.'[145] From these two short works we find a concern with the relationship of memory to printed matter, but, more importantly, we find the utilization of the printed material as both an aid and augmentation/supplement to memory. Thus, in Hugh of St Victor we begin to see how reading the written text can expand and help build one's memory, but also how the text can be used in place of memory. We often talk, today, about not being able to remember 'everything', and many now use their personal libraries as stand-ins for memory; although they have read the material, it is impossible to retain all of the information, and the books are used as aids.

Nevertheless, Hugh is quick to dismiss those who spend their days engrossed in study but, because they have not mastered the art of memorization, really do not learn anything: 'we find many who study but few who are wise.'[146] Students are 'not to rejoice a great deal' because they have read many texts, 'but because you have been able to retain them'.[147] 'Memory', he claims, 'retains through gathering', and from this it is not difficult to move to the *florilegia* and anthologies that collected texts throughout the Middle Ages.[148] This retention through gathering makes *legere* the conduit to *memoria*.

This leads us to what Hugh says about reading itself. In the *Didascalicon* he writes that 'Aptitude gets practice from two things – reading and meditation. Reading consists of forming our minds upon rules and precepts taken from books, and it is of three types: the teacher's, the learner's, and the independent reader's. For we say, "I am reading the book *to* him", "I am reading the book *under* him", and "I am reading the book."'[149] It is with the third, what Hugh calls 'the independent reader', that I am concerned, because this reader has presumably moved beyond the stage of the learner – which is the condition of the first two readers – and has assumed a posture of reading that implies a mind that is self-sustaining and growing under its own powers. This is the glossing mind, the mind that reads with an eye to making connections and relationships to previously read materials and knowledge, a mind actively engaged in the type of thinking replicated by hypertext. This is the reader who has integrated *legere* and *lectio*, producing what we might perhaps term a third activity: *glōssā*. The act of glossing, whether literally with a pen or figuratively with one's memory, is more active than merely *lectio* or *legere* because it involves the reader putting his *memoria* into action instead of merely filing away what he is reading; this is a retrieval process and a compilation more than merely filing. 'Re-collection is not passive, but rather an activity involving human will and thought.'[150] This contributes to the phrase 'make memory' – memories are indeed constructed and reconstructed, producing a layered psychic phenomenon. When a reader encounters a new text, his memory is reactivated and new layers of memory are added with the new reading.

Even in the early Church, reading, education and memory were innately related. In many instances, such memory was cultivated by repeated reading of a particular phrase or sentence, thus connecting the activity to meditation. As Hugh of St Victor writes, 'Meditation takes its start from reading but is bound by none of reading's rules or precepts.'[151] The 'consummation' of learning 'lies in meditation'.[152] This is certainly education as contemplation, and it recalls the phrase used by early monks who called their meditation practice *mneme theou* or 'memory of God'.[153] Of course, in the early Church and throughout the Middle Ages, the goal of education was closeness to God through contemplative, sometimes ascetic, practice. How, then, do reading and glossing a text fit into this contemplation? We only have to look to Augustine who clearly tells us that reading is a form of celebrating God, particularly when one is reading and memorizing Scripture. So reading and memory are, for Augustine, intimately related.

Memory for Augustine 'is the locus of the self':[154] 'In my memory . . . I meet myself – I recall myself, what I have done, when and where and in what state of mind I was when I did it.'[155] O'Donnell notes the 'perceived decay' of memory techniques 'in the face of literacy and of artificial devices to counterfeit their restoration'.[156] Nevertheless, as Brian Stock writes, reading is one avenue to self-improvement in Augustine: 'The key to self-improvement lies in replacing one type of patterned behaviour with another and, in Augustine's view, in attaching improvement through memory to a nonpersonal framework through the institution of reading.'[157] Although he rarely refers to a written text, it is clear that Augustine's memory is both compiled by and aided by his reading. Particularly in books 10–12 of the *Confessiones*, Augustine outlines his ideas on memory, some of which are elaborated on in *De Doctrina Christiana*. For Augustine, 'reading is a "manifesting", a making apparent, of his self.'[158]

Both Hugh of St Victor and Augustine owe great debts to Plato, whose *Phaedrus* outlines a Socratic/Platonic theory of memory. Socrates implores Phaedrus to recite a speech from memory, but Phaedrus pleads that he 'did not memorize the speech word for word' but instead could give 'a careful summary of its general sense'.[159] In Socrates' narrative, Thamus worries that writing 'will introduce forgetfullness into the soul of those who learn it: they will not practice using their memory because they will put their trust in writing.'[160] Writing 'will enable them to hear many things without being properly taught, and they will imagine that they have come to know much while for the most part they will know nothing. And they will be difficult to get along with, since they will merely appear to be wise instead of really being so.'[161] This sounds a great deal like Hugh of St Victor's fear that 'many study but few are wise,' and this fear persists throughout the Middle Ages in many texts where book learning is placed below experience in an educational and spiritual hierarchy.

2.13 The Glossa Ordinaria *as 'Printed Memory'*

The type of memory embraced by the Middle Ages, and earlier, was, one might say, replaced by the written text and augmented by the act of glossing. Memorization of Scripture eventually metamorphosed to use of the printed text of the Bible, particularly with the addition of marginal and interlinear notation. I argue here that glossing in some ways replaced the process of formal memorization, filling a role as the book culture developed and mere volume of material to be memorized surpassed any single individual's abilities to do so. The glossator replaces the lector; glossing improves upon the collecting and gathering of *legere*. If we consider a 'reader' in Hugh of St Victor's time, we realize that he is someone who has developed a keen ability to memorize, to gather information into a personal memory palace. He is able to file and retrieve information and texts with astonishing accuracy. The majority of his 'file space' is taken up by biblical materials – either the Bible texts themselves or a select number of commentaries. As the patristic era moved toward a close, and the number of manuscripts throughout Europe increased, the ability for this individual to keep track of the volume of material was challenged. Give this individual a pen and permit him to write in the text – and then, importantly, keep the text in his possession – and you have just increased his memory perhaps a hundredfold. His memory can now be inscribed on the page, reinforcing, concretizing, and perhaps employing Hugh of St Victor's method of diagramming as an aid to memorization.

Such a 'reader' has the ability to link texts and ideas in his mind, joining together memorized texts or information in much the same way that a hypertext system does electronically. The modern-day computer user is, cognitively, the beneficiary of the medieval reader. That reader accomplished intangibly/psychically what the modern computer user does with bytes and electrical current. As Mary Carruthers has duly noted, the medieval mind did not distrust memory as we do today; in fact, memory was valued over some written texts because, it was believed, an individual's memory could be more accurate than a faulty text.[162] 'Having a good memory is virtually as good as having the book itself.'[163] This argument is similar to Socrates'. And as we move through the Middle Ages and into the English Renaissance, the process of glossing texts became more commonplace, leading, in fact, to the commonplace book. As the volume of material increased, it became clear to the reader that holding – and retaining – all of the read information would be increasingly unlikely. Glossing personal copies of texts then became a way of individualizing copies of works, leading to the popular practice of keeping a commonplace book.

2.14 The Printed Edition

Many factors contributed to the first printed edition of the *Glossa Ordinaria* in 1480/1. Although *Glossa Ordinaria* material had circulated throughout Europe for close to 500 years, all was, of course, in manuscript. The first printed edition is a landmark in incunabula. It has been noted not only for its content but for its typography and for the mysterious shroud over its origins. Descriptions of the volumes litter bibliographic studies of the eighteenth and nineteenth centuries. Karlfried Froehlich's history of the printed *Glossa Ordinaria*, in the introduction to the facsimile edition, is so thorough that I have used it liberally throughout this section. Additionally, Froehlich has published a series of indispensable articles on the printer, Adolph Rusch, and the edition.

As early as 1776, Andreas Gottlieb Masch's *Beiträge zur Geschichte merkwürdiger Bücher* noted that the 1480/1 edition is the only one to present the complete Latin Vulgate with the double gloss. As printed in 1480/1, the work comprises 1,211 leaves gathered in 155 quires and printed in folio format. The bound volumes take up more than a foot and a half of shelf space. Significant is the impressive number of extant copies which Froehlich notes: between 180 and 250. The first edition was expensive – between 23 and 30 guilders – but it nevertheless achieved impressive sales and, Froehlich writes, 'had a general appeal that went beyond the ordinary';[164] even the 1992 facsimile edition sold for more than US$1,000. No doubt there was a certain pride associated with owning one of the original sets, something akin to owning the entire set of Harvard Classics, the complete works of Dickens in an impressive edition, or Audubon's *Birds of America* in the elephant folio edition. This does however pose a nagging question: how many of those who purchased and owned that first edition of the *Glossa Ordinaria* actually used it or even cracked its spine? Was it like one of our contemporary 'best-sellers', a book everyone has to own but few actually read? We cannot know, but we have yet to surmise the work's influence on the European intellectual world which can, in some ways, be related to its use.

The printed edition of 1480/1 has an interesting history of its own. With few exceptions, scholars have been unable to trace the different books to specific manuscripts with any certainty. As Karlfried Froehlich has noted, the first printed edition 'signaled a veritable revolution with respect to the availability of one of the most important sources of patristic exegesis for medieval theologians'.[165] Prior to 1480/1, if one wanted to consult what was commonly called the *Glossa Ordinaria*, one would have only a particular manuscript of perhaps four or five books. A complete set of the glossed Bible would have filled between nineteen and twenty-three volumes.[166] Such a collection was not unheard of, as Christopher De Hamel has shown, but it is not the rule by any means.

Because of its size, clearly someone reading the 1480/1 edition still required the use of a lectern, or at least a table, in order to hold the massive volumes. Whether or not readers of the printed edition themselves glossed the text is not known. Froehlich writes: 'I have not yet found an actual copy from the personal library of an academic theologian although there may be some, just as we know of *Glossa ordinaria* manuscripts which were annotated by university teachers.'[167] We could point to individual copies of texts in libraries and extrapolate to make the statement that readers continued to gloss the printed text, but that would neither be good scholarship nor would it be accurate. It is more likely that, well past the age of the patristics, readers of the printed edition treated it as they treated most early printed books – with a certain degree of reverence that would discourage or even prohibit them from writing in the text, particularly if the text were held in a monastic or academic library. Nevertheless, it is a curiosity, as Froehlich reports, that no copies of the book have been found in the personal library of a theologian. Whereas it is commonplace today for readers to mark personal copies of texts as they read, no evidence survives, whether textual or visual, that medieval readers pored over texts with pens in hand.

The history of the first printed edition offers insight into the workings of an early printer. The edition was printed by Adolph Rusch, a 'fairly well educated' printer in Strassburg who was able to correspond in Latin.[168] A paper merchant, Rusch also bought and sold books and manuscripts. When he married the daughter of Jacob Mentelin, Strassburg's first printer, Rusch inherited the printing shop. It is in the so-called Amerbach correspondence that we find the clearest evidence to construct a history of how and perhaps why this volume was printed and why it was printed by Rusch.

The right to ownership of printing the *Glossa Ordinaria* was apparently disputed in contention over printing the volumes, indicating their cost and value. In the correspondence between Rusch and Johann Amerbach, the celebrated Basel printer who first used Roman type, we discover Rusch wondering whether Amerbach is preparing an edition of the work himself:

> Honorable Master, there is a great rumor going around here that you now want to publish the *Glossa ordinaria*. Although I hardly believed that it was true, nevertheless, because many people were saying it with such confidence, I have decided to write you this brief letter expressing my concern ... This business could be ruinous for me and would bring you little or no profit. You see, I have to confess that I have kept approximately a hundred copies of the *Glossa* at my place.[169]

Rusch used four different movable types, borrowing 'the type he needed from [Johann] Amerbach and printed under a contract with Anton Koberger of Nuremberg'.[170] Froehlich also believes the volumes were sold unbound in folded sheets. That the paper was in fact 'unusually strong' with 'wide margins' perhaps did allow for – or even encourage – future illumination and/or annotation by owners.[171] However, there is little evidence that any printed edition of the *Glossa Ordinaria* was illuminated. And whether or not owners or users did annotate the printed edition is unclear; no evidence exists in a printed copy to indicate this.

If sales were brisk, as Froehlich indicates, little evidence survives of the buyers. Froehlich tells us that 'Both Rusch and his distributor Koberger must have envisioned a reading public whose willingness to buy this convenient tool they judged optimistically enough to warrant the investment.'[172] The volumes must have been available in most monastic libraries throughout Europe, but records of individual ownership are lacking. De Hamel writes: 'Many monastic libraries seem deliberately to have set about building up stocks of the various volumes of the Gloss.'[173] The availability of a printed edition would have met this need. It is clear that a tool such as the *Glossa Ordinaria* would indicate a tremendous advance in patristic study and exegesis. However, at the time of the initial printing, study of the patristics throughout Europe was unstable at best. With the Reformation on the horizon, the use of Church Fathers in study of the Bible was under fire. And the Reformation may be the single reason few individually-owned copies of the *Glossa Ordinaria* survive: they were perhaps destroyed, either by their owners or by the authorities. As study of the Fathers deteriorated, by the mid-seventeenth century, there was diminishing demand for the *Glossa Ordinaria*; thus the last printed edition appeared in Antwerp in 1634.

The physical act of compiling the text must have been strenuous to say the least. 'Rusch achieved this feat by figuring out the exact ratio of Vulgate text and marginal glosses appropriate to each page, linking the latter to the Vulgate by giving a lemma for each, and inventing a system of visual symbols to connect each interlinear gloss to its proper reference in the Vulgate text on the line below.'[174] The process may have taken years to complete. Even today, with the help of computers, such a layout for a text this large would take days, if not months.

We must wonder how Rusch succeeded. There is no indication that he had scholarly assistance, and Froehlich suggests that Amerbach, from whom he borrowed the type, may have also assisted in acquiring texts, 'probably borrowed from several libraries'.[175] Instead, Karlfried Froehlich suggests that 'Rusch relied on his own experience and common sense, not on any expert.'[176] Given the tenacity with which scholars have attempted to trace the source of Gutenberg's Bible texts, it is rather astonishing that Rusch, no scholar himself, seems to have compiled the texts for his edition of the *Glossa Ordinaria* without external expert assistance.

Rusch's edition was never reprinted, but the next edition of the *Glossa Ordinaria* was printed in Venice in 1495 by Paganinus de Paganinis. This text, printed in four volumes, added Nicholas of Lyra's *Postilla*. Froehlich suggests that for the Vulgate text and the *Glossa Ordinaria* Paganinus 'followed quite closely the Rusch edition'.[177] Of particular importance, 'The marginal gloss also follows Rusch in every textual detail.'[178] Only three years later, in 1498, the Basel printers Johann Froben and Johannes Petri printed an edition of the Vulgate, the Gloss and Nicholas of Lyra's *Postilla* in six volumes. Froben and Petri made one important change to the Rusch text: the layout was more navigable as they introduced relationships between the Vulgate text and the corresponding gloss by using small superscript letters to direct the reader from a scriptural word to the related gloss. This 'ingenious solution to the problems of typographical logistics' proved fruitful: the 1498 edition would become the typographic model for future reprints of the *Glossa Ordinaria*.[179]

Also in Basel, in 1502, the Baslers reprinted the work, a printing that spawned often vicious correspondence between printers as they argued over profits. This was followed by another edition, this one in 1508 with a slightly revised and corrected text. Two improvements were introduced in this edition: many sections now began with woodcut initials which, the volume's title announces, 'was intended to ease the reader's orientation';[180] the other improvement was the introduction of symbols to distinguish between the gloss (a hand), Lyra's *Postilla* (a rosette), and his *moralitates* (a star).

The Lyon edition of 1520 is a copy of the Basel edition of 1580; the Lyon 1528–9 edition reprints the 1520 Lyon edition. The edition printed at Lyon in 1545 is a 'large, beautiful set of six volumes plus index volume'.[181] The 1588 Venice edition is most important to the modern understanding of the *Glossa Ordinaria* as hypertext. It is with this edition that some patristic quotations were more explicitly identified.

The Paris edition of 1590 is referred to as such because it was published by the Paris theologians; in reality, it was printed in Lyon (see illustration 4). This was to be a scholarly revision, including more thorough and accurate patristic references. In the end, Froehlich writes, 'the new work was nothing less than a "revised" version of the medieval Gloss in form and content.'[182] This edition was meant to expunge and amend the previous editions by removing many of the pagan references. We should remember that by 1590 a 'book culture' had begun to arise throughout Europe, spurring the need for a thoroughly accurate and documented *Glossa Ordinaria* text. The volumes would be used not only as polemical tools but as sources for literary and theological criticism and scholarship:

> The argument from Scripture *and Tradition* which the Council of Trent had opposed to the seemingly reductionist and privatistic *sola scriptura* of the Reformation demanded the availability of a tool such as the Gloss, albeit in a form critically sifted according to the most advanced methods of textual scholarship available.[183]

Notably, it was with the 1590 edition that Strabo's name became associated with the printed text: *Biblia Sacra cum Glossa Ordinaria primum quidem a Strabo Fuldensi collecta*.

The Douai/Antwerp edition of 1617 had perhaps two goals: to produce the most complete and accurate text; and to produce the most helpful materials for the contemporary writer, a writer engaged in polemical mud-slinging. We should recall that Douai was the site of the first Catholic edition of the Old Testament in 1609. But this edition continues to propagate the myth that Strabo wrote the *Glossa*. As Froehlich recounts: 'The Benedictine monk Walafrid Strabo wrote the marginal gloss in the ninth century; another Benedictine, Anselm of Laon, added the interlinear gloss, a "new and unusual form of commentation", under Henry IV around 1100.'[184]

The 1634 edition printed at Antwerp closes the history of the printed *Glossa Ordinaria*. This edition, not really a revision in any way, is perhaps the one extant in the largest numbers, with several dozen copies available worldwide.

The 1865 edition of the *Glossa Ordinaria*, included in Migne's *Patrologia Latina*, has been criticized and with due reason.[185] The *Glossa Ordinaria* is included as part of the work of Walafrid Strabo, with Migne mistakenly failing to question Tritheim's assumption that Strabo is the work's author. As a result, Migne omitted the entire interlinear gloss as well as the text of the Vulgate itself; the gloss for Ezekiel, Daniel, and the Minor Prophets is missing. Froehlich clearly outlines Migne's motivations:

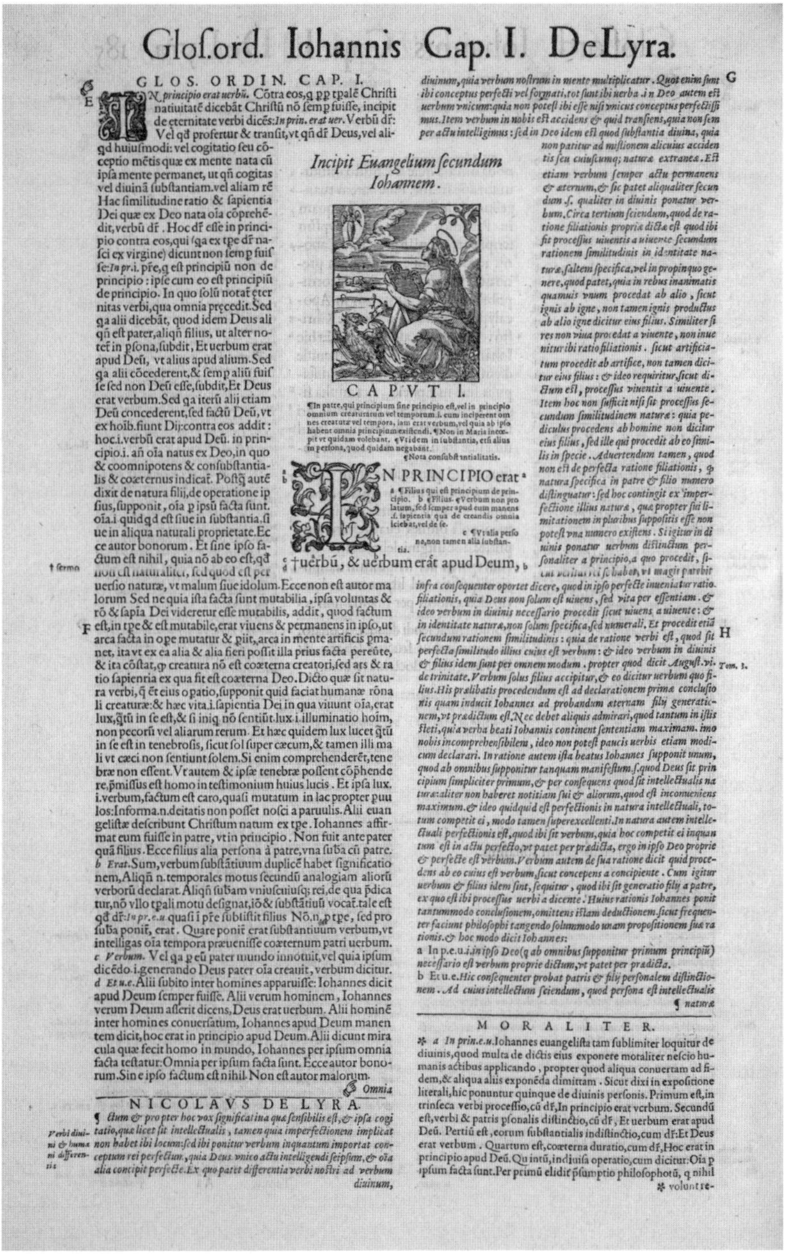

Glof.ord. Iohannis Cap. I. DeLyra.

GLOS. ORDIN. CAP. I.

IN principio erat uerbū. Cōtra eos,q pp tpalē Christi natiuitatē dicebāt Christū nō semp fuisse, incipit de æternitate verbi dicēs: In prin. erat uer. Verbū dr: Vel qđ profertur & transit,vt qñ dr Deus,vel aliqd huiusmodi: vel cogitatio seu cōceptio mētis quæ ex mente nata cū ipsa mente permanet, ut qñ cogitas vel diuinā substantiam.vel aliam rē Hac similitudine ratio & sapientia Dei quæ ex Deo nata oīa cōprehēdit,verbū dr. Hoc dr esse in principio contra eos,qui (qa ex tpe dr nasci ex virgine) dicunt non semp fuisse: In pr.i. pře,q est principiū non de principio: ipse cum eo est principiū de principio. In quo solū notat ęternitas verbi,qua omnia pręcedit.Sed qa alii dicebāt, quod idem Deus ali qñ est pater,aliqñ filius, ut alter notet in psona,subdit, Et uerbum erat apud Deū, vt alius apud alium.Sed qa alii cōcederent,& semp aliū fuisse sed non Deū esse,subdit,Et Deus erat verbum.Sed qa iterū alii etiam Deū concederent,sed factū Deū,vt ex hoib.fiunt Dii:contra eos addit: hoc.i.verbū erat apud Deū. in principio.i. añ oīa natus ex Deo,in quo & coomnipotens & consubstantialis & coæternus indicat. Postq̃ autē dixit de natura filii,de operatione ip sius,supponit, oīa p ipsū facta sunt. oīa.i quidqd est siue in substantia.si ue in aliqua naturali proprietate.Ec ce autor bonorum. Et sine ipso factum est nihil, quia nō ab eo est,qđ non est naturaliter, sed quod est per uersio naturæ, vt malum siue idolum.Ecce non est autor ma lorum Sed ne quia ista facta sunt mutabilia, ipsa voluntas & rō & sapia Dei videretur esse mutabilis, addit, quod factum est,in tpe & est mutabile,erat viuens & permanens in ipso,ut arca facta in ope mutatur & piit,arca in mente artificis pmanet, ita vt ex ea alia & alia fieri possit illa prius facta pereūte, & ita cōstat,q creatura nō est coæterna creatori,sed ars & ratio sapientia ex qua fit est coæterna Deo.Dicto quæ sit natura verbi,q̃ ēt eius opatio,supponit quid faciat humanæ rōna li creaturæ:& hæc vita.i.sapientia Dei in qua viuunt oīa,erat lux,q̃tū in se est,& si iniq nō sentiūt lux.i.illuminatio hoim, non pecorū vel aliarum rerum. Et hæc quidem lux lucet q̃tū in se est in tenebrosis, sicut sol super cæcum,& tamen illi ma li vt cæci non sentiunt solem.Si enim comprehenderēt,tenebræ non essent.Vt autem & ipsæ tenebræ possent cōphende re,pmissus est homo in testimonium huius lucis. Et ipsa lux. i.verbum,factum est caro,quasi mutatum in lac propter puu los: In forma.n.deitatis non posset nosci a paruulis.Alii euangelistæ describunt Christum natum ex tpe. Iohannes affirmat eum fuisse in patre, vt in principio. Non fuit ante pater quā filius. Ecce filius alia persona à patre,vna suba cū patre. *b Erat*.Sum,verbum substātiuum duplicē habet significationem,Aliqñ n.temporales motus secundū analogiam aliorū verborū declarat.Aliqñ subam vniuscuiusq rei,de qua pdicatur,nō vllo tpali motu designat,iō & substātiuū vocat.tale est qđ dr: In pr.e.u quasi i pře subsistit filius Nō,n,p tpe, sed pro suba ponit, erat. Quare ponit erat substantiuum verbum,vt intelligas oīa tempora præuenisse coæternum patri uerbum. *c Verbum*. Vel qa p eū pater mundo innotuit,vel quia ipsum dicēdo.i.generando Deus pater oīa creauit, verbum dicitur. *d Et u.e.* Alii subito inter homines apparuisse: Iohannes dicit apud Deum semper fuisse. Alii verum hominem, Iohannes verum Deum asserit dicens, Deus erat uerbum. Alii hominē inter homines conuersatum, Iohannes apud Deum manentem dicit,hoc erat in principio apud Deum.Alii dicunt mira cula quæ fecit homo in mundo, Iohannes per ipsum omnia facta testatur:Omnia per ipsum facta sunt. Ecce autor bonorum.Sine ipso factum est nihil. Non est autor malorum.

Omnia

NICOLAVS DE LYRA.

Etum & propter hoc vox significat ina quæ sensibilis est,& ipsa cogitatio,quæ licet sit intellectualis, tamen quia imperfectionem implicat non habet ibi locum:sed ibi ponitur verbum inquantum importat conceptum rei perfectum,quia Deus vnico actu intelligendi seipsum,& oīa alia concipit perfectè.Ex quo patet differentia verbi nostri ad verbum diuinum, [margin: *Verbi diuini & humani differentia*]

Incipit Euangelium secundum Iohannem.

CAPVT I.

In patre,qui principium fine principio est,vel in principio omnium creaturarum vel temporum.i. cum inciperent omnes creaturæ vel tempora, iam erat verbum,vel quia ab ipso habent omnia principium existendi. Non in Maria incœpit vt quidam volebant. Videm in substantia, etsi alius in persona,quod quidam negabant.

Nota consubstantialitatis.

IN PRINCIPIO erat [a] uerbū, & uerbum erat apud Deum, [b]

a Filius qui est principium de principio. b Filius. Verbum non prolatum, sed semper apud eum manens .s. sapientia qua de creandis omnia iciebat,vel de se.

c Vt alia perso na,non tamen alia substantia.

diuinum,quia verbum nostrum in mente multiplicatur. Quot enim sunt ibi conceptus perfecti vel formati,tot sunt ibi uerba .i n Deo autem est uerbum vnicum:quia non potest ibi esse nisi vnicus conceptus perfectissimus.Item verbum in nobis est accidens & quid transiens,quia non sem per actu intelligimus: sed in Deo idem est quod substantia diuina, quia non patitur ad mistionem alicuius acciden tis seu cuiuscumq; naturæ extraneæ. Est etiam verbum semper actu permanens & æternum,& sic patet aliqualiter secundum .s. qualiter in diuinis ponatur verbum.Circa tertium sciendum,quod de ratione filiationis propriæ dicta est quod ibi sit processus uiuentis a uiuente secundum rationem similitudinis in identitate naturæ,saltem specifica,vel in propinquo genere,quod patet,quia in rebus inanimatis quamuis vnum procedat ab alio, sicut ignis ab igne, non tamen ignis productus ab alio igne dicitur eius filius. Similiter si res non viua procedat a viuente, non inuenitur ibi ratio filiationis. sicut artificiatum procedit ab artifice, non tamen dicitur eius filius: & ideo requiritur,sicut dictum est, processus viuentis a uiuente. Item hoc non sufficit nisi sit processus secundum similitudinem naturæ: quia pediculus procedens ab homine non dicitur eius filius, sed ille qui procedit ab eo similis in specie. Aduertendum tamen, quod non est de perfecta ratione filiationis, q naturæ specifica in patre & filio numero distinguatur: sed hoc contingit ex imperfectione illius naturæ, quæ propter sui limitationem in pluribus suppositis esse non potest vna numero existens. Si igitur in diuinis ponatur uerbum distinctum personaliter a principio,a quo procedit, sicut ... habet, vt magis patebit infra consequenter oportet dicere, quod in ipso perfectè inueniatur ratio. filiationis, quia Deus non solum est uiuens, sed vita per essentiam. & ideo verbum in diuinis necessario procedit sicut uiuens a uiuente: & in identitate naturæ,non solum specifica,sed numerali. Et procedit etiā secundum rationem similitudinis: quia de ratione verbi est, quod sit perfecta similitudo illius cuius est verbum: & ideo verbum in diuinis & filius idem sunt per omnem modum. propter quod dicit August.vi. de trinitate. Verbum solus filius accipitur,& eo dicitur uerbum quo filius.His prælibatis procedendum est ad declarationem primæ conclusionis quam inducit Iohannes ad probandum æternam filii generationem,vt prædictum est.Nec debet aliquis admirari,quod tantum in istis fleti,quia verba beati Iohannis continent sententiam maximam. imo nobis incomprehensibilem, ideo non potest paucis uerbis etiam modicum declarari. In ratione autem ista beatus Iohannes supponit unum, quod ab omnibus supponitur tanquam manifestum.s.quod Deus sit principium simpliciter primum,& per consequens quod sit intellectualis na turæ:aliter non haberet notitiam sui & aliorum,quod est inconueniens maximum.& ideo quidquid est perfectionis in natura intellectuali, totum competit ei, modo tamen superexcellenti.In natura autem intellectuali perfectionis est,quod ibi sit verbum,quia hoc competit ei inquantum est in actu perfecto,vt patet per prædicta, ergo in ipso Deo proprie & perfecte est verbum.Verbum autem de sua ratione dicit quid procedens ab eo cuius est verbum,sicut concepens a concipiente. Cum igitur uerbum & filius idem sint, sequitur, quod ibi sit generatio filii a patre, ex quo est ibi processus uerbi a dicente. Huius rationis Iohannes ponit tantummodo conclusionem,omittens istam deductionem,sicut frequenter faciunt philosophi tangendo solummodo unam propositionem suæ ra tionis.& hoc modo dicit Iohannes:

a In p.e.u.i.in ipso Deo(q ab omnibus supponitur primum principiū) *necessario est verbum proprie dictum,vt patet per prædicta.*

b Et u.e.*Hic consequenter probat patris & filii personalem distinctionem. Ad cuius intellectum sciendum, quod persona est intellectualis*

naturæ

MORALITER.

a In prin.e.u. Iohannes euangelista tam sublimiter loquitur de diuinis,quod multa de dictis eius exponere moraliter nescio humanis actibus applicando, propter quod aliqua conuertam ad fidem,& aliqua aliis exponēda dimittam. Sicut dixi in expositione literali,hic ponuntur quinque de diuinis personis. Primum est,in trinseca verbi processio,cū dr,In principio erat verbum. Secundū est,verbi & patris psonalis distinctio,cū dr, Et uerbum erat apud Deū. Pertiū est, eorum substantialis indistinctio,cum dr:Et Deus erat verbum. Quartum est,coæterna duratio,cum dr,Hoc erat in principio apud Deū.Quintū,indiuisa operatio,cum dicitur:Oīa p ipsum facta sunt.Per primū elidit psumptio philosophorū, q nihil

volunt re-

Illustration 4 The opening page of St John from *Biblia Sacra cum Glossa Ordinaria . . . et Annotationibus de Nicolaus a Lyra*, 2A1v, published in Venice, 1588 ediition, illustrates how page layout in printed editions of the late sixteenth and early seventeenth centuries attempted to accommodate the growing commentary, now employing an elaborate system of signs and symbols, including some spilling into the narrow margins of this printed page. This item is reproduced by permission of The Huntington Library, San Marino, California.

Migne's generation was blind to the possibility still keenly felt by the Paris theologians of 1590, the insight that the *Glossa Ordinaria* of the Bible is not a 'text' in the usual sense, answering to all the 'normal' questions about authorship, original, and distortions. Rather it is the expression of a living tradition, and, in this sense, no more than a textual tool – the 'Glossed Bible'.[186]

Migne's goals in publishing the *Patrologia Latina* were twofold: broad access to the texts of the Church, provided at a moderate cost. As R. Howard Bloch has written in his study of Migne, 'Migne saw his mission as that of saving the "patrimony of the Church".'[187] Migne himself wrote, 'We will have as ours the consolation of having rendered the *Patrologia* accessible and intelligible to all.'[188] However, much of Migne's text was printed from other editions or reproduced without the attending critical apparatus. As Bloch points out, Migne often printed with mistakes and a lack of editing.

In some way Migne fits well into the history of the *Glossa Ordinaria* tradition: 'he participated in a long tradition going back to at least the twelfth century of copying the Fathers in collections.'[189] In fact, with the *Glossa Ordinaria* at least, Migne did more than merely copy: he excised and made pseudo-editorial decisions that were faulty if not wholly incorrect. His attribution of the text to Strabo might be forgiven were it not for the omission of all of the interlinear notation in the text. One should certainly not use the *Patrologia Latina* edition of the *Glossa Ordinaria* as a reliable scholarly tool.

As already noted, in 1992, a group of scholars, led by Karlfried Froehlich and Margaret Gibson, published a four-volume facsimile of the 1480/1 edition, for the first time making available to modern scholars the printed *Glossa Ordinaria* as it appeared before emendation and erroneous attribution. The importance of this facsimile cannot be overstated, as it replaces the only other widely available copy of the text in Migne. This does not overlook the fact that, between 1481 and 1634, there is evidence for no fewer than a half-dozen printed editions of the *Glossa Ordinaria*.

We still have to address the question of buyers. Although De Hamel has shown us clearly that Prince Henry collected glossed books of the Bible, we are still left to wonder who, apart from the wealthy royals, bought the *Glossa Ordinaria* in its printed edition? Certainly monastic libraries would have had a copy, as would the wealthier academic libraries. The persistent question remains: did individuals purchase a copy, and, if so, for what purpose? The *Glossa Ordinaria*, like many early printed books, would have been a status symbol for the wealthy. The entire text certainly was majestic, and just as many today purchase books merely to fill their shelves and not to read, it is probable that many of the earliest buyers of the *Glossa Ordinaria* put the book on their new bookshelves where they remained unopened and unread. I have found no evidence, in sifting through surviving library catalogues, of personal ownership of the *Glossa Ordinaria*.

But the present study is more interested in the reading of the text than in the mere purchasing. As a result, I will take it as *a priori* that the reader of the *Glossa Ordinaria* was either a monastic or an academic whose goal was a better and more complete understanding of the Bible text and perhaps of the Fathers. As such, the reader was confronted with a complex page and a rather elaborate system of signs and referents.

3

Reading, Theory, and Reading Theory

3.1 What is Reading in the Middle Ages?

Because so much of our understanding of the *Glossa Ordinaria* hinges on how the text may have been read, it is important for us to understand the nature of reading theory for readers of the text in the Middle Ages. While we have ample evidence for the content of their reading, few medieval writers actually tell us much about the ways in which texts were read. Did they read standing or sitting, did they annotate, did they consciously memorize? What we today call 'reading theory' is confined to explications of the ancients or modern observations of how writers wrote about texts, extrapolating how they read from that material. There do not seem to have been any theorists like Roland Barthes or Stanley Fish in the Middle Ages. In fact, the academic study of reading is a relatively new endeavour. Because reading is first a physical activity, the only other evidence can be culled from the illuminations in medieval manuscripts, some of which may indicate the physical poses and postures involved in reading in the Middle Ages. Nevertheless, as one might expect from the rest of the present study, much of medieval reading theory is culled from Augustine. This chapter therefore surveys Augustine's reading theory, both as it developed in the *Confessiones* and then in his critical and exegetical work, particularly *De Doctrina Christiana*, and then examines the influential *Didascalicon* of Hugh of St Victor. What we now call 'reading theory' in contemporary critical literature did not exist as such in the early Middle Ages, that is, there was no holistic or organized system to consult. Cassiodorus' *Introduction to Divine and Human Readings* offers some advice, but, because the majority of the general public were unable to read, the locus of reading and developing hermeneutic theory was the monastery. It is from the writing within the monastic walls that we extrapolate a type of theory of reading. And most of that is to be found in writing about Latin grammar.

The study of Latin grammar was a cottage industry in the Middle Ages, an industry that developed out of the Carolingian manuscript culture. Latin grammar study grew from Bible study itself because, in order to gain a fuller understanding of Scripture, it was necessary to understand the language of the Bible. Thus, the study of Latin grammar was conducted in the service of study of the Bible and was itself viewed in some circles as a form of devotion. As Brian Stock has written, in the Middle Ages, 'Latin was the unique language of both grammar and scripture. To teach grammar was to teach the letter of the Word.'¹ Latin is so important that Augustine equates the earliest rational activity of a child with learning a few words of Latin.

The study of grammar in the Middle Ages was substantially different from similar study today: whereas today students learn grammar to communicate in the language (in largely prescriptive terms), in the Middle Ages the goal was quite different. M. B. Parkes describes the four functions of grammatical studies in the early Middle Ages: *lectio, emendatio, enarratio* and *iudicium*.² As Parkes describes it, '*Lectio* was the process whereby a reader had to work out the text . . . by identifying its elements of letters, syllables, words and sentences.'³ *Emendatio* required the reader to 'correct the text in his copy'; *enarratio* looked at vocabulary and rhetorical devices with the goal of interpreting the text; *iudicium* exercised aesthetic judgements.

Of course, it is with *lectio* that I am most concerned here. But that 'working out', as Parkes calls it, had one goal: 'in order to read it aloud'.⁴ The age of silent reading, so well documented by Paul Saenger, had yet to begin. Readers read aloud for the spiritual edification of others (and the self), most often a church congregation or monastic community. However, what did *lectio* mean in the context of the early Middle Ages? Interestingly, many of the words in Latin and English used to denote reading first appear relatively late. As Ian Frederick Moulton notes, 'In English, "literate" is a late medieval term – it first appears in texts from the 1450s.'⁵ At some point, and I believe that point occurs between 1200 and 1400, the Latin *legere* and the English 'to read' finally shift from referring to reading aloud to silent reading; with that move to silent reading, the word used to denote reading changed to *lectio*, implying a more reflective activity.

Paul Saenger has written the seminal discussion of silent reading as a development of the Middle Ages, refuting earlier scholars such as Pierre Chantraine and Bernard Knox who argued that silent reading had already been adopted by the ancient reader. One way to trace this shift is linguistic and another is contextual. In the first, we trace the development of *lectio* and, later, 'reading', to surmise when the denotative change occurred. Another way is to examine texts and look at context for the term in order to determine whether the author refers to reading aloud or reading to oneself, silently. The lexicographic meaning of the word and the cultural meaning are important because it is perhaps the biggest piece in a puzzle so large and difficult that it seems to have pieces of identical size that have been printed on both sides.

The sense that reading is also gathering, ordering, reordering and, by extension, sorting is reflected in the meaning of *legere*. Therefore, reading is not merely a passive activity which one experiences, but it is more an active endeavour which one makes happen. Selection, choice and compilation all fall under the *legere* umbrella. That *legere* shifted to *lectio* at some point and, as a result, when we discuss *lectio divina*, as we shall later in this chapter, we begin to see how reading is an active pursuit which one, in the case of *lectio divina*, initiates and controls in an effort to gain clearer understanding of Scripture. *Lectio* becomes an activity in which the reader truly searches for meaning.

Contrary to the *lectio* of the monastic writers of the Middle Ages, the Romans chose the word *legere* to denote the verb 'to read'. In fact, *legere* is the word most often used by Augustine to describe the act. In the *Confessiones*, *legere* is used ninety-two times while *lectio* is only used six times to describe the action of reading. Eventually *legere* came to include *lectio*. As Svenbro explains, the word actually means 'to pick, gather, collect', and he explains the word's relationship to *lex*, law.⁶ It is more interesting to me that the word originally had meanings related to collection because, as I have shown, the *Glossa Ordinaria* is just that: a collection of readings. And for ecclesiastical Latin, the verb *lego* does in fact have the dual meanings of 'read' and 'recite', as well as to 'gather' and to 'choose'. Extrapolating that verb to the monastic practice of *lectio divina*, we discover that for the Middle Ages, *lectio*, reading, was apparently related also to the act of both gathering texts and choosing them, significant activities for the compilation of the *Glossa Ordinaria*.

The connection between reading and knowing God is made clear in a ninth-century treatise by a Frankish noblewoman named Dhuoda. In the *Liber manualis*, written for her son William, Dhuoda writes, 'In holy reading you will learn how you must pray and what you should avoid, be wary of, or seek out – what you should do in all matters.'[7] So, for Dhuoda, reading leads one to prayer. Nevertheless, reading still appears to be an oral activity for Dhuoda. As Parkes reiterates, in Dhuoda's handbook, 'one learns about God from reading books.'[8] The goal of reading here is only edification; one could argue that it is not even contemplative because the goal is not to understand oneself more completely but to edify one's soul as an end in itself. This is not *lectio* for educational or even exegetical purposes.

In most cases such reading involved application of an interpretative tradition woven into grammatical studies so apparent in the literature of the ancient world. Cavallo and Chartier note that by the fifth to fourth centuries BC reading theory had moved towards 'a reading style capable of reading "through" a text', the reader having achieved the ability to consider, examine, interpret and ultimately understand the material.[9] Most often, as I argue here, that reading 'through' a text would imply a network: the reader's ability to make connections between texts in order ultimately to construct a knowledge base from which he could continually draw. The metaphor of reading 'through' presents the text as a window through which the reader makes discoveries not only about the text (the window) itself, but about texts (and the world) beyond the one at hand.

In many ways, then, the text acts as a window/mirror through/into which the reader discovers the self. Caroline Walker Bynum asks 'Did the Twelfth Century Discover the Individual?', and she notes 'the discovery within oneself of human nature made in the image of God'.[10] The 'development of the self', she further notes, 'was toward God'. The development of the book and the nascence of a reading public are consistent with this self-reflection, a process that reading invites and encourages.

Indeed, the very concept of hypertext requires an individual who has the ability to read far and wide, to store that information in an organized and accessible way, and to retrieve often disparate items of information and make connections. If this is not the development of the self, what is? The self as mind is certainly indicated by an ability and willingness to explore new ideas and relate and situate oneself amidst those new ideas.

In what sounds like modern reader-response theory, Svenbro writes of *epilegesthai*, a Greek verb whose literal meaning is 'to add something said' to something: 'The reader adds his voice to the writing, which is incomplete in itself . . . without the reader, writing would remain a dead letter.'[11] According to Svenbro, the Greeks thought writing was itself incomplete: 'If a text must be read in order for it to be complete, it follows logically that reading is an integral part of the text.'[12] Because ancient Greek texts, and even most early European texts in the Middle Ages, lacked spacing, every reading became a voiced experience. The text, as Svenbro continues, 'becomes the sounded realization of writing, and without the reader's voice, writing would have no way of being distributed or expressed'.[13] Without authorial end punctuation, sentencing and paragraphing, the reader/listener had to rely on individual understanding. The sentence unit itself becomes reliant on the reader's understanding of the Latin (or Greek) grammar and syntax. This type of uninterrupted reading – for lack of another way of describing reading print without word, sentence and paragraph breaks – perhaps more closely mirrored the reader's own thinking process, a process more likely to make seemingly random associations than to think in a linear fashion.

This mode of reading implies that when the reader brings his personal voice to the text, he not only completes the text, but he amends it. This would also imply that every reading of the text, completed by the personal voice of the reader, not only changes the text but results in a reading different from any other reader's. The resulting chaotic panoply of readings seems impossible – every text becomes a network of millions of different readings dependent upon individual readers. And, in my interpretation, this is not exactly the case. The text itself does in fact remain static, and the readers do change, but that does not necessarily change the text, only the interpretation and understanding of it. The glossed text, however, does change as the glossator adds his comment, thereby creating a network, not unlike a computer network, in which readers serve as individual nodes connecting to one another to create, as it were, a type of intellectual internet.

Although the reader does engage in an active way with the text, the text itself remains a passive participant in the activity – unless the reader changes the static and physical text itself, either through emendation or omission. It is here – and only here, I argue – that the reader has any type of permanent and indelible influence on further readings of the text. And it is here that the *Glossa Ordinaria* text experienced its transformations with subsequent readings. To understand the distinction we must understand the connotations of two important medieval phrases: 'I read' and 'I write'.

3.2 *'I Read' and 'I Write'*

Although Walter Ong has argued that 'there is no way directly to refute a text' since the author 'cannot be reached in any book,' it would seem that glossing perhaps comes closest to the type of refutation Ong dismisses.[14] In fact, one can easily, through the gloss, refute a text although indeed the author still cannot be reached. Because such glossing, in the manuscript stage, becomes a type of layering of one commentary upon another, the glosses themselves become refutations of both the main/original text and the commentaries that have preceded them. Like peeling an onion, one would have to peel back the layers of commentary in order to see each one on its own, and finally find the original text itself. Behind/beneath the main text, one might find the author. This is confused in the *Glossa Ordinaria* because the glossing itself is part of, or is itself, the main/original text. But since 'writing is in many respects like reading,' the processes, while superficially different, are actually quite similar.[15]

In the modern world, we work under the assumption that reading is a very personal, perhaps the most personal, introspective act. We often read alone, in silence, and that solitude, physical and spiritual, is often what results in an individual 'entering' the text, displaying itself in readers' descriptions of being 'sucked into' the world of the text, becoming involved in the narrative, and perhaps even feeling that they themselves are living in the world of that text. But this type of interaction with the text has only really been possible since the development of silent reading and, some might argue, with the development of the modern novel, though its beginnings do appear in medieval romance. Prior to silent reading and the novel form, most reading was religious reading with the purposes of prayer, devotion or teaching. And even early medieval readers who prayed by reading texts still did so through oral recitation of the text, whether aloud to a group or to themselves. Reading was indeed a more physical act, often beginning with the heft of a volume that was either chained to its shelf or so heavy that holding it up to read (as moderns do) was impossible. The physical aspect of reading, then, might have included standing in front of the text or sitting on a high stool with the volume propped on a lectern. As M. T. Clanchy notes, 'Reading was a physical exertion, demanding the use not only of the eyes, but of tongue, mouth and throat. Writing was a similar act of endurance, requiring three fingers to hold the pen, two eyes to see the words, one tongue to speak them, and the whole body to labour.'[16] Such physicality in reading survives today in the Jewish practice of 'davening'[17] when praying, rocking back and forth in rhythm with the spoken prayer. Curiously, many Jews do this even when praying alone, without a group in a synagogue. Similarly, many modern Christians pray accompanied by genuflection, prostration or other physical movement.

In the modern world reading has become emblematic for acts of contemplation and reflection. From Shakespeare to Charlotte Brontë, the mention of a character reading conjures images of an individual pensively considering his or her own existence. We recall the suggestion in *Hamlet* that Ophelia 'read on this book' since it will 'colour her loneliness'. Similarly, in *Jane Eyre* Jane's withdrawal into her own world, a world over which she herself is in control, is suggested when she, particularly in the opening chapters of the novel, escapes through reading. In some sense, the act of silent reading, alone, is also an indication of the development of the individual. As Burt Kimmelman notes, the trope of reading 'tells us how selfhood was understood', demonstrating 'how the fourteenth-century version of selfhood was a formulation of individual autonomy that looked ahead to the modern concept of the ego'.[18] We perhaps find this gleaned in the earlier writing of Augustine where scholars have glossed Augustine's intellectual development as the evolution of ego and its requisite machinations; Brian Stock's *Augustine the Reader* clearly elaborates its subtitle: 'Meditation, Self-Knowledge, and the Ethics of Interpretation'. By the fourteenth century, 'the idea that *to read* is *to become oneself* is taken quite seriously.'[19]

Eric H. Reiter refers to the 'reader/scribe' in fifteenth-century book production: 'Individual clerics, university students, parish priests, and others increasingly produced books themselves for their own personal use, and these readers eagerly sought popular devotional and pastoral works, sermons, and the like to fill their books.'[20] The idea that the reader would also be the scribe is one borrowed largely from the Carolingian manuscript culture. That the reader would 'talk back' to the text by inscribing his own reactions, and thus make his ideas a part of the permanent text (at least his copy of it), presages contemporary reader-response theory. And, I will argue in this chapter, both sentiments are valid in our understanding of reading theory in the Middle Ages. There are, as we will see, problems with applying reader-response theory to medieval reading, particularly to manuscripts, because the theory assumes a fixed text, and medieval manuscripts were in a state of constant change – one copy of a text might and often did vary greatly from another copy.

By the time the various *Glossa Ordinaria* manuscripts were gathered to form a coherent whole, the text had become a bridge, as Brian Stock writes, 'between *ratio* and *auctoritas*. Through the interior dialogue, a summary of biblical and patristic authority becomes a "text" before actually being written down.'[21] For Anselm, particularly, 'the text acts as an intermediary for discussion within his own mind.'[22] The same process makes the *Glossa Ordinaria* 'work', i.e., the marginal and interlinear notes operate in lieu of that 'discussion' within the reader's mind and allow him literally to go off the page into the ether of his own knowledge and understanding. The abstract text, the entire epistemology of reading, begins to shift back and forth from the page to the mind. For the first time, as we truly enter the age of print, what had been exclusively abstract, confined to memory and thought process, now becomes tangible on the printed page. That shift is seismic, and its aftershocks continue to be felt throughout the Middle Ages and into the early Renaissance throughout Europe.

The medieval Christian physical activity of praying is seen most often in monastic depictions of monks engaged in *lectio divina*. Owing to the unwieldy size of the books, the monks are depicted seated at an oversized desk or on a stool in front of a lectern. They are most often hunched over and are conventionally shown with hands on the page they are reading, undoubtedly using their fingers to follow the lines of the page. Did they read aloud when doing this? We cannot be sure. Paul Saenger has argued that the practice of silent reading did not arise until text began to be separated on the page. So we can assume that most monastic reading, whether in private or with the community, was conducted aloud.

The effects of this reading aloud are quite different from the effects of reading silently. And often the goals are also different. It is only with the development of silent reading that we really begin to see the analogies of writing the body that arise in medieval mystical literature. Such writing, which is indicative of the *corpus mysticum*, begins to appear only when the act of reading transformed from a public and vocal act to a more internal and contemplative act. In some sense, the act of glossing a text became the act of glossing the body. When a reader glossed a text, he was also glossing, inscribing, the body/*corpus* with his own ideas and reactions. In this way, the text transformed into an individual and personal mode of discourse through which and by which the reader understands his self. It is in this way that we see that reading, such as Augustine's, can actually change the individual in substantive ways. As Brian Stock tells us, Augustine's objective is 'a better understanding of the self and its relationship to God through the medium of scripture'.[23] So the text becomes a tool to transform the soul of the reader. The cognitive function of reading is then secondary to the spiritual function. In this scenario, the text has little use as a text: it is a tool, a medium, through which the individual develops self.

The role of commentary in the cognitive sequence of reading occurs as an interruption or intervention in the reading process. The act of glossing, whether physically with a pen or intellectually with a psychic hyperlink, constitutes an important stage in the process. All reading is commentary as the reader engages in an ongoing process of interpretation and glossing in the psychological space reserved for working out complex problems and sorting through and filing data. The modern practice of hypertext annotation is merely the logical next stage in the processes of writing and reading, now (in the twenty-first century) advanced by the introduction of computer technology. However, to think that hypertext only developed with Ted Nelson's coinage of the term in 1965 is not only a mistake: it grossly underestimates the capabilities of the human mind. Hypertext glossing has gone on for as long as people have been engaged in silent reading. As Augustine writes, 'Meditating day and night, at least when time permits, I pin down my thoughts with my pen, lest, through forgetfulness, they vanish for ever.'[24] Augustine realized, then, that he could not hold those thoughts in his mind for ever; the inscription on his memory was not enough and had to be extended through his pen to the page.

For a modern, the acts of reading and writing are paired; when we speak of a 'literate' individual, we assume the abilities to both read and write. For the medieval that was not the case. The ability to read no doubt preceded the talent of writing, if only because the materials used to write were so expensive. But the hermeneutic of reading in the Middle Ages does seem to have linked reading with writing, in that writing (in) the text was an integral part of the interpretative process. This is perhaps the reason that so many early printers laid out pages with wide margins, ample space for the reader to jot down his own ideas or response to the text. The semiotics of that space of the page indeed invite the reader to join in the discussion, adding his voice to whatever debate is already in progress. In the case of the *Glossa Ordinaria* that debate involves some serious sacred issues. But we should recall at this point that the reader who glosses a text such as the *Glossa Ordinaria* is not only glossing the biblical text, but is responding to those who came before, most often Church Fathers. The interpretative debate invites the reader to join in, and that debate concerns the already extrapolated issues of the text. More often than not, the reader's response would be to Augustine's comment on a verse in Genesis, and not to the Genesis verse itself. In this way, the reader is not in danger of blaspheming or defaming the sacred text.

3.3 Augustine and Memory

More than any other writer of the Middle Ages, Augustine has influenced theories of learning, reading, writing and thinking. From his own experiences, recounted in the *Confessiones*, to his doctrinal and theoretical writing, most significantly in *De Doctrina Christiana*, Augustine gives us a sense of the life of the medieval mind. However, it is just a sense. Because pedagogy did not yet exist as a going academic concern, the Middle Ages produced no complete and self-contained theory of education. And this learning involved a good deal of reconfiguring of the classical ideas of the mind as well as the developing field of psychology, a field that would not come to complete fruition until the English Renaissance and then the indulgences of Sigmund Freud and C. G. Jung in the late nineteenth and early twentieth centuries.

Of course, the chief aid in learning for the Middle Ages was memory. The role played by memory, as outlined notably first by Frances Yates and more recently by Mary Carruthers, in the reading process, and indeed in the hermeneutics of interpretation, cannot be understated. At a time, during the Middle Ages, when texts were not necessarily widely available, the reader depended more upon retrieving facts and actual texts from his memory than from written works he may have owned. That is one of the most significant shifts in approaches to reading and studying between the Middle Ages and the modern period. With texts so available – and so affordable – student learning has shifted from memorization to glossing or annotating a text. Such students may not know the answer to a particular question from memory, but more often than not they know where to find it in their printed books. Some cognitive scientists and psychologists have argued that, in this way, the modern has made more 'space' in his mind for higher-level, more abstract, thinking. The ability to write down important information and save it for posterity affords the individual the luxury of not having to remember that morsel of information. Instead he is able to utilize that part of his brain for more complex thinking.

It is this approach which Vannevar Bush envisaged when he postulated his 'memex' in his 1945 article 'As We May Think'. In that influential piece, Bush writes, 'our methods of transmitting and reviewing the results of research are generations old and by now are totally inadequate for their purpose.' Because memory is transitory, Bush argues, we are in need of a device that would transform memory to a stable and permanent medium. The machine he theorizes, the memex, would be 'an enlarged intimate supplement to [the individual's] memory'. What Bush proposed, in 1945, would seem the mechanical fulfilment of what Augustine, in the fifth century, first suggested.

The importance of memory in reading is noted as early as Augustine's *Confessiones* where memory, 'a spacious palace, a storehouse for countless images of all kinds', is highlighted as the key pedagogical tool in reading.[25] The 'storehouse' of memory itself is imaged as a type of book, 'which in some indescribable way secretes them [sensations] in its folds'.[26] We must remember, however, that for Augustine, memory itself is a text onto which experiences and sensations are inscribed for later retrieval. Without a multitude of printed volumes to store on his shelf, Augustine must rely on this storehouse, what the Jesuit Matteo Ricci would later refer to as a 'memory palace'. But the metaphor of a palace or library ends there, since it is not arranged as a physical library would be. This is no card catalogue organized by authors' last names in a linear fashion. Instead, this is an associative system into which memories have been dispersed or broadcast as seed. When he wishes to retrieve them, Augustine, writes, 'I have to collect them again, and this is the derivation of the word *cogitare*, which means *to think* or *to collect one's thoughts*. For in Latin the word *cogo*, meaning *I assemble* or *I collect*, is related to *cogito*, which means *I think.*'[27] These two sentences are vital to an understanding of medieval theories of the mind and, for present purposes, to medieval theories of reading. The Latin word for *think* summons the act of collecting or assembling or, by extension, organizing.

This rearranging and reordering of ideas and information forms the core of the reading experience. The reader calls from his memory previously read and/or learned ideas and begins the process of reordering his own ideas in order to put them more in line with the newly acquired information. It is as if the reader's alphabetical index receives new information that requires an entire overhaul of the catalogue already in existence.

Reading is clearly not an innate function acquired at birth. In the *Confessiones* Augustine notes in Book 1 that he was sent to school to learn to read, even though he 'was too small to understand what purpose it might serve'.[28] After recounting his early exploration of the 'empty romances' of classical literature in Latin, Augustine recalls the pear-tree incident, in Book II, concluding that 'it is still alive in my memory', indicating the 'storehouse' nature of memory and summoning the image of the memory as a library, filled as it is with sensations and experiences that can be recalled and re-collected (*cogitare*) at any time by their owner.

Reading functions as the compelling tool of conversion in Augustine's young life. And in the autobiography, Augustine consistently relates his intellectual and spiritual development to his reading. His reading of Cicero 'altered [his] outlook on life'.[29] But, of course, his reading of the Scriptures catalysed his intellectual development. At first 'a child',[30] Augustine discovered the categories of sin and began to formulate a theodicy by reading Scripture. Significantly, when Augustine strayed from his mother's desires for a Christian life, a priest who was called to visit Augustine told her, 'From his own reading he will discover his mistakes.'[31] There is a sense of discovery and exploration in Augustine's reading, and, although most of his reading is unguided by a teacher or mentor, it is the very nature of associative thinking that seems to be guiding his intellectual development. It is Augustine himself who is in control of the direction his reading takes.

Augustine's break with the Manichees and the acquisition of Ambrose as a teacher truly brought his Christianity to full development, and as is the case with the rest of Augustine's biography, this feat was accomplished largely through reading. With Ambrose as his guide, Augustine begins to understand the existence and importance of a variety of exegetical modes. He discerns, for example, the difference between a figurative interpretation and a literal one:[32] 'I was glad too that at last I had been shown how to interpret the ancient Scriptures of the law and the prophets in a different light from that which had previously made them seem absurd.'[33] He begins also to understand the layers of meaning in Scripture: 'it seems to me all the more right that the authority of Scripture should be respected and accepted with the purest faith, because while all can read it with ease it also has a deeper meaning in which its great secrets are locked away. Its plain language and simple style make it accessible to everyone, and yet it absorbs the attention of the learned.' Again, later: 'I can see now that the passages in Scripture which I used to think absurd are not absurd at all. They can be understood in another sense, quite fairly.'[34]

The written text, then, is vital to the intellectual and spiritual development of the individual. It is through books that Augustine is prompted 'to return to my own self'.[35] But when Augustine reads the letters of Paul, his understanding of the Word of Christianity is enriched through the theories of the Platonists and – much more – set down in a clearer and Christian context. Thus Augustine ascertains the kind of layered meaning mentioned earlier through a type of layered reading: reading Platonism through Paul allows Augustine better to understand both. By extension, this is the type of understanding gleaned by reading the *Glossa Ordinaria* text: greater clarity of Scripture through a layered reading of the Church Fathers' readings of the text.

And Augustine's focus on reading is not confined to his own experience. He notes that one monk in the Milan monastery read the life of St Antony, and 'even before he finished reading he conceived the idea of taking upon himself the same kind of life and abandoning his career in the world'.[36] When he read, 'you alone could see, a change was taking place,'[37] thereby reflecting the transformative possibilities and effects of reading. This brings us to the recollection of the voice telling Augustine '*tolle lege*' ('Take it and read').[38] This phrase, however, should be at the head not only of the *Confessiones* but of the collected works of Augustine, as it is reading that guides his development. To be sure, Augustine's approach here, 'to open my book of Scripture and read the first passage on which my eyes should fall', is not exactly associative reading. Instead, it indicates a mind hungry for enrichment and eager to respond to the command to read. Reading these few passages, mostly from Paul, is enough for Augustine to exclaim, 'You converted me to yourself, so that I no longer desired a wife or placed any hope in this world but stood firmly upon the rule of faith, where you had shown me to her in a dream so many years before.'[39] Though it does not seem that unusual to experience conversion through hearing, particularly Scripture, Augustine's conversion experience here is notable for its relationship to reading a written text. As he noted earlier, referring to his observation of Ambrose reading silently, 'He read on and in his heart, where you alone could see, a change was taking place'.[40] Such reading inscribes the heart (and soul) of the individual, effecting substantive change. The cognitive connection between reading and the soul is magnified in the ancient Greek *nous*, which denoted both soul and mind. Thus, like Ambrose, Augustine read 'and in his heart . . . a change was taking place'.

> 'Memory' as 'heart' was encoded in the common Latin verb *recordari*, meaning 'to recollect'. Varro, the first-century BC grammarian, says that the etymology of the verb is from *revocare* 'to call back' and *cor* 'heart'. The Latin verb evolved into the Italian *ricordarsi*, and clearly influenced the early use in English of 'heart' for 'memory'.[41]

Even Augustine's early acts of faith are exhibited in the form of writing: 'Once we were there I began at last to serve you with my pen.'[42] Writing becomes a devotional act in the lives of such later medieval mystics as Hildegard of Bingen, Margery Kempe and Richard Rolle. They, and others like them, record their experiences for the edification of others, as an act of devotion and thanksgiving to the God who granted them the experiences in the first place. The action is much the same. God has inscribed the experience on the mind and body of the individual, and that individual then in turn, acting as a type of amanuensis, inscribes his experience on the page. Memory is fleeting and transient; the written page, presumably, carries with it a degree of permanence. Indeed, Hildegard is reluctant to record her experiences in writing until she is given approval and encouragement to do so by her spiritual adviser.

However, much of what Augustine is doing in the *Confessiones* seems to involve conversion as reading, and reading as conversation. Hence the relationship between reading and the community, something Brian Stock notes in *Listening for the Text*. Reading, he notes, from 'about the middle of the eleventh century on . . . begins to carry on an interpretive conversation with its own textual past'.[43] This eventuates itself in 'social organization' which 'itself becomes a text worthy of commentary and interpretation'. When Augustine enters into conversation, in this case with God, that conversation draws Augustine into a community of believers, a community organized on the principles of texts, reading and textual interpretation. Consistency of the text binds the early Christian Church together – one reason why the development of Jerome's Vulgate was so vital to the Church's prospering and growth.

If reading is conversation, then the act of glossing a written text naturally grows from reading, as the act of glossing is the tangible product of the conversation. This is especially true if that conversation is conducted with God through the scriptural text itself.

The reader 'speaks' to the text and responds to the Divine Word by glossing the margins. Glossing is not merely the act of interpreting; it is also vital to understanding and to response. With Augustine we first find the building of textual communities as he conducts his conversation with God in the *Confessiones* and with that textual community that is the Holy See of the Church. As Stock notes, 'What was essential for a textual community, whether large or small, was simply a text, an interpreter, and a public.'[44] The text here is obviously the Bible. The interpreter is Augustine, and the public, in this case, is the extended Christian community of readers. 'Through the text, or, more accurately, through the interpretation of it, individuals who previously had little else in common were united around common goals ... The essential bond was forged by means of belief; its cement was faith in the reality of belonging. And these in turn were by-products of a general agreement on the meaning of a text.'[45] A collective – and collected – memory was also part of that bond. The common memory of the textual community, evident not only in the common texts they shared, but in the sharing of the Eucharist (the literal *corpus mysticum*), catalysed and grew that community. Thus memory is a shared concern which, while personal, is also communal. The development of a textual community is integral to a reading culture. Without that community, the culture of reading stagnates and emaciates. Through such a community the history of ideas becomes grounded and is permitted to grow. 'The essential element is the community, the living people whose minds are peopled and shared by thoughts, intentions, and potential actions. The normal hermeneutic activity is the experience of the text along with individual interpretations.'[46] Texts and their interpretations open new worlds, and in the context of Christianity, these worlds are often outgrowths of conversion experiences, such as Augustine's.

Augustine explains that his first inclination after the '*tolle lege*' experience was to 'retire quietly from the market where I sold the services of my tongue'.[47] This act of contemplation and reflection then led him to the pen himself. And perhaps his most organized and clearly written hermeneutic statement is found in *De Doctrina Christiana*. The command *tolle lege* might be the motto of the medieval Church – even in the monastic world reading was at the centre, as is evident in Benedict's Rule. This reading naturally led to questions and discussion about interpretation, which gave rise to works like *De Doctrina Christiana*, which purports to be a discussion of, as Augustine writes in the opening sentence, 'certain rules for interpreting the Scriptures'.

3.4 Writing as Spiritual Practice

It is with Augustine that the act of reading becomes central to the faith, and central to one's spiritual and intellectual development. In the faith of a Church built on the Word, reading had always been central, but it is in the *Confessiones* and *De Doctrina Christiana* that we really begin to see the centrality of reading to an individual's faith and spiritual development. This shift from the public to the private, from the aural to the visual, to the read and written word, is encapsulated in *tolle lege* and expanded in the corpus of Christian hermeneutic literature that followed, beginning in the Middle Ages and continuing today. One of the most important sites of the medieval hermeneutic debate was the *Glossa Ordinaria*, with the debate taking place, literally, between the lines and in the margins. The margins as site of discussion mirror the margins of society, where some of the most important debate often takes place. The written page, and by 1481, the printed page, was an ideal medium in which this debate might germinate and grow.

The very concept of glossing a text develops from the combined acts of reading and writing. Historically, the ability to read predates the ability to write, and it is the combination of the two that produces what Reiter calls the 'reader/scribe', the reader who also acts as author. And I will argue here that glossing is an activity born of the monastic life and in some ways fundamentally related to the Rule of St Benedict and the conventions he set down for conducting oneself in a cloistered relationship with God. That Rule formed the basis of Christian spiritual life in the Middle Ages, and the secular scholar, himself an outgrowth of the monastic life, seems to have adapted many of the tenets of Benedict's Rule to life outside the monastery – the monastery itself largely replaced by the late Middle Ages by the academic institution of the university. It should come as no surprise to us that the spiritual practices of the monastic life, including daily reading, should have transformed and adapted to life in the university. In order better to understand this adaptation, we need greater insight into the practices of Augustine, in many ways the first true scholar of the Christian faith.

Augustine's reading experience is particularly instructive because the reader does not necessarily encounter the learned teacher disseminating his knowledge. Instead, he journeys with Augustine as he embarks on a mission of discovery that is his life. Thus, when Augustine tells us how he learned to read the Bible, the reader is able to read with him as a peer. The reader is intimately involved in Augustine's first-person narrative, and the education of Augustine is, as with Frederick Douglass's narrative of his own educational growth, both history and example. The text, the *Confessiones*, serves both as history and as example of its own narrative. Augustine seems to be inviting the reader, as did Socrates, on a co-operative search for the truth/Truth.

Augustine notes the centrality of reading in the preface to *De Doctrina Christiana*: 'So the person who knows how to read, on finding a book, does not require another reader to explain what is written in it.' In this way, the reader may 'arrive at the hidden meaning for himself'.[48] The importance of individual interpretation, interpretation that can only come about through individualized reading, reaches through the Reformation and into the postmodern theory of the late twentieth and early twenty-first century. It gives the reader the ability to reflect, contemplate and understand in ways not available through oral transmission of the text because such interpretation is the result of a very personal and subjective reading. Even those who appreciate audio books today often note that actual reading is quite different in that the audio book does not permit one to stop easily, reflect and even return to a paragraph for rereading (indeed, the whole notion of paragraphing loses its meaning in an audio book). Reading not only permits but encourages understanding that is beyond the superficial. Of course, for Augustine the most important text is Scripture, and, building on the exegetical theories of Origen and others, Augustine understands the importance of looking beyond the literal and searching for the 'hidden meaning'.

The logical next step after reading is writing. But the patristics have surprisingly little to say on the subject. It is my argument here that the act of reading transforms into the act of writing by the ninth and tenth centuries, and that the process of glossing combines reading and writing the text by the twelfth century. When an individual reads a text such as the Bible, there is an almost constant process of glossing, whether this presents itself in actually writing in the margins and creating a type of hypertext or in the creation of that network in the reader's own mind. This was evident originally in the kind of figural reading of the New Testament that was so popular in the early Church. Christ carrying the cross to his own crucifixion in John 19 is prefigured in Isaac carrying the thicket of wood to his own sacrifice in Genesis 22. The congregant listening to that section of the Gospel is expected, in this scenario, to make the connection to the story of Abraham sacrificing his son in Genesis 22:7–18, and thus further his understanding of the nature of Scripture and, ultimately, God's ultimate plan for salvation. Of course, this was particularly important in the early days of the Church, when new members and converts were in abundance; making such figural ties between the new and the old increased the Church's ability to embrace those who believed in the old. As time progressed into the age of print, printed Bibles tended to give the reader such figural references in the margins,[49] prompting the reader to go, if you will, off the page, one of the guiding principles of hypertext theory. Before the age of print, the reader needed to work out such connections in his mind. But now that books could be printed in a permanent and fixed state, functions such as cross-references and word glosses could be tucked into the margins of the page, thus freeing the reader to contemplate the more important spiritual message conveyed in the text, a message that Augustine notes is often 'hidden'. The search for and discovery of that hidden message was in many ways the goal of the monastic life, and a précis for that search and discovery can be found in Benedict's Rule.

3.5 St Benedict

It is in the Rule of St Benedict, written for the organization and administration of monastic life, that we find clear indications that reading was a central monastic activity. It is, nevertheless, curious that Benedict discusses reading only in conjunction with the manual labour of daily life. Though the type of reading Benedict requires is what is now termed *lectio divina*, the meaning of the term for the Middle Ages appears to have been quite different from the modern monastic use. By the period of the printed *Glossa Ordinaria*, *lectio divina* had become a generic term meaning 'spiritual reading'. Chapter 48 of the Rule states: 'Idleness is an enemy of the soul. Therefore, the brothers should be occupied according to schedule in either manual labour or holy reading [*lectione divina*] . . . Each monk shall receive a book from the library [*singulos codices de bibliotheca*], which he should read [*legant*] carefully cover to cover.'[50] We should note the apparent equality with which Benedict wrote about 'manual labour or holy reading', almost implying that reading was as physical, or at least as strenuous, an act as manual labour in the fields. Benedict is sure to separate reading from talking, not only, presumably, because talking would disrupt the reading of other monks, but because reading is a more highly personal and devotional activity than talking. Thus, 'If someone wishes to read, let him do so to himself in such a way as to disturb no one.'[51]

Anscari Mundo and Terrence Kardong have, in separate studies, pointed out that the reading may not always have been biblical. Nevertheless, Kardong notes that Chapter

73 'recommends the reading of the Fathers in the same breath as it commends the Bible'.[52] One might then imagine the monk's *lectio* of both the Bible and the Fathers resulting in a gloss, which applies his knowledge of the latter to gain a clearer understanding of the former. Nevertheless, Kardong argues that 'books given out for *lectio* were really fascicles of the Bible. When the popularity of the Bible declined in the late medieval period, *lectio divina* became something else – usually "pious reading".'[53]

Kardong also notes that 'The movement from public to private *lectio* is a very important step toward restoring the privacy of the individual, a thing that was very precious to the Desert Fathers, but almost totally unknown to the Master.'[54] With little privacy, *lectio divina* and, in fact, any type of reading was essentially a public activity, engaged in with the group. Whether this indicates reading aloud is unclear. In Benedict, however, *lectio divina* 'seems to be strictly a group activity, but Benedict considers it a private affair'.[55] In other words, although the monks read together as a group, that reading was a private activity for each individual monk; the group did not imply a congregation praying – or studying – in unison.

Thomas Keating has noted that modern exegesis no longer has the concerns that the medieval reader did when reading Scripture: 'In the Middle Ages there was a highly developed teaching on the various senses of Scripture. Modern exegesis does not have much regard for it.'[56] To be sure it is with St Benedict's Rule that we gain our first insights into the nature of *lectio divina*, though what we glean from Benedict is slight indeed. Although there are strains of *lectio divina* running through the writings of many of the writers of the early Church, it remains wholly unclear what, other than the Scripture itself, the subject of that *lectio* is to be. It is not until the age of print that curricula of texts begin to be produced, though Cassiodorus does provide a type of early list. Did the *Glossa Ordinaria* readers use this text as a tool for *lectio divina*? I do not believe they did. The *Glossa* was, instead, a reference work, a functional tool; although it was used for devotional study, the stress is more properly placed on the word *study* in that phrase. While one might use a printed Bible as a tool for devotion and contemplation, the *Glossa Ordinaria* was used more as an educational and intellectual tool than as a spiritual or devotional one.

Ultimately, then, I am suggesting two different modes of reading: a devotional one and an intellectual one. While the two need not be mutually exclusively, I do believe that in the Middle Ages there had been a clear distinction. The former has as its sole and focused goal a coming closer to God while the latter is more interested in a fuller understanding of one's faith and relationship with God; the one is based in the heart, the other in the mind. The one is more devotional while the other is more academic-minded. Medieval reading theory for both would vary greatly, if it existed. No handbooks of the type we now understand seem to have been produced in the Middle Ages. Both Augustine's *De Doctrina Christiana* and Hugh of St Victor's *Didascalicon* frustrate anyone looking for a handbook on reading, exegesis or preaching although both do provide a skeleton for reading procedure, if not theory. As Margaret Gibson has written, Hugh's work 'is not a complete survey of knowledge; it is what you need to know for a higher purpose'. Eileen Sweeney and others have argued for the influence, albeit not the presence, of Augustine's *De Doctrina Christiana* in Hugh's work.[57]

What I am working towards here is a separation of *legere* from *lectio* in which *lectio* is the more developed and more personal mode of reading, one used for edification rather than education. Although the words often seem interchangeable, the context in which they are used (by Benedict and Augustine, particularly) is telling, and is worthy of consideration.

3.6 From Legere to Lectio in Augustine

Clearly the early Church considered its members to be readers. Augustine indicates in *De Catechizandis Rudibus*, as Brian Stock notes, that 'The educated who enter the church are members of *a new reading community.*'[58] But just what it meant to Augustine to be a member of a 'reading community' is not very clear. Stock argues that 'above all they must learn how "to hear the divine writings," that is, how to listen to the Bible as it is read aloud to them.'[59] This listening becomes a type of reading in which the catechumen must develop an interpretative and hermeneutic sensibility in order to listen properly. One recalls the famous study of John Ciardi called *How does a Poem Mean?* (in which listening is as important as reading), and it is easy to extrapolate a similar study that might be titled *How does the Bible Mean?* Monographs on how to read the Bible seem to self-reproduce in the contemporary world. Few if any similar works appeared in the medieval world.

The idea of the Church as a community of readers is prevalent throughout Augustine's work. 'Christianity', Brian Stock writes in *Augustine the Reader*, 'emerges as a textual community built around shared principles of interpretation.'[60] The community of the Church, then, is an explicitly hermeneutic one, based as it is on a common understanding of interpretative approaches. But how to achieve this common understanding? Clearly, this is to be done through a type of shared hermeneutic, a hermeneutic that encourages its members to make meaning, to assimilate a variety of interpretative techniques in order to arrive at a commonly shared understanding of the text. In many ways, the *Glossa Ordinaria* is an attempt to express that commonly shared understanding in print form. The *Glossa Ordinaria*, however, is not necessarily prescriptive but is instead suggestive of particular readings. In the burgeoning age of print, the responsibility (and the power) of interpretation sits on the individual reader's shoulders, and it is for him to search out the marginal and interlinear sources and construct a complete (and often complex) meaning for himself.

How then is such listening related to either *legere* or *lectio*? In fact, in *Listening for the Text*, Brian Stock argues for what he terms 'textual communities', 'microsocieties organized around the common understanding of a script'.[61] Individuals in such communities 'existed in a halfway house between literacy and nonliteracy'. As literacy rates began to rise, individuals moved from rearranging text (*legere*) – written or aural – instead to reading (*lectio*) as a reflective act. If meaning is cultivated through the interior, and spoken/written language is the representation of that meaning, then Boethius (building on Plato, in *Consolatio Philosophiae*) leads us to argue that words are imperfect copies of ideas (and, by relation, language is a construct and an imperfect one). As a result *legere* is more about processing ideas, and *lectio* is more about articulating them.

We discover the move from *legere* to *lectio* centred in the work of Augustine, both in practice, in *Confessiones*, and in theory, in *De Doctrina Christiana*; and this movement establishes a practice of reading for personal edification and education that was later ingrained in the production of the *Glossa Ordinaria*. Prior to the age of print, reading centred on one of two goals: oral reading to a group, i.e., congregants or students; or solitary reading of manuscripts, whose goal was often, in the monastic world, the copying of such manuscripts. The movement from *legere*, reading purely for a practical purpose, to *lectio*, reading for edification and contemplation, is first noted clearly in Augustine.

In the *Confessiones*, what James O'Donnell calls an 'ascent from ignorance to illumination' is clearly linked to the development of both the content and form of Augustine's reading.[62] In *De Doctrina Christiana*, the preferred term is *legere* with *lectio* used only once. The issue involves the metaphorical language used to describe the act of reading. Whether it is *lectio*, *legere* or even *ruminatio* (as it is in Gregory the Great), we must realize that, particularly in the earliest stages of silent reading and reflection, the word used to describe the act is innately linked into the attitude toward the act itself. Is it passive or active? Is it a gathering, as in the sense of *legere*, or a type of mastication and, by result, digestion, as in *ruminatio*?

Indeed, *legere* is what George Lakoff and Mark Johnson call a 'spatial metaphor'.[63] Since 'we typically conceptualize the nonphysical *in terms of* the physical,' it is easy to understand how the verb *legere*, meaning 'to gather' is often used to stand in for 'to read'. The act of reading is an act of gathering information and data in the space of the mind. Because human beings visualize so readily, again according to Lakoff and Johnson, the mind is conceptualized as a container into which the individual places gathered information, data, ideas. This metaphorical gathering, *legere*, is realized in texts such as the *Glossa Ordinaria* where the information is presented in a somewhat unformed medium, awaiting the reader's *lectio*, processing that information, transforming it into knowledge.

3.7 Gregory the Great

The exegetical methods of Gregory the Great became the dominant hermeneutic for biblical study in the Middle Ages, in many ways replacing the fourfold method of Origen. Henri de Lubac even refers to 'the Gregorian age', since Gregory's exegetical method was adopted and adapted by so many in the period. I am not as interested in Gregory's method here as I am in its implications for glossing and the use of glosses in reading the Bible. For Gregory, 'The meaning of a text was as much the creation of its reader as it was determined by the text.'[64] And it is this approach to scriptural meaning that empowers the glossator in his work on the *Glossa Ordinaria* – that the text's meaning might change for each reader and that there is no one, concrete and indisputable, meaning. Meaning is dependent on the approach, background and goal/intent of the reader. We see this type of reading reflected in what Robert Scholes calls 'centrifugal reading'. Such a reading 'sees the life of a text as occurring along its circumference, which is constantly expanding, encompassing new possibilities of meaning'.[65] An approach which 'privileges the margin', centrifugal reading refuses to come to a fixed meaning, assuming as it does that meaning changes with reading, and that reading is an ongoing, ever-changing process itself.

The idea that Scripture contains two levels of meaning, the literal and the allegorical (or spiritual), contributes to glossing the text as glossing may permit the reader to penetrate the literal meaning to reach the more important allegorical meaning. Gregory implies that the spiritual interpretation 'illuminates what is concealed by the letter of the Law'.[66]

3.8 Robert of Melun

Robert of Melun (*c*.1100–67), a significant but understudied contemporary of Peter Abelard, made some interesting remarks on glossing, and although these remarks do not seem to be the norm for the period, they are nevertheless important. Put simply, Robert objects to the practice. What exactly were Robert's objections? First, he felt that glossed Bible texts had attained a degree of authority themselves, discounting perhaps the importance of the Scripture at the centre of the work. Second, he was concerned that readers were studying texts such as these in order 'to be considered studious', but in reality 'they prefer not understanding to not reading.'[67] This concern, as Constant Mews puts it, that 'reading had become an end in itself,' is seen later in such authors as Richard Rolle, the fourteenth-century English mystic, who was concerned that reading was being substituted for learning and for spiritual development. Robert of Melun is merciless when it comes to the glossators themselves: 'It is clear that the masters of the glosses – for this is the name by which they are known – lack understanding of the glosses as much as of their text, even though they can distinguish glosses and divide them with full stops and assign a gloss to the text to which it belongs.'[68] The charge seems to be that the glossators are merely clerks, adept at compilation and formatting but virtually clueless when it comes to the content of their work. This is akin to a student who may be able to translate his Latin or French literally but has no real understanding of the content of those translations. Robert of Melun is clearly more interested in the content: 'Robert emphasises the importance of grasping the *sententia*, the thought or opinion behind a text. A book of *sententie* or thoughts about issues raised by scripture he thought of more value than simple glosses on the scriptural text.'[69]

3.9 The Importance of Grammar Study to Biblical Exegesis/Reading

It is difficult to discern which came first: study of grammar in the service of study of Scripture or vice versa. One thing is clear: because the Church felt that Latin was the divine language, it was imperative that anyone desiring a deeper understanding of Scripture must study Latin and its grammar. In this sense, the study of Latin grammar itself grew to a devotional practice by the high Middle Ages. As Vivien Law writes, 'To play any part in the life of the Church – to gain access to the Scripture, to read the writings of the Church Fathers, even to comprehend the liturgy – a knowledge of Latin was essential.'[70] Studies of grammar and manuscript transmission of the grammars of Priscian and Donatus, to name just two, flourished throughout the Middle Ages. The reputation of these two grammarians was no doubt enhanced by their citation in later Church Fathers. Jerome, for example, refers to Donatus as *praeceptor meus* ('my instructor').[71] Along with Isidore's *Etymologiae*, Donatus and Priscian 'formed the core of the early mediaeval grammarian's library'.[72] By the time of Augustine, it was not uncommon for the patristic *œuvre* to include a Latin grammar.[73] These Christian authors clearly felt that an understanding of Latin grammar was key to a fuller understanding and reading of Scripture, and the examples often used in these grammars are culled from the Old and New Testaments.

Nevertheless, in Cassiodorus' *Introduction to Divine and Human Readings*, which may be the earliest ecclesiastical handbook, grammar is still directly linked to spoken language: 'Grammar is skill in the art of cultivated speech.'[74] In John of Salisbury's *Metalogicon*, grammar is viewed as the first and perhaps most important of the seven liberal arts, necessary for ascending the hierarchy of learning and reading the higher levels of ethics and theology. In order to understand God's Word, theology, one must first understand the language of God's word, Latin.

The practice of the Latin gloss is evident throughout both patristic literature and early vernacular literature, as glossing of Latin patristic texts occurred as often as glossing of vernacular texts in Latin. Even Erasmus' first edition of the Greek New Testament included glosses and annotations in Latin. Clearly even today, if one wants to be a serious exegete, one must learn and understand Latin. But my point in mentioning this practice here is to suggest that the critical and analytical tools required to learn Latin and then to gloss in Latin are the same tools one might use to decipher and better understand a complicated Latin text such as the *Glossa Ordinaria*, particularly when that text has, at its heart, the Latin Vulgate.

3.9 Augustine and Hugh of St Victor

Certainly, more than any other texts of the Middle Ages, it is in the *De Doctrina Christiana* of Augustine and the *Didascalicon* of Hugh of St Victor that we find the best evidence for a handbook related to reading and reading theory. As Eileen Sweeney has noted, 'Hugh turns reading into a moral project.'[75] Hugh writes: 'Twofold is the fruit of sacred reading, because it either instructs the mind with knowledge or it equips it with morals.'[76] Augustine's intention in the *De Doctrina Christiana* is to 'set out the rules to guide the faithful in the reading and teaching of Scripture'.[77] Both Hugh and Augustine encourage multiple interpretations of a text. Of course, this also confuses the issue as this would require acceptance of multiple interpretations of Hugh's and Augustine's own texts, but that is another issue.

The very notion of reading any text, especially Scripture, literally is dismissed by Hugh of St Victor: 'I know that the Divine Scripture, more than all other books, is compressed in its text ... There are certain places in the divine page which cannot be read literally.'[78] Later he explains how literal readings may produce contradictions: 'Even so the Divine Page, in its literal sense, contains many things which seem both to be opposed to each other and, sometimes, to impart something which smacks of the absurd or the impossible.'[79] Augustine agrees: 'Sometimes not just one meaning but two or more meanings are perceived in the same words of scripture.'[80] In fact, Augustine consistently stresses the more mystical nature of language, that is, authors are not always able to say what they want using the tools of human language. As a result, meaning is often unclear or hidden: 'Perhaps the author too saw that very meaning in the words which we are trying to understand.'[81] This multiple meaning is a gift from

God: 'Could God have built into the divine eloquence a more generous or bountiful gift than the possibility of understanding the same words in several ways, all of them deriving confirmation from other no less divinely inspired passages?'[82] But Augustine warns against taking a meaning 'which cannot be verified by unequivocal support' and relying on it for interpretation. The suggestion that the reader seek understanding of such words or passages by looking beyond Scripture is strongly disputed: 'But this practice is dangerous; it is much safer to operate within the divine scriptures.'[83] As a result, neither Augustine nor Hugh treats the scriptural text as if it had only one meaning, literal or otherwise. The freedom with which each endows the text is evident, then, in the practice of glossing the text and reading the glosses based upon a variety of interpretative models.

In the *Confessiones* we witness the maturation of Augustine's intellect as he moves from naive child to rational and analytical, and eventually faithful, adult. Augustine uses reading not only as education and edification, but it is also presented as a solution to problems. In *Confessiones* 3.12 Augustine explains that when he was a child his mother was told: 'Just pray to God for him. From his own reading he will discover his mistakes and the depth of his profanity.'[84] Reading then is self-discovery and an opportunity for self-correction. The reading of Augustine's text itself is, he says, intended as instruction: 'But when others read of those past sins of mine, or hear about them, their hearts are stirred so that they no longer lie listless in despair, crying "I cannot". Instead their hearts are roused by the love of your mercy and the joy of your grace.'[85] As Ralph Flores puts it, 'by Augustine's instruction, the reader, too, is instructed.'[86] Although moderns assume the importance of reading not only to intellectual development but to emotional maturity, medieval people relied more on the spoken word, most often received, of course, in a church. So Augustine's experience is not only important, it is perhaps one of the first such reading experiences to be recorded. And the shift from orality to literacy is moved further forward to the age of silent reading via Augustine's observation of Ambrose.

The relationship between silent reading – and silence itself – and contemplation is striking.[87] It is not until Augustine is able to filter out the noise of sin and daily life that he is truly able to come to the heart of existence. It is that achievement, an achievement accomplished through reading, that marks the most important stage in Augustine's intellectual and spiritual development. It is the piercing of the word/Word itself, the realization that allegorical reading, what Augustine refers to in *De Doctrina Christiana* as the 'hidden meaning', is an integral part of understanding.[88] That realization is achieved in silence, a fact that Benedict knew all too well. The broad subject of Chapter 6 of Benedict's Rule is silence (*taciturnitas*), and Benedict addresses silence as the solution to 'evil speech' (*malis verbis*). In other places, Benedict orders 'profound silence' (*silentium*) at meals so that the reader may be heard.[89] Later, in Chapter 42, he orders that 'Monks ought to strive for silence at all times.' Finally, in Chapter 48, Benedict relates silence to reading: 'After Sext, however, and they have risen from table, let them rest on their beds in total silence (*omni silentio*). If someone wishes to read (*legere*), let him do so to himself in such a way as to disturb no one.'

4

Reading the *Glossa Ordinaria*: Genesis 1:1, 3:1 and John 1:1

4.1 *The* Glossa Ordinaria *Incipit/Genesis Preface*

The preface to Genesis in the *Glossa Ordinaria* also serves as a general preface for the entire work. In actuality, it is a cobbled-together collection – almost a collage, a post-modern pastiche – of passages, mostly from Augustine, held together with the glue of an assembler, a redactor or, as Augustine might call him, a *cogitator*, that is, one who re-collects memories.[1] If, as Cicero and Quintilian first suggest, the memory is a landscape, a forest, then the reader searches for the various sites of information (*loci*) in that landscape. The analogous space of the page affords us the opportunity to search for the various *loci* in an effort to re-collect information and construct an entirely new, personal space. The redactor of the Genesis preface has searched the collective landscape of Christian exegesis and selected appropriate *loci* for this new space, offering it as a personal space for the reader to adapt to his own knowledge, purposes and understanding.

The preface opens with a passage from *De Genesi ad Litteram* (*The Literal Meaning of Genesis*) in which Augustine encourages careful selection in one's searching of the landscape: 'When we read the inspired books in the light of this wide variety of true doctrines which are drawn from a few words and founded on the firm bases of Catholic belief, choose that one which appears as certainly the meaning intended by the author.'[2] Augustine continues, but the redactor omits, that if the choice is not clear, one should always choose 'in harmony with our faith' texts 'which our faith demands'. While encouraging his reader to engage in selection, he compels him to choose, if not wisely, then faithfully, i.e., with faith. Such an approach speaks against a too rational (and too literal) approach to reading Scripture, something with which Augustine is greatly concerned. If reason does not provide an acceptable interpretation, the reader should always repair to faith.

The next passage which the redactor notes as taken from 'Aug.' also comes from *The Literal Meaning of Genesis*. Again the concern is the nature of interpretation and selection, and here Augustine notes that 'different interpretations are sometimes possible'.[3] However, if an interpretation proves contrary to faith or doctrine, the reader is implored not to 'rush in headlong' but instead to hope that interpretation should 'conform to that of Sacred Scripture'. The redactor is clearly concerned from the start with issues related to a hermeneutic of biblical interpretation. In the first words not from another source, he writes: 'Notandum qi hæc scriptura ita allegoricis verbis texit ut allegoricum sensum contineat: et hystoricam fidem rerum gestarum non omittat' ('It should be noted what this writing conceals with allegorical words: the reader should not lose faith in historical things'), concerned particularly with the allegorical interpretation of Scripture and, echoing Augustine, noting that a faithful interpretation should not be dismissed in lieu of an allegorical one. In other words, a spiritual reading may sometimes be preferable to a literal one. Although Augustine's own work implores the reader to 'consider the eternal truths' in the text, he does not dismiss the real possibility that the reader will require multiple interpretative tools with which to decipher and understand those truths.[4] Such an approach would seem, *sub rosa*, to be the thread that holds the entire *Glossa Ordinaria* together. Without multiple interpretative approaches, the *Glossa Ordinaria* would be much less useful. That the redactor has given us a wide variety of interpretations and approaches is what made this text so important for centuries, indeed through the English Renaissance and into the eighteenth century. Given the ability of memory to re-collect 'is the foundation of all moral training and excellence of judgment', a text that re-collects carries even greater weight.[5]

While choice is key to reading and understanding, informed choice is even more important. Particularly when a multiplicity of texts or interpretations exist, the process by which one chooses to read becomes vital to that individual's understanding and faith. The distinction, for example, between reading a diplomatic edition of a Dickens novel and a scholarly edition, complete with apparatus, can mean the difference between a basic understanding of the plot and a more complete understanding of the critical, historical and theoretical issues inherent in that same text. With the dangers of heresy, the medieval reader needed to be aware of the possibly specious texts he might encounter. Partial responsibility for textual choice and direction lay in the redactor's hands and his careful selection of textual glosses.

The redactor goes on to give an overview of Scripture, noting the collection to come. A cursory look reveals, not surprisingly, reliance on the word of the Gospel authors: '*sicut Evangelium*'. The *Glossa Ordinaria* functions figurally in many ways, chiefly by using patristic writers, in addition to New Testament allusions, in the glosses on Old Testament texts. The redactor joins together disparate elements to present a pastiche of Christian biblical theology in the Middle Ages. In next citing a passage from Jerome's *Hebrew Questions on Genesis*, the redactor offers an excellent example of the hermeneutics of translation. Jerome notes that 'most people' think the opening of Genesis reads, 'In the Son, God made heaven and earth,' but he tells us that the Septuagint 'translated it as *In the beginning*; and in the Hebrew is written *bresith*'.[6] Thus 'the verse can be applied to Christ more in respect of its intention than following its literal translation.' This is vital to the hermeneutic principle of the entire *Glossa Ordinaria*, and it sits on Augustine's shoulders, upon which the literal and the allegorical have an interesting symbiotic relationship. Where some may think them antithetical, the redactor sees them as working in union to a common end as reading allegorically can assist with the literal meaning of the text.

After a citation from Jerome, our redactor briefly explains the four approaches to interpreting Scripture: *historia, allegoria, tropologia* and *anagoge*. As an example of this hermeneutic, the redactor uses the opening verse from John 1: 'In principio erat Verbum.' He implies that connecting John 1:1 to Genesis 1:1 anticipates other verses from the Gospels of Luke and Matthew, not only with the Son present at Creation but with Adam as a prefiguration of Jesus. The preface is an introduction for the reader of what is to come throughout the work: a weaving together of original insight, patristic commentary and Scripture. As a weaver, the redactor works with an array of fabric and colour to weave a dynamic and intricate tapestry. A stress on *verbum* is the focus of the gloss on John 1:1, as explained later in this chapter.

When our redactor gives us a patristic reference or marker (e.g., 'Strabus' or 'Aug.'), we are to be particularly reverent of the authority and *auctoritas*. However, often no such marker is indicated, and one has to wonder whether the imprimatur of the source's author is omitted with intent or by accident. On this opening page, the redactor not only refers the reader to patristics, but he also invokes Plato and Aristotle[7] in his discussion of 'In principio', appealing to the ancient Greeks on the subjects of time and beginning. Amazingly, nothing is left out here, making this preface historically, philosophically and theologically encyclopaedic. We seem to be voyeuristic readers, peering over the shoulder of a great mind who himself is attempting to referee centuries of other great minds. Particularly, the acknowledged importance of pagan Greeks in what is essentially a Christian framework reflects the acceptance, especially in light of the later Scholastics and Aquinas, that those Greeks serve a vital function for Christian philosophy, if not theology.

Often, the redactor pauses to give a paragraph of '*Mystice*', noting the specially hidden meaning in the text, a more mystical reading (from the Latin *mysticus*). Augustine, Isidore and Bede are noted here as providing the '*mystice*' explanation for a figural connection between Genesis 1:1 and John 1:1, and so the redactor moves from 'Primo in verbo' to Adam and Noah. The preface continues with a narrative of Noah and Abraham, moves through David, Saul and the 'transmigratio in babilone', i.e., the Babylonian transmigration. We can see the formation of the forty-two generations of Jesus mentioned in Matthew 1:17.[8] Another '*mystice*' interpretation details the question of *anima* and *corpora*, the conflict between soul and body that arises from the Genesis description of God creating man in his likeness. Citing Augustine's *Two Books on Genesis against the Manichees* (without attribution), the redactor explains that Peter clarified the distinction in the Acts of the Apostles.[9] When he recounts the seven days of creation, we get a thumbnail sketch of the entire *Glossa Ordinaria* on Creation. Nevertheless, these are presented as '*mystice*' interpretations, and this label is used throughout the *Glossa Ordinaria* to provide some of the more interesting and important exegetical points.

Lewis and Short trace this use of *mystice* to Ambrose's commentary on Luke.[10] Ambrose notes that, if one were to read the Genesis text 'mystically',[11] it would be possible to argue that the whole race of man descended from the three sons of Noah in Genesis 10. It is in this '*mystice*' reading of the text that I am most interested. Given that interpretation of the biblical text can often be shrouded in the mystical, looking for hidden meaning and having the Church Fathers upon whom to rely for that meaning forms one of the vital functions of the *Glossa Ordinaria* text as a whole. We would do well here to recall Origen's hermeneutics and consider the relationship to medieval hermeneutics regarding biblical interpretation.

Origen's teaching on mystical tropology implies 'speech turned around'.[12] The mystical tropological approach does in fact take a biblical text and, more importantly, its interpretation and turn it around, looking it at, and within it, from different angles in order to lead the reader to a more evocative and satisfying understanding. As always, the ultimate goal is edification, meditation, contemplation and closeness with God. When the *Glossa Ordinaria* redactor explains a particular interpretation as '*mystice*', we understand that the reading may not be obvious but instead require that we read off the page into the Church Fathers and into faith. The use of the word '*mystice*' to denote this type of reading is not unusual, particularly in Augustine, where it is used in *De Doctrina Christiana* to refer to an especially spiritual approach to reading Scripture: 'Numerorum etiam imperitia multa facit non intelligi translate ac mystice posita in scripturis' ('An unfamiliarity with numbers makes unintelligible many things that are said figuratively and mystically in scripture').[13]

As noted earlier in the present study, this type of reading developed out of monastic practice, particularly the Benedictine Rule. As Henri de Lubac notes, the practice is picked up by Bernard of Clairvaux, but I argue here that this hermeneutic of reading Scripture was already ingrained in the *Glossa Ordinaria*, centuries before Bernard. In fact, if the reader approaches the biblical text with only a literal eye, there is no need for the *Glossa Ordinaria* at all – the text itself, as Fundamentalist Christians today argue, is enough. Augustine himself, who encouraged us to read with multiple interpretations, would have appreciated the multilayered *Glossa Ordinaria*, with its multitude of readings peeled like the skins of an onion, each revealing a new, exciting and fresh approach to the text. Whether one reading is more valid than another is almost entirely up to the individual reader, who is going to assemble his own reading of the text based on the different skins he has chosen to peel back. One way to see those onion skins is to examine particular verses as examples. Indeed, a '*mystice*' reading of the text will reveal in the same way that 'Jesus Christ was once held hidden under the letter of the ancient Scriptures, and one could not discover him in them until the hour of his advent.'[14] Michel de Certeau argues that much that is 'mystical', i.e., hidden from regular view and thus marginal, was by the sixteenth century pushed off the metaphorical page, into the margins and even off the page completely. A hermeneutic that combines the reader's memory and knowledge with the gathered knowledge of the Church Fathers reveals the light in the darkness. Such exegesis reveals 'The secret and hidden sense of Christ itself'.[15]

4.2 Genesis 1:1

'In the beginning God created the heavens and the earth.' *In principio*. This verse begins the journey into the text of the Bible and of the *Glossa Ordinaria* proper. And we might even suggest 'in the beginning' as an appropriate epigraph for the entire text, a text concerned with beginnings, the past, and how those beginnings feed the present. How does the Christian present fulfil the Hebrew (and even Greek) past? Once the peeling of the skins has begun, the onion reveals complexities, nuances and the wonders of what the Church Fathers refer to as 'the mystery' (*mysterium*). And it is a mystery sometimes cloaked in language allegorical, obscure and even obtuse.

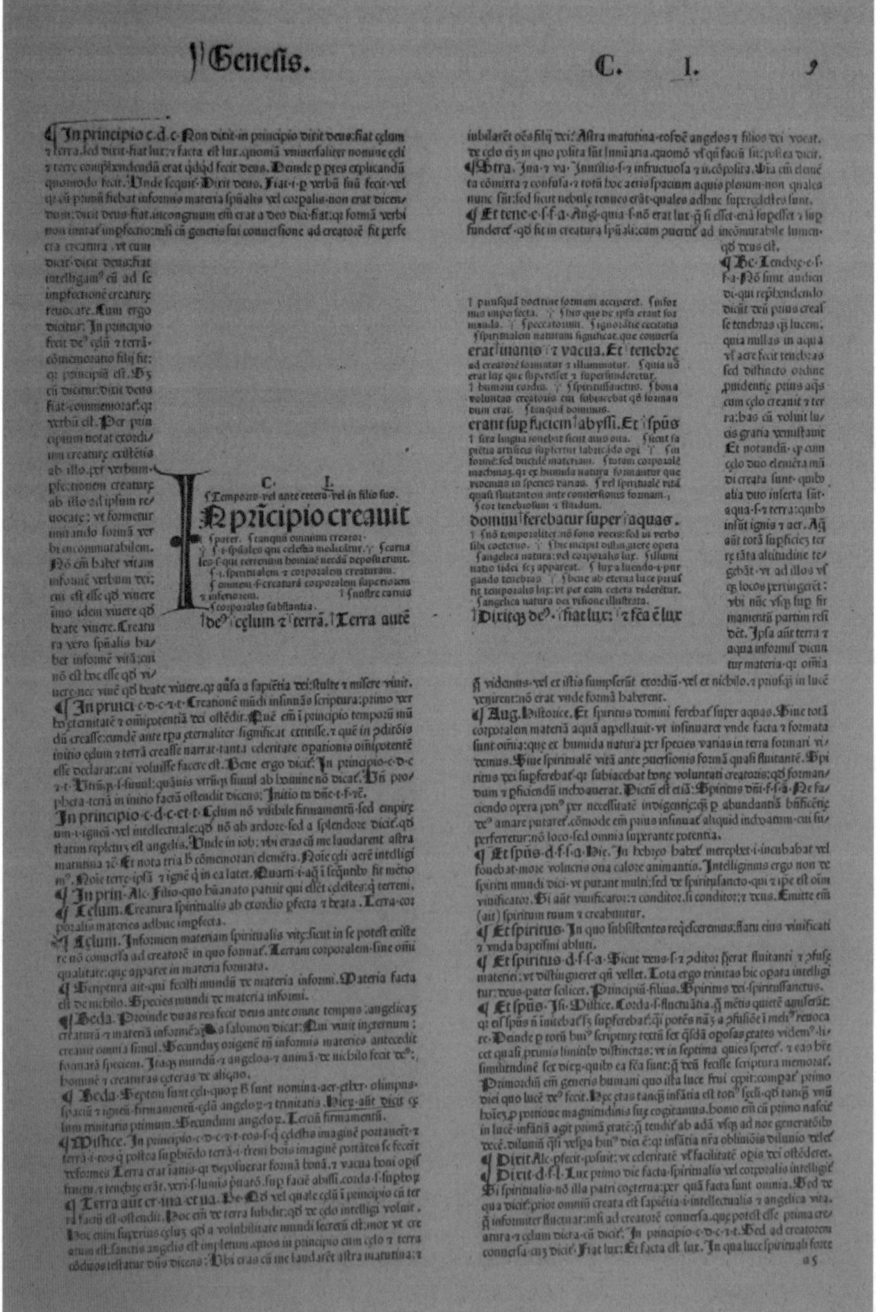
Genesis. C. I.

In principio creauit deus celum et terram. Terra autem erat inanis et vacua. Et tenebre erant super faciem abyssi. Et spiritus domini ferebatur super aquas. Dixitque deus fiat lux: et facta est lux

Illustration 5 Genesis 1:1 from *Biblia Latina cum Glossa Ordinaria: Facsimile Reprint of the Editio Princeps Adolph Rusch of Strassburg 1480/81*, introduction by Karlfried Froehlich and Margaret T. Gibson (1992). Photo courtesy of Brepols Publishers, Turnhout, Belgium.

The first marginal gloss on Genesis 1:1 notes that God did not actually 'say' but instead created by '*fiat*', i.e., he commanded that the heavens and the earth come into existence. In fact, this initial gloss is much concerned with the notion of creation by fiat, even offering an alternate as '*In principio fecit deus caelum et terram*' ('In the beginning God caused the heaven and earth to exist'). In this sense, God is noted as the fashioner or maker (from the Latin *facere*). As we might expect, much of the concern here involves language and word (*verbum*) choice. There is a clear distinction between *verbum* and *verbum dei* (the word of God). Words signify, as we have seen in Augustine (and understand from modern linguistics and structuralist theory), but only the Word of God has the power to create. As Augustine tells us in *De Doctrina Christiana*, ambiguity (*ambiguitas*) is present throughout Scripture, and it is the responsibility of the reader to develop a hermeneutic with which he will resolve such ambiguity. Confusions resolved by punctuation[16] are not as difficult as 'the ambiguities of metaphorical words'.[17] As Augustine notes throughout his work, 'one must take care not to interpret a figurative expression literally.'[18] One who reads the text literally is trapped in 'a miserable kind of spiritual slavery' (*animae servitus*) and is 'incapable of raising the mind's eye above the physical creation so as to absorb the eternal light'.[19] Thus, Augustine is able to read Genesis 1:1 as an allusion to the '*verbum*' of John 1:1 and weave the texts – Old Testament and New – together, something the *Glossa Ordinaria* redactor does more explicitly in the glosses on John 1.

The marginal glosses on this opening Genesis verse indicate the depth with which the *Glossa Ordinaria* reads the biblical text. With a focus on both *verbum* and *auctoritas*, the text provides its reader with a rounded but open-ended interpretation, encouraging further exploration but also providing what would be sufficient for either *lectio divina*, *lectio spiritualis* or academic reading. One truly gets the feeling that one is reading the text over the shoulders of the authorities who have preceded, whether they are explicitly referenced or not. Thus, Seneca, never explicitly noted in the *Glossa Ordinaria,* seems present in a variety of ways that imply his ancient oral-based textual hermeneutic. As Michel Foucault notes, Seneca 'said we should alternate between reading and writing'.[20] What surfaces is a new hermeneutic of reading, a hypertextually theoretical approach to reading in and outside the text. As time progressed, by the 1480/1 edition especially, there is a wealth of knowledge and writing on Scripture, and the *Glossa Ordinaria* text certainly seems to encourage its reader not only to acknowledge but also to utilize that knowledge and writing in his own reading and interpretation.

To be sure, it is Augustine as *auctoritas*[21] who looms over the Genesis text, with no fewer than two explicit and at least a half-dozen implicit references on the first page of the preface. Other *auctores* mentioned on that first page include 'Tertullianus', 'Hieronymus', 'Strabus', 'Isidorus', 'Beda', 'Aristoteles' and 'Plato'. Such a multitude of interpretations of and comments on Genesis, particularly the opening verses of the first chapter, would appear open and inviting of a hypertext reading. Later printed Bibles, such as the Geneva, first published in 1560, employed the use of extensive marginal notations and footnotes, using superscript letters to refer readers to the relevant marginalia. The *Glossa Ordinaria* is not as explicit in making connections between particular passages and the annotations. Instead the reader is clearly intended to work from the centre of the page out, first reading the Vulgate verse, then the interlinear notation and finally the significant and sometimes extensive marginal notation. However, I argue, the reader may also be encouraged to read beyond the margins of the text, breaking through the boundary of the printed page into the more abstract space of understanding, memory and intellect. The space of the page in particular becomes a site for contention, dissension and dispute. It becomes, in Michel de Certeau's words, 'habitable, like a rented apartment. It transforms another person's property into a space borrowed for a moment by a transient.'[22] When the page can no longer accommodate or contain its ideas, those ideas have nowhere to move but beyond the boundaries of that page. 'The production of a space. Not merely a space of ideas, an ideal space, but a social and a mental space.'[23] This space 'established itself during the Middle Ages' and 'was by definition a space of exchange and communications, and therefore of networks'.[24] Michel de Certeau similarly notes: 'Every story is a travel story – a spatial practice.'[25] Any narrative activity is continually concerned with marking out boundaries.[26] Thus emerge a legitimate space and an alien space; the legitimate space endorsed by the authority or, in the case of the *Glossa Ordinaria*, the *auctoritas* – it is the margins of the page that present the imprimatur for centuries of patristic comment. The alien space is individualized, cleared and colonized by the solitary reader. Thus we see the transformation of the public space of the page into the private space of the reader's mind. Again, de Certeau is astute on this point: the reader 'combines their fragments and creates something un-known in the space organized by their capacity for allowing an indefinite plurality of meanings'.[27] Each reader and each reading of the *Glossa Ordinaria* thus becomes an individualized experience owned by the individual. Influenced by the *auctoritas* in the margins, the reader constructs in the abstract spaces of the mind, integrating memory in ways Socrates wished for, in order to create meaning. The negotiations the reader engages in with the text result in understanding, interpretation, elaboration. As de Certeau again notes, 'the text has a meaning only through its readers; it changes along with them; it is ordered in accord with codes of perception that it does not control.'[28] The author, in this scheme, has little control over a multivalent text as the reader builds and constructs meaning.

In the case of Genesis 1:1 the reader has much to work with, given the cultural importance of the opening verse. The *Glossa Ordinaria* text forces the reader to consider, contemplate, indeed to meditate on the meaning of 'In principio' in order better to understand the nature of time and God's relationship to it. This is, in some ways, a new hermeneutic for the age of print; in other ways, I argue, it is an old hermeneutic applied to a new medium in that it mimics the type of associative thinking described by the ancients. The text demands a non-linear approach as a panoply of interpretative constructs bombards the reader with choices and encourages exploration and even collaboration.

But it is the reader who brings his own faith and experience to the page. This follows Augustine, who, as Marcia Colish notes, argues that 'the words on the sacred page would have no meaning for the reader without his anterior faith.'[29] The text then mediates the author's intended meaning with the reader's understanding. However, this is more than reader-response theory because of the nature of the text. Scripture offers itself to the reader in such a way that he may come with a preconceived notion of the phrase 'In principio' but never have truly reflected on the meaning of the phrase both in and out of the context of the Creation narrative. The glosses in the *Glossa Ordinaria* prompt the reader to enter the meditative, intellectual and spiritual spaces of his mind in order to produce a space open to the interpretative possibilities of the text. As Augustine taught us in the *Confessiones*, memory plays a vital role here. The text is invited into the memory palace, the storehouse of memory, the cloisters of memory – all Augustine's phrases. Its power is 'prodigious', and the process of *cogitare* does indeed collect and (re)arrange the thoughts of the individual to make sense of what it already knows in light of the new information coming in. Augustine even goes so far as to say: 'the mind and the memory are one and the same.'[30] As in Hugh of St Victor, the entire process of reading and learning centres in meditation.[31] The reader in this case need not be a cleric or a scholar, though those are the classes most likely to be exposed to and have access to the text at the time.

The redactor goes to great lengths to relate Genesis 1:1 to John 1:1, indicating that the Son was present at Creation. The perfecting of the creator (*perfectionem creaturae*) recalls the unchangeable word (*verbum incommutabile*). In his work *On Genesis against the Manichees*, Augustine argues that Christ was present at Creation. In that work he also professes that 'there was no time before the beginning of time. For God also made time, and thus there was no time before he made time.'[32] Although there is other patristic commentary on Genesis, it is significant here that the *Glossa Ordinaria* redactor chooses an Augustinian approach to the text,[33] perhaps revealing his connection to an Augustinian order.[34]

4.3 Genesis 3:1

Any attempt to compile a complete reading of the *Glossa Ordinaria* will fail. The book is tremendous, and has so many various strands that reading it at times feels like handling an unruly sea of hydras. Because of this, I selected one of the more familiar texts, Genesis 1:1, as a first example for this primer. Using Genesis 3:1, I now illustrate the hermeneutic principles behind reading this complex and important text.

Both our cultural and theological interpretation of Genesis 3, the Fall narrative, is largely indebted to the theology of Augustine. As a result, it is no surprise that the *Glossa Ordinaria* text for Genesis 3 is littered with Augustine references, both explicit and allusive. The central text of Genesis 3 begins on the twenty-fifth page of the *Glossa* text, and only contains three lines of verse on its first page: 'Sed et serpens erat callidior cunctis animantibus terre que fecerat dominus deus. Qui dixit ad mulierem.' If we ignore the interlinear glosses for the moment, these opening lines offer four extensive marginal glosses. In fact, Augustine's *De Genesi ad Litteram* is the primary source for most of the marginal glosses on Genesis 3. The idea that the serpent was the most subtle of the creatures is undoubtedly a debt to earlier creation mythologies and pagan systems in which serpents were symbols of wisdom. Augustine writes that 'it is in a figurative sense that the serpent is called "the most subtle" (*prudentissimus*) or, according to many Latin manuscripts, "the wisest" (*sapientissimus*).'[35] The marginal gloss summarizes this Augustinian text, but it fails to refer to it explicitly, not giving the reader a direct reference.

Augustine is clear in his text that the serpent is the Devil in disguise: 'The serpent signifies the devil who was certainly not simple.'[36] This explicitly Christian reading of the verse is then itself glossed by Augustine when he refers his reader to the Hebrew: 'I leave it to experts in Hebrew to say what the proper meaning of the word is in that language and whether in that language men may be called wise and understood to be wise in a bad sense not by a misuse, but by the proper use, of the word.'[37] As Brenda Deen Schildgen notes, Augustine suggests in *De Doctrina Christiana* that 'Meaning cannot be fixed because it is fragmented or scattered throughout a large range of possible meanings.'[38] Augustine suggests instead a 'textual community' in which interpretations live and change according to the historical and social context of members of that text's community. Such a textual community is suggested throughout Brian Stock's scholarship on Augustine. Stock suggests that 'The bishop of Hippo is the first genuine theorist in the field' of reading hermeneutics.[39]

As a result, when the *Glossa Ordinaria* redactor employs Augustine as his prime marginal operator, he is by a natural relationship suggesting application of Augustine's hermeneutics of reading to the *Glossa Ordinaria* text. In some sense, the redactor tells the reader: 'This is not what is important; what is important is that you leave this text.' The reader thus becomes a traveller with an open access pass; he is able to come and go as he pleases, to follow his whim in what he observes outside the bus and chooses to explore, but he always has the option and invitation to return to the bus. This hypertextual journey operates not in the actual space of the city, as in the spatial theory of Henri Lefebvre, but in the abstract space of the reader's mind. Through associative-type linking, the reader is presented with myriad options; pursued to their fullest – e.g., reading the entirety of Augustine's work on Genesis – will most likely return the reader to the *Glossa Ordinaria*. However, as with the medieval pilgrimage, it is the process, the journey, that becomes more important than the destination. What the pilgrim/reader learns along the way will serve as, in Wordsworth's words, 'food / For future years' in the reader's growing understanding and memory. This is indeed reading for self-exploration, contemplation, rumination. The reader is not confined to the text of Genesis 3:1 but has the freedom to read into the margins and beyond the page. Meditation, meditative reading, is not only encouraged, but it would seem that Augustine models such reading in the *Confessiones*. This type of reading also falls in line with *lectio divina* as prescribed by Benedict in the Rule. '*Lectio divina* and its cognates do not describe a method of interpretation or hermeneutics but a slow, tranquil, and deliberative type of reading that is chiefly grounded in the voice of the reading subject.'[40]

As an example of this 'deliberative type of reading' that might encourage a type of meditative reading, we need only look at the first gloss on Genesis 3:1. The gloss focuses on the use of the word *callidior* to describe the serpent. The marginal gloss is directly from *The Literal Meaning of Genesis* where Augustine reflects on the meaning of the word '*sapientia*' in this context. The chapters from *The Literal Meaning of Genesis* referred to and excerpted are indeed an exploration, a slow rumination, on the meaning of *sapientia* as it relates to a serpent who speaks. Wisdom, Augustine writes, is usually meant 'in a good sense' ('in bonum accipi') when it refers to angels or 'anima rationalis' (the rational soul). The fact that the Greek Fathers had already made *sapientia* a synonym for *sophia* and, by extension, *logos* connects this early passage with the New Testament. Augustine gives us no real indication of that semantic/linguistic connection here, instead focusing on the philosophical nature of wisdom and the rational soul. His gloss almost seems intended to answer the simple, but arguable, question, 'How can a snake speak?' In fact, Augustine's response suggests the kind of ruminative reading endorsed by St

Benedict and Gregory the Great and discussed by Jean Leclercq. Augustine writes that 'we speak of wise bees or ants because their works suggest an imitation of wisdom.' It is here that Augustine introduces the reading of the serpent as Satan: 'This serpent, however, could be called the wisest of all the beasts not by reason of its irrational soul but rather because of another spirit, that of the Devil, dwelling in it.'[41]

In truth, that Jerome chose *callidior* for the Vulgate is telling because the word is indeed multidimensional in meaning. Jerome is a bit more detailed on this verse in his own explanation of the Greek word *phronimotatos* ('wisest') used in the Septuagint and the Hebrew *arum* ('crafty'). It can mean not only skilful but artful or sly. It also has connotations of having been taught by experience or practice, thus endorsing the Augustinian reading that the serpent is sly by means of some transfer of experience by Satan. As a result, the gloss peels back meaning, revealing the complexity of a simple word as it relates to an entire theology and doctrine. In this way, the text encourages deeper meaning and, potentially, heresy.

The *Glossa Ordinaria* redactor gives us only the Augustinian gloss that *callidior* is the 'most prudent of translated words'. He then goes on to discuss that the serpent is not a rational spirit, but that a devilish spirit may be able to speak 'the wisest things'. Is this beast intended to function as a rational being? Is the serpent's 'subtlety' equivalent to intelligence? The text here only suggests the questions, leading questions, to encourage the reader to explore the answers himself, primarily in other texts and in his own cultural and educational memory.

The next reference, which the redactor claims is to 'Strabus' (i.e., Strabo), seems instead to come from Peter Lombard, who is citing Augustine where he suggests the serpent is given voice in the same way that the Devil gives voice to the possessed, in other words, unknowingly, thus absolving the serpent as a species of the sin. The redactor notes that the Devil 'was speaking with the serpent unknowing', thus absolving the serpent as a species of the temptation about to be offered.

The next gloss, again from Augustine, notes the '*inexcusabilis*' nature of the lie of the woman. Because the woman was 'mindful' (*memor*) of the precept not to eat the fruit, hers is a 'damnable fault' (*negligentia damnabilis*). A patriarchal reading, to be sure, that reinforces the knowingness of Eve – she was 'mindful' – thus reinforcing the justification of her punishment. What becomes clear as one scans the glosses to Genesis 3:1 is the construction of a general patristic reading of the text. Although we may see this as a particularly misogynstic reading, given the extraordinary blame placed on the woman, the text follows from Augustine's reading of the Fall narrative, thereby endorsing a particular theology.

4.4 John 1:1

The text begins with the Monarchian Prologue attributed to the Spanish theologian and heretic Priscillian (d. 386). The prologue, not included in Jerome's Vulgate, establishes the *auctoritas* and foundation for the authority of the evangelist.[42] This prologue also explicitly links the 'incorruptible beginning' (*incorruptibile principium*) in Genesis to 'the incorruptible end' (*incorruptibilis finis*) – the alpha and the omega. The gloss on the prologue is taken from Augustine's tract on John.[43]

The redactor begins with a defence for those who argue that Christ was not always in existence from the 'eternitate verbi dicens' ('speaking of the eternal word), i.e., Creation. The spoken word ('verbum dicit') is a reflection of the mind of God. The wisdom of God ('sapientia dei') is the result of the word of God, which is equated with Christ. Thus, Christ is present at Creation since 'in the beginning was the word.' The 'eternity of the word' ('eternitas verbi') precedes all. The resulting conclusion is that both the word of God and Christ are co-omnipotent, co-substantial and co-eternal (*coomnipotens et cosubstantialis et coeternus*). The sentiment, and the language, comes directly from the Fourth Lateran Council, held in 1215.[44] Overall, John 1:1 is read here, as it is throughout biblical exegesis, as a rewriting or fulfilment of Genesis 1:1.

5

The *Glossa Ordinaria* and Hypertext

The few verses reviewed in the previous chapter reflect the ethos of the entire text, an invitation – almost oddly – to leave the text, to explore beyond the margins. In this sense, the *Glossa Ordinaria* operates as a medieval version of modern hypertext. Ted Nelson, often credited with coining the term 'hypertext', writes almost exclusively of the concept in the context of the growing world of electronic media in the 1960s. However, other theorists, most recently including literary theorists such as George P. Landow, cultural critics such as Henri Lefebvre and Michel de Certeau, and psychologists such as Rand J. Spiro have helped advance our understanding of the concept to ways of thinking in the abstract. Spiro, for example, has argued for cognitive flexibility in learning, which posits that the successful learner is flexible in his learning modalities and has the ability to reorganize and restructure his knowledge.[1] In fact, I would like to advance the idea even further, taking into account the centuries of patristic thinking on reading, hermeneutics, memory and contemplation/rumination that I have offered in the preceding chapters.

In his seminal 1980 work *Literary Machines*, and building on Vannevar Bush's 1945 essay 'As We May Think' on the memex (which Nelson includes in full in his work), Nelson writes: 'Our Western cultural tradition is a great procession of writings, all with links implicit and explicit between them.'[2] Nelson's driving idea is that 'Literature is an ongoing system of interconnecting documents.'[3] Because such writing relates in insightful ways, Nelson suggests a 'linkage structure between documents' that might 'hold the thoughts together between documents'.[4] The suggestion adapts the print modality to the cognitive process through electronic media. Nelson feels that the burgeoning new electronic media can be structured so that information may be delivered in a way that more closely models the thought process of the human brain.

Hypertext, which Nelson described in 1965 succinctly as 'non-sequential writing', is more about pathways than explicit form: 'in hypertext we may create new forms of writing which better reflect the structure of what we are writing *about*; and readers, choosing a pathway, may follow their interests or current line of thought in a way heretofore considered impossible.'[5] Focused on the future and the utilization of the computer to effectuate this system, Nelson fails to look back and realize that the cognitive process of hypertext has existed since the Middle Ages, indeed, since human beings began to write and read, perhaps even to think. Spiro agrees that 'much of the work on computer hypertext systems has been driven by the power of technology, rather than by a coherent view of the cognitive psychology of nonlinear and multidimensional learning and instruction.'[6] Cognitive flexibility encourages 'the ability to spontaneously restructure one's knowledge' based on new information and understanding.[7] What Spiro has called 'ill-structured domains' seems to layer nicely with Nelson's 'non-sequential writing'.

In an earlier paper, delivered at the Association for Computing Machinery's Twentieth National Conference in 1965, Nelson noted: 'it is almost everywhere necessary to deal with deep structural changes in the arrangements of ideas and things.'[8] His focus, however, in this early paper is on hypertext writing, not reading. Late in the paper, though, in a section subtitled 'Philosophy', he writes that hypertext 'may contain annotations, additions and footnotes from scholars who have examined it. Let me suggest that such an object and system, properly designed and administered, could have great potential for education.'[9] Hypertext, then, empowers the reader with freedom of choice, the freedom to explore the text at hand in the context both of his own previous individual knowledge and the knowledge of the culture at large. To be sure, as Peter Foltz argues, this is 'partly dependent on the amount of background knowledge of the reader'.[10] However, I would argue, the medieval reader had many tools at his beck and call, mostly through memory, that he was perhaps more culturally-aware of the religious milieu in which he lived, and that he was more adept at making the kinds of hypertextual links Nelson recommends, those links being made cognitively instead of on the page or on the screen. In this way, I suggest that knowledge becomes even more personal, empowering the reader with a greater sense of ownership of ideas.

Hypertext systems, like any computer system, work as networks of connecting nodes. A node is, simply, any device connected to a computer network. If we reposit the concept of a node as any *person* connected to a network through a textual medium, we begin to see how the *Glossa Ordinaria* – indeed, any glossed text – might operate in that the reader himself is one of the nodes, a connection point, defined as either a redistribution point or an endpoint along a network of communication. Many of the reader's own links in that node are to memory, the subsequent connection points in the network therein contained. The redactor has provided the reader with the initial links – from the Genesis text to an excerpt from Augustine – and the reader can then make the choice (choice being a concept so integral to hypertext theory) to follow that link to nodes that extend not only off the printed page but into the reader's/Augustine's memory. When Augustine outlines for us his own reading in the *Confessiones*, he explicitly outlines a hermeneutic of reading that includes the use of memory. Each gloss, in this Barthesian world, is a node in the network. But, in some sense, the *Glossa Ordinaria* itself is nothing more than a large node in a larger intellectual network.

Texts such as these are open systems, what Roland Barthes calls 'the writerly text': '*ourselves writing*, before the infinite play of the world ... is traversed, intersected, stopped, plasticized by some singular system ... which reduces the plurality of entrances, the opening of networks, the infinity of languages.'[11] A hypertext, whether literal or figurative, is a gateway into the vast intellectual inheritance/expanse of humanity, a potential text, a text in a continual state of becoming that, once it becomes fixed, once it 'is', has in essence ceased existing in an organic sense. It instead has become, at that point, a corpse, frozen, still and lifeless.

While many hypertext theorists, particularly Nelson and Landow, are clear that their concepts of hypertext are related only to electronic media and the electronic links between texts, I endorse hypertext as a more abstract and cognitive concept, not only a physical and electronic one. Associative thinking, the basic building block of hypertext, is a characteristic of the mind, not of the page or the screen. For the Middle Ages, and armed with Augustine's ideas on memory and his reading hermeneutics, would it not be possible to view reading of a glossed text such as the *Glossa Ordinaria* as conducive to hypertext theory? Most hypertexts are, as Barthes says, 'writerly texts', i.e., texts whose meaning is governed not by the author but by the reader who continually writes (on) the text in order to add dimensionality. I often recall printed encyclopaedia articles on the human body that employed plastic templates for each of the body's systems; when laid one over the other, the complete 'meaning' of the body comes into view. Each of the layers of meaning is governed by the viewer who chooses through which layers he will understand the body. Similarly, the reader who writes on the text of the *Glossa Ordinaria* is making new meaning with each subsequent writing. 'Texts are able to be revisited and reinterpreted by the different audiences that they reach or create.'[12]

For example, using a scholarly article on Joyce's *Ulysses* as his example, Landow writes,

> In each case, the reader can follow the link to another text indicated by the note and thus move entirely outside the scholarly article itself. Having completed reading the note or having decided that it does not warrant a careful reading at the moment, one returns to the main text and continues reading until one encounters another note, at which point one again leaves the main text.[13]

I think Landow stops short here. The reader may not only conduct 'a careful reading' of the note; he may decide to pursue that reference beyond the note to the entire text to which the note refers. In the case of the *Glossa Ordinaria*, this may mean reading all of Augustine's work on Genesis or, more likely, combing through memory for everything the reader may have already learned about Genesis, Augustine, and Augustine's reading of Genesis. The result is a multifaceted and multilayered reading of the text at hand. The verse in Genesis fades into the background as what was in the margins of the printed page becomes more central for the reader.

Let me offer a personal example. As an undergraduate, I fell in love with Milton's *Paradise Lost*, carrying the old Merritt Hughes edition with me as Linus carried his blanket in the Peanuts comic. Hughes's extensive footnotes and glosses were not only enlightening and informative: they were, for me, instructive. When Hughes referred repeatedly to a text by Dante called *The Divine Comedy*, I not only went and looked up the relevant references: I realized that I should be reading Dante if I wanted a better understanding of Milton's text. So I bought a dog-eared copy of Dante at a used bookstore and began reading. When I returned to Milton, that reading of Dante added another layer to my understanding of *Paradise Lost*. Add to that my prior understanding of the Fall narrative, as I had grown up Jewish with the Judaic reading of that text filed in memory. The result was a cultural/academic/intellectual reading enriched by marginal reading, compelling me (as the reader) to read off the page of Hughes's edition of Milton (already a kind of hypertext layer in and of itself) and climb out on to the myriad branches Hughes invited me to explore. The choice, whether to stay with Milton, to read

Hughes's commentary or to go off the page to Dante or Augustine, was entirely mine as the reader.

As Landow writes, 'As a reader, you must decide whether to return to my argument, pursue some of the connections I suggest by links, or, using other capacities of the system, search for connections I have not suggested. The multiplicity of hypertext, which appears in multiple links to individual blocks of text, calls for an active reader.'[14] To be sure, no passive reader will navigate a page of the *Glossa Ordinaria*. The text demands that the reader engage it on multiple levels, employing a variety of reading hermeneutics and the full complement of that reader's background and knowledge, including his previous reading. This has less to do with the back-and-forth concerns of contemporary hypertext theory – much of which fills Landow's work – and more to do with a cognitive process related to memory and the way the mind processes information in the light of previously established knowledge, the kind of cognitive flexibility suggested by Spiro. The links in this case are formed not electronically, not in the space of the cyberuniverse, but in the space of the reader's own mind. The mind is the universe here. Though Landow is writing about the electronic link, he notes well the significance of such a system:

> Electronic linking shifts the boundaries between one text and another as well as between the author and the reader and between and the teacher and the student. It also has radical effects upon our experience of author, text, and work, redefining each. Its effects are so basic, so radical, that it reveals that many of our most cherished, most commonplace, ideas and attitudes toward literature and literary production turn out to be the result of that particular form of information technology and technology of cultural memory that has provided the setting for them.[15]

In fact, that 'cultural memory' forms the integral centre of the *Glossa Ordinaria* and the type of system I am endorsing. Without such a memory, the text degrades to words merely printed on a page. The reader with no knowledge, understanding or even awareness of the Bible or the Church Fathers will come to the *Glossa Ordinaria* page and process nothing; analogously, the reader who has not studied Russian comes to a page of Tolstoy in the original and can process nothing. He does not understand the language. And I suggest that this is in some ways the reading of a different type of language, a different type of reading altogether.

This reader is Augustine's reader; he is an active reader continually searching memory for pertinent information and ideas to relate to the work at hand. In this way, he is the author of his own text, creating a new text, an individual text, a text personal to him and his past. The gathering, the re-collection or *legere*, of information from the text filters through the understanding of memory to produce that new text. Thus each text, each reading of the text, yields distinctive results. No two readings are alike, just as no two readers are, but the readings, though different, may add to each other to have a cumulative effect.

The useful application of hypertext to analogue textuality has been noted by Anders Klitgaard, who writes: 'the concept of reading in the plain old-fashioned sense is still relevant to digital textuality.'[16] To be sure, the model for hypertext's theoretical approach to the digital text is analogue textuality. Any new model bases itself in some ways on the old.[17] Thus, it is not a stretch for us to think backwards and realize that hypertext – and the linking of one text to another – is realized in electronic form based on what the mind was already capable of doing in the abstract. Cognitively, this may not be the linking of text to text but of text to idea and idea to idea, the mind lacking the facility to file tangible works into folders and cabinets.

Michel Foucault described medieval space as 'the space of emplacement', writing that Galileo 'opened up' that space to reveal an 'infinitely open space. In such a space the place of the Middle Ages turned out to be dissolved, as it were: a thing's place was no longer anything but a point in its movement.'[18] In many ways, the space of the *Glossa Ordinaria* foreshadows Galileo's revolution, and the types of social spaces, some of them written, discussed in the work of Henri Lefebvre, spaces defined by a lack of boundaries and extensive use of the margins and the marginal. Coincidentally, such spaces are what Foucault and Derrida call 'nodes' in a greater 'network' of thought. This wide-ranging network is the medieval world itself, one in which boundaries are continually broken to create spaces for new ways of thinking about old issues, theological, philosophical, social and historical. In the growing age of print, the writers of the *Glossa Ordinaria* try to transfer the abstract of those new spaces to the tangible of the printed page. It is, I believe, no coincidence that the printed edition of 1480/1, as well as later printed editions, leaves ample open space in the margins for the reader to add his own comments and glosses. In other words, 'the centre cannot hold': the text spirals out from the centre, an organic and always mutating organism.

As a result, the *Glossa Ordinaria* combines the notion of hypertext – a network of linked nodes – with Vannevar Bush's memex, a tool, in this case a tool for biblical exegesis and understanding. In this context, then, it is interesting that both Bush's memex and the hypertext systems it preceded have so often signalled 'the death of the book'. The *Glossa Ordinaria*, as an early prototype for hypertext, comes at the birth of the printed page but in some ways even then presages the death of the printed page. If the *Glossa Ordinaria* redactor had had access to the modern computer, it would seem he would have employed it to make tangible what he could only theorize, not unlike Galileo's telescope proving what Copernicus could only theorize. However, in many ways I would argue that the medieval mind's ability to think about this text abstractly and reach out and connect texts intellectually, creating a network in the space of the mind, is a human achievement to marvel at.

In his prophetic article outlining his concept of the 'memex', Vannevar Bush notes that the human mind 'operates by association. With one item in its grasp, it snaps instantly to the next that is suggested by the association of thoughts, in accordance with some intricate web of trails carried by the cells of the brain.' The memex, Bush suggests, 'is a device in which an individual stores all his books, records, and communications, and which is mechanized so that it may be consulted with exceeding speed and flexibility'. The *Glossa Ordinaria* is, in effect, an early realization of Bush's conception. With its extensive marginal and interlinear remarks and references, the *Glossa Ordinaria*, like the memex, 'is an enlarged intimate supplement to [the user's] memory'. This massive text operates both as a supplement and a complement to memory, and, like the *Glossa Ordinaria*, the memex affords the user the ability to 'add marginal notes and comments'.

In Bush's suggestion, 'the process of tying two items together is the important thing,' illustrating the conceptual principle behind hypertext linking. If we envisage the medieval scholar poised at his desk, open copy of the *Glossa Ordinaria*[19] in front of him, we can think of the book as a memex for exegetical use. A discussion of a twentieth-century invention – only in theory – and a fifteenth-century printed Bible text might seem anachronistic, but both are really only tools for accessing knowledge. As Jerome McGann points out in a discussion of the printed versus digital book, 'they are just tools designed to manage knowledge and information at different scalar levels.'[20] In several ways, that is the point I am making in this study. The *Glossa Ordinaria* is merely a tool for accessing biblical and exegetical knowledge. Whether in its manuscript versions, its early print editions or Migne's edition in the *Patrologia Latina*, the information remains largely the same; what changes is the way we access that information and the effectiveness of turning that information into knowledge.

In searching for new ways to organize information and transmit knowledge, the medieval mind displayed a startlingly modern understanding of cognitive theory. All the way back to Augustine and his discussions of memory and the hermeneutic of reading, we find many of the same theories discussed in contemporary criticism, but the medieval lacked the technical ability to effectuate what he theorized. The practice was lacking. With the invention of the computer and the advances made in programming, we can now, using modern reading and hypertext theory, fulfil the desires of the medieval who looked for new ways to index and access knowledge. Augustine himself wonders if this is possible: 'I can see the possibility that if someone suitably qualified were interested in devoting a generous amount of time to the good of his brethren he could compile a monograph classifying and setting out all the places, animals, plants and trees, or the stones and metals, and all the other unfamiliar kinds of object mentioned in scripture.'[21] However, it is not merely the compilation that is at stake here, but it is the organization of such material and how one can access it. Cassiodorus also remarks that such works would be helpful. Thomas O'Loughlin has noted the importance of manuals for understanding the Book of Genesis where 'the basic understanding of the role of the commentator was that of teaching.'[22]

In 1965 Ted Nelson noted that hypertext 'could have great potential for education . . . Such a system could grow indefinitely, gradually including more and more of the world's written knowledge.' What Nelson envisaged was an electronic version of what the Middle Ages had already established: a glossed text, one with ample space on the page continually to add more glosses, and one which would be 'linked' to the user's personal knowledge and understanding. It is in this way that the *Glossa Ordinaria* is a cognitive and hermeneutic revolution. In much the same way that Galileo revolutionized our understanding and, more importantly, our way of understanding the universe, the *Glossa Ordinaria* did not necessarily change our understanding of the Bible, but it did amend our way of understanding that text.

Jay David Bolter refers to the electronic book as a 'potential text' in 'a perpetual state of reorganization'.[23] In his ground-breaking work, *Writing Space*, Bolter explains that in the acts of writing and thinking 'it becomes difficult to say where thinking ends and writing begins, where the mind ends and the writing space begins.'[24] Why can we not posit that the mind writes and that we indeed write the mind? That is, writing is a loop of endless thinking in which the mind is continually written as it also advances new thoughts. Such an argument would advance our notions of what 'I' actually means, as Douglas Hofstadter has recently suggested in *I am a Strange Loop*. Thus, Augustine's thinking and use of memory, Bolter's writing and Hofstadter's individuality are tied together with the cognitive hypertext providing the connective tissue of the organism. This is text as conversation, and it is also body as text, conversing with itself, furthering its intellectual development. The text is an extension of the body, the extended memory of the individual, working as a cognitive loop. Bolter suggests that writing's 'reflexive character gives the writer a new awareness of self'.[25] However, this is really no different from Augustine suggesting that memory fulfils the same function. Replace Augustine's 'memory' with Bolter's 'writing', and we find that both are integral to the individual's intellectual and, in Augustine's case, spiritual development.

Notes

Introduction

1. Elizabeth Eisenstein, *The Printing Press as an Agent of Change: Communications and Cultural Transformations in Early Modern Europe* (Cambridge: Cambridge University Press, 1979).
2. Beryl Smalley, *The Study of the Bible in the Middle Ages* (Notre Dame: University of Notre Dame Press, 1964), p. 230.
3. Christopher De Hamel, *Glossed Books of the Bible and the Paris Book Trade* (Woodbridge: D. S. Brewer, 1984), p. xii.
4. William W. E. Slights, *Managing Readers: Printed Marginalia in English Renaissance Books* (Ann Arbor: University of Michigan Press, 2001), p. 256.
5. Jay David Bolter, *Writing Space: The Computer, Hypertext, and the History of Writing* (Hillsdale, NJ: Lawrence Erlbaum Associates, 1991), p. 2.

Chapter 1

1. Beryl Smalley, 'La Glossa Ordinaria: quelques prédécesseurs d'Anselme de Laon', *Recherches de Théologie Ancienne et Médiévale*, 9 (1937), 371.
2. Samuel Berger, *Histoire de la Vulgate pendant les premiers siècles du Moyen Âge* (Paris: Hachette et Cie, 1893), p. 133.
3. De Hamel, *Glossed Books of the Bible*, p. 9.
4. In *A Latin Dictionary* (Oxford: Oxford University Press, 1879).
5. Ausonius, 'Epigrams on Various Matters', in *Ausonius*, with an English translation by Hugh G. Evelyn-White (Cambridge: Cambridge University Press, 1921), p. 1.204.
6. The Revd A. L. Mayhew and Revd Walter W. Skeat, *A Concise Dictionary of Middle English* Oxford: Clarendon Press, 1888).
7. *Oxford English Dictionary*.
8. Hugh of St Victor, *The Didascalicon of Hugh of St Victor: A Medieval Guide to the Arts*, trans. Jerome Taylor (New York: Columbia University Press, 1961), Book 4, Chapter 16; p. 119.
9. See Hermann Kantorowicz (ed.), *Studies in the Glossators of the Roman Law* (Cambridge: Cambridge University Press, 1938).
10. Such as *Liber Extra* (1234), the *Liber Sextus* (1298) and the *Clementines* (1317).
11. Kathy Eden, *Hermeneutics and the Rhetorical Tradition* (New Haven: Yale University Press, 1997), p. 60.
12. Hermann Kantorowicz, 'Note on the development of the gloss to the Justinian and the Canon Law', in Smalley, *Study of the Bible*, p. 53.
13. Ibid.

14 H. J. Jackson, *Marginalia: Readers Writing in Books* (New Haven: Yale University Press, 2001).
15 Slights, *Managing Readers: Printed Marginalia in English Renaissance Books*.
16 H. J. Jackson, *Marginalia: Readers Writing in Books* (New Haven: Yale University Press, 2001), p. 6.
17 Robert Scholes, *Protocols of Reading* (New Haven: Yale University Press, 1989), p. x.
18 Michel de Certeau, *The Practice of Everyday Life*, trans. Steven Rendall (Berkeley: University of California Press, 1984), p. 117.
19 Henri Lefebvre, *The Production of Space*, trans. Donald Nicholson-Smith (Oxford: Oxford University Press, 1991), p. 31.
20 Michel de Certeau, *The Mystic Fable*, I: *The Sixteenth and Seventeenth Centuries*, trans. Michael B. Smith (Chicago: University of Chicago Press, 1992), p. 19.
21 De Hamel, *Glossed Books*, p. 1.
22 Anthony Grafton, *The Footnote: A Curious History* (Cambridge, MA: Harvard University Press, 1997), p.1.
23 Grafton, *The Footnote*, p. 27.
24 Henri de Lubac, *Medieval Exegesis*, II: *The Four Senses of Scripture*, trans. E. M. Macierowski (Grand Rapids: W. B. Eerdmans, 2000), p. 20.
25 Michael Camille, *Image on the Edge: The Margins of Medieval Art* (London: Reaktion, 1992), p. 16.
26 M. B. Parkes, 'Reading, copying and interpreting a text in the early Middle Ages', in *A History of Reading in the West*, ed. Guglielmo Cavallo and Roger Chartier, trans. Lydia G. Cochrane (Amherst: University of Massachusetts Press, 1999), p. 99.
27 I had many graduate school professors who could do this as party tricks, but it was always astounding to the new generation.
28 Literacy rates for the period are difficult to pin down. For some discussion, see Harvey J. Graff, 'The legacies of literacy: continuities and contradictions in Western culture and society', in Suzanne De Castell, Allan Luke and Kieran Egan (eds), *Literacy, Society and Schooling* (New York: Cambridge University Press, 1986), p. 106.
29 Brian Stock, *The Implications of Literacy: Written Language and Models of Interpretation in the Eleventh and Twelfth Centuries* (Princeton: Princeton University Press, 1983), p. 26.
30 Ibid., p. 53.
31 Ibid., p. 326. Stock also notes: 'as the influence of textual culture spread, so did conflicts over the relationship between language, texts, and reality' (p. 327). So the central subject of that relationship provided much fodder for conflict.
32 Ibid., p. 333.
33 Ibid., p. 335.
34 Scholes, *Protocols*, p. 8.
35 Ibid, p. 10.
36 I have chosen, in this study, to focus on the marginal annotation to the text. The interlinear annotation, while significant, requires a greater degree of sophistication in reading – both Latin and reading in general – as well as a greater understanding of the elaborate system of signs developed for the text. I hope to tackle this question in a later study, particularly as that system of signs relates to the work of the early thirteenth-century thinker, Robert Grosseteste.
37 De Hamel, *Glossed Books*, p. 5.
38 Ibid., p. 12.
39 Karlfried Froehlich, 'Introduction', in *Biblia Latina cum Glossa Ordinaria: Facsimile Reprint of the Editio Princeps Adolph Rusch of Strassburg 1480/81* (Turnhout: Brepols, 1993), p. xii.
40 Peter Robinson's 'The Canterbury Tales Project' has been surveying extant copies of Chaucer's work. The numbers are relatively small: 'What we actually have are some eighty-four manuscripts of the *Tales* and four early printed editions dating before 1500' ('The history, discoveries, and aims of the Canterbury Tales Project', *The Chaucer Review*, 38, 2 (2003), 126).
41 Quoted in Froehlich, 'Introduction', p. xiii.
42 Smalley, *Study of the Bible*, p. xxvii.

[43] Johannes Quasten, *Patrology*, II: *The Golden Age of Greek Patristic Literature from the Council of Nicaea to the Council of Chalcedon* (Westminster, MD: Newman Press, 1960), p. 135.
[44] Ibid.
[45] Cyril of Alexandria, Third letter to Nestorius, p. 29.
[46] Cyril, Second letter to Nestorius, p. 5.
[47] See illustration 2.
[48] Richard H. Rouse and Mary A. Rouse, *Preachers, Florilegia and Sermons: Studies on the Manipulus Florum of Thomas of Ireland* (Toronto: Pontifical Institute of Medieval Studies, 1979), p. 4.
[49] A. J. Minnis, *Medieval Theory of Authorship: Scholastic Literary Attitudes in the Later Middle Ages*, 2nd edn (Philadelphia: University of Pennysylvania Press, 1988), p. 4.
[50] Ibid., p. 9.
[51] Minnis, *Medieval Theory*, p. 1.
[52] Ibid., p. 9. Minnis goes on to note that 'The converse often seems to have been true: if a work was good, its medieval readers were disposed to think that it was old.' This would make the medieval attribution of authors such as Pseudo-Dionysius more understandable.
[53] Quoted ibid., p. 11.
[54] Notably, God is often referred to as 'author' (*auctor*).
[55] Augustine, *De Doctrina Christiana*, ed. and trans. R. P. H. Green (Oxford: Clarendon Press, 1995), p. 199. Hereafter cited as *DDC*.
[56] Minnis, *Medieval Theory*, p. 47.
[57] Quoted ibid., p.50.
[58] Quoted ibid., p.52.
[59] See Richard Salomon, *Opicinus de Canistris; Weltbild und Bekenntnisse eines avignonesischen Klerikers des 14, Jahrhunderts von R. G. Salomon mit beiträgen von A. Heimann und R. Krautheimer* (London: Warburg Institute, 1936).
[60] Henri de Lubac, *Corpus Mysticum: The Eucharist and the Church in the Early Middle Ages*, trans. Gemma Simmonds (Notre Dame: University of Notre Dame Press, 2006).
[61] Brian Stock, *Augustine the Reader: Meditation, Self-Knowledge and the Ethics of Interpretation* (Cambridge: Harvard University Press, 1996), p. 6.
[62] Noted by Augustine in *Confessiones*, 1.6.49–52.
[63] Minnis, *Medieval Theory*, p. 42.
[64] Minnis notes a collection of four Psalter prologues in Cambridge, Corpus Christi College, MS 217, fols. 21r–22v (*Medieval Theory*, p. 236, n. 20).
[65] Ibid., p. 42.
[66] This fact is also noted by E. Ann Matter in 'The Church Fathers and the *Glossa Ordinaria*', in Irena Backus (ed.), *The Reception of the Church Fathers in the West: From the Carolingians to the Maurists* (Leiden: E. J. Brill, 1997), I, p.86.
[67] Augustine, *LMG* 1.21.41; p. 45.
[68] Cassiodorus, *An Introduction to Divine and Human Readings*, trans. Leslie Webber Jones (New York: Columbia University Press, 1946), p. 124.
[69] Augustine, *LMG* 1.18.37; p. 41.
[70] Augustine, *DDC*, p. 169.
[71] See the landmark work by such scholars as James O'Donnell and Brian Stock.
[72] See Rosamond McKitterick, *The Carolingians and the Written Word* (Cambridge: Cambridge University Press, 1989), especially ch. 5.
[73] St Benedict, *Benedict's Rule: A Translation and Commentary*, trans. Terrence Kardong (Collegeville, MN: Liturgical Press, 1996). This reference is from ch. 9, my translation. Subsequent references to *The Rule of St. Benedict* are from this edition.
[74] *Rule*, p. 106.
[75] Pieter Roose, '*Lectio divina* among the monks', *Communio*, 13, 4 (Winter 1986), p. 369.
[76] *Rule*, prologue, p. 43.
[77] Roose, '*Lectio divina*', p. 371.

NOTES

[78] Jean Leclercq, *The Love of Learning and the Desire for God: A Study of Monastic Culture*, trans. Catharine Misrahi (New York: Fordham University Press, 1961), p. 14.
[79] Ibid., p. 14.
[80] Ibid,, p. 15.
[81] Quoted in Parkes, 'Reading, copying', p. 92.
[82] Quoted ibid., p. 93.
[83] See Ivan Illich, *In the Vineyard of the Text: A Commentary to Hugh's Didascalicon* (Chicago: University of Chicago Press, 1993), p. 25.
[84] Ibid., p. 57.
[85] Ibid., p. 58.
[86] Smalley, *Study of the Bible*, p. 37.
[87] Mary Carruthers, *The Book of Memory: A Study of Memory in Medieval Culture* (Cambridge: Cambridge University Press, 1990), p. 159.
[88] M. A. Rouse and R. H. Rouse, 'The development of research tools in the 13th century', in *Authentic Witnesses: Approaches to Medieval Texts and Manuscripts* (Notre Dame: University of Notre Dame Press, 1991), p. 221.
[89] Ibid., p. 221.
[90] Ibid., p. 223; cf. Mary A. Rouse and Richard H. Rouse, 'Statim invenire: schools, preachers, and new attitudes on the page', in *Renaissance and Renewal in the Twelfth Century*, ed. Robert L. Benson, Giles Constable and Carol D. Lanham (Toronto: University of Toronto Press, 1991), pp. 202ff.
[91] Theresa Gross-Diaz, *The Psalms Commentary of Gilbert of Poitiers: From Lectio Divina to the Lecture Room* (Leiden: E. J. Brill, 1996), p. 25.
[92] Ibid.
[93] The text is Petrarch's *Secretum*; quoted in Carruthers, *Book of Memory*, p. 163.
[94] Quoted ibid., p. 163.
[95] Illich, *In the Vineyard*, p. 5.
[96] Stock, *Augustine the Reader*, p. 111.
[97] Brian Stock, *Listening for the Text: On the Uses of the Past* (Baltimore: Johns Hopkins University Press, 1990), p. 7.
[98] See, for example, Henry Abramson, *Reading the Talmud: Developing Independence in Gemara Learning* (New York: Feldheim, 2006).
[99] Augustine, *DDC*, p.11.
[100] Ibid.
[101] Augustine, *Confessions*, trans. R. S. Pine-Coffin (New York: Penguin, 1961), p. 146 (7.10). Hereafter cited as *Conf*. I have included book and chapter numbers after each citation for ease of reference.
[102] Augustine, *Confessions*, p. 114 (6.5).
[103] Paul Saenger, *Space between Words: The Origins of Silent Reading* (Stanford: Stanford University Press, 1997), p. 8.
[104] Stock, *Augustine the Reader*, p. 18.
[105] Augustine, *Confessions*, p. 58 (3.4).
[106] See John Hammond Taylor, SJ, 'St. Augustine and the *Hortensius* of Cicero', *Studies in Philology*, 60 (1963), 487–98.
[107] Cicero, *De Inventione*, in *Cicero on Invention, Best Kind of Orator, Topics*, trans. H. M. Hubbell (Cambridge, MA: Harvard University Press, 1949), p. 117.
[108] Kathy Eden, *Hermeneutics and the Rhetorical Tradition* (New Haven: Yale University Press, 1997), p. 18.
[109] Ibid., p. 54.
[110] Augustine, *The Literal Meaning of Genesis*, trans. John Hammond Taylor (New York: Newman Press, 1982), I, p. 19. Hereafter cited as *LMG*.
[111] Augustine, *Confessions*, p. 116 (6.4).
[112] Augustine, *DDC*, p. 165.

[113] Jesse M. Gellrich, *The Idea of the Book in the Middle Ages: Language Theory, Mythology, and Fiction* (Ithaca: Cornell University Press, 1985), p. 129.
[114] Stock, *Augustine the Reader*, p. 109.
[115] Thomas F. Martin, 'Augustine's *Confessiones* as pedagogy: exercises in transformation', in *Augustine and Liberal Education*, ed. Kim Paffenroth and Kevin L. Hughes (Aldershot: Ashgate, 2000), p. 31.
[116] Stock, *Augustine the Reader*, p. 38.
[117] Ibid.
[118] Stock, *Augustine the Reader*, p. 39.
[119] Martin, 'Augustine's *Confessiones*', p. 32.
[120] Guglielmo Cavallo, 'Between *volumen* and codex: reading in the Roman world', in Chartier and Cavallo, *A History of Reading in the West*, p. 71.
[121] Grafton, *Footnote*, p. 5.
[122] Ibid., p. 15.
[123] Nicholson Baker, *The Mezzanine* (New York: Vintage, 1988).
[124] Jacques Derrida, 'Tympan', in *Margins of Philosophy*, trans. Alan Bass (Chicago: University of Chicago Press, 1982).
[125] Camille, *Image on the Edge*, p. 10.
[126] Ibid.
[127] Ibid., p. 16.
[128] Some manuscripts of the *Glossa Ordinaria* do include more elaborate notation systems, though I would hesitate to refer to any of those manuscripts as 'illuminated'.
[129] Camille, *Image on the Edge*, p. 21.
[130] See the fine work of Michel de Certeau in his *Mystic Fable*.
[131] See Michael Fishbane, *Biblical Interpretation in Ancient Israel* (Oxford: Oxford University Press, 1989).
[132] Michael Fishbane, 'Inner-biblical exegesis' in his *The Garments of Torah: Essays in Biblical Hermeneutics* (Bloomington: Indiana University Press, 1992), p. 3.
[133] See, for example, Daniel Boyarin's *Intertextuality and the Reading of Midrash* (Bloomington: Indiana University Press, 1994).
[134] Alfred W. Pollard, 'Margins', *The Printing Art*, 10, 1 (1907), 17.
[135] Jackson, *Marginalia*, p. 2.
[136] Ibid., p. 6.
[137] Ibid., p. 85.
[138] Pollard, 'Margins', 17.
[139] A more detailed discussion of page layout and lining will come in chapter 2.
[140] See http://www.ebook.com.
[141] Jackson, *Marginalia*, p. 87.
[142] Leclercq, *Love of Learning*, p.120.
[143] See John Contreni, *The Cathedral School of Laon from 850 to 930: Its Manuscripts and Masters* (Munich: Arbeo-Gesellschaft, 1978).
[144] Hugh of St Victor, *Didascalicon*, p. 144.
[145] Jerome Taylor, 'Introduction', in *The Didascalicon of Hugh of Saint Victor*, p. 7.
[146] Hugh of St Victor, *Didascalicon*, p. 115.
[147] Quoted in Parkes, 'Reading, copying', 92.
[148] Guy Lobrichon, 'Une nouveauté: les gloses de la Bible', in *Le Moyen Âge et la Bible*, ed. Pierre Riche and Guy Lobrichon (Paris: Beauchesne, 1984), p. 96.
[149] Ibid., pp. 96–7.
[150] *Oxford English Dictionary*.
[151] Ann Moss, *Printed Commonplace-Books and the Structure of Renaissance Thought* (Oxford: Oxford University Press, 1996), p. 13.
[152] Macrobius, *The Saturnalia*, trans. Percival Vaughan Davies (New York: Columbia University Press, 1969), pp. 26–7.

153 Moss, *Printed Commonplace-Books*, p. 15.
154 Rouse, 'Florilegia', p. 165.
155 Matter, 'The Church Fathers and the *Glossa Ordinaria*', p. 109.
156 See *The Cambridge History of the Bible*, ed. Peter R. Ackroyd, Christopher Francis Evans, G. W. H. Lampe and S. L. Greenslade (Cambridge: Cambridge University Press, 1970), III, pp. 204–9.
157 Froehlich, 'Introduction', p. xii, n. 1.
158 In his introduction to the facsimile edition, Froehlich summarizes the known biography of Rusch and his printing house.
159 Manuel Castells, *The Rise of the Network Society* (Malden, MA: Blackwell, 1996), p. 35. It is not my intention here to recall the history of Rusch or his press. Suffice it to say, 'specific social conditions foster technological innovation that itself feeds into the path of economic development and further innovation' (Castells, *The Rise*, p. 37).
160 Froehlich, 'Introduction', p. xv.

Chapter 2

1 See, for example, Smalley, *Study of the Bible*, and 'La Glossa Ordinaria: quelques prédécesseurs d'Anselme de Laon', *Recherches de Théologie Ancienne et Médiévale*, 9 (1937), 365–400.
2 Gross-Diaz, *Psalms Commentary*.
3 *Glossa Ordinaria in Canticum Canticorum: Pars 22*, ed. Mary Dove (Turnhout: Brepols, 1997).
4 See, especially, 'The printed gloss', in *Biblia Latina cum Glossa Ordinaria*, pp. xii–xxvi; and 'An extraordinary achievement: the Glossa Ordinaria in print', in *The Bible as Book: The First Printed Editions*, ed. Paul Saenger and Kimberly Van Kempen (London: The British Library, 1999), pp. 15–21.
5 See Matter, 'The Church Fathers and the Glossa Ordinaria,' pp. 83–111.
6 See, especially, 'The glossed Bible' in *Biblia Latina cum Glossa Ordinaria*, ed. Karlfried Froehlich and Margaret T. Gibson (Turnhout: Brepols, 1992), pp. vii–xi; 'The twelfth-century glossed Bible', *Studia Patristica*, 23 (1990), 232–44; and 'The place of the Glossa Ordinaria in medieval exegesis', in *Ad Litteram: Authoritative Texts and their Medieval Readers*, ed. Kent Emery Jr and Mark D. Jordan (Notre Dame: University of Notre Dame Press, 1992), pp. 5–27.
7 Gibson, 'The place of the Glossa', p. 5.
8 J. de Blic, 'L'œuvre exégétique de Walafrid Strabon et la Glossa Ordinaria', *Recherches de Théologie Ancienne et Médiévale*, 16 (1949), 5–28.
9 See D. E. Luscombe, *The School of Peter Abelard: The Influence of Abelard's Thought in the Early Scholastic Period* (Cambridge: Cambridge University Press, 1970), esp. ch. vi.
10 Quoted in Stephen C. Jaeger, *The Envy of Angels: Cathedral Schools and Social Ideals in Medieval Europe, 950–1200* (Philadelphia: University of Pennsylvania Press, 1993), p. 230.
11 G. R. Evans, 'Masters and disciples: aspects of Christian Interpretations of the Old Testament in the eleventh and twelfth centuries,' in *Hebrew Bible/Old Testament: The History of Its Interpretation*, ed. Magne Sæbo (Göttingen; Vandenhoeck & Ruprecht, 2000), 1, 2, p. 238.
12 *Study of the Bible*, p. 49.
13 See Luscombe, *The School of Peter Abelard*, p. 179.
14 See Laura Cleaver, 'Grammar and her children: learning to read in the art of the twelfth century', *Marginalia*, 9 (2009), http://www.marginalia.co.uk/journal/09education/cleaver.php.
15 Contreni, *The Cathedral School of Laon*.
16 Evans, 'Masters and disciples', p. 238.
17 Jaeger, *The Envy of Angels*, p. 116.
18 Charles Homer Haskins explains the shift well in his *The Renaissance of the Twelfth Century* (Cambridge, MA: Harvard University Press, 1927), pp. 47–54.
19 Jaeger, *Envy of Angels*, p. 4.
20 Ibid.
21 Contreni, *The Cathedral School of Laon*, p. 34.
22 Ibid., p. 37.

[23] Leclercq, *Love of Learning*, p. 3.
[24] Ibid., p. 71.
[25] Ibid., p. 77.
[26] John O. Ward, 'From antiquity to the Renaissance: losses and commentaries on Cicero's *Rhetorica*', in *Medieval Eloquence: Studies in Theory and Practice of Medieval Rhetoric*, ed. James J. Murphy (Berkeley: University of California Press, 1978), p. 31.
[27] Leclercq, *Love of Learning*, p. 113.
[28] John J. Contreni, 'A propos de quelques manuscrits de l'école de Laon au IXe siècle: découvertes et problèmes', *Le Moyen Âge*, 78 (1972), 5–39.
[29] Contreni, *The Cathedral School of Laon*, p. 41.
[30] Ibid., p. 46.
[31] W. M. Lindsay, 'The Laon AZ-type', *Revue des Bibliothèques*, 24 (1914), 15–27. Also see Contreni, *The Cathedral School of Laon*, pp. 47ff.
[32] Dom A. Wilmart argues there is no evidence that Anselm studied under St Anselm of Canterbury. The assumption nevertheless continues to be made (see Wilmart's 'Un commentaire des Psaumes restitué à Anselme de Laon', *Recherches de Théologie Ancienne et Médiévale*, 8 (1936), 341, n. 58).
[33] Valerie I. J. Flint, 'The school of Laon: a reconsideration', *Recherches de Théologie Ancienne et Médiévale*, 43 (1976), 91; and Smalley, *Study of the Bible*, p. 50.
[34] Quoted in Smalley, *Study of the Bible*, p. 50.
[35] Jean Leclercq, 'Le commentaire du Cantique des cantiques attribué à Anselme de Laon', *Recherches de Théologie Ancienne et Médiévale*, 16 (1949), 29–39; Flint, 'School of Laon', 91.
[36] J. Ghellinck, SJ, 'The Sentences of Anselm of Laon and their place in the codification of theology during the XIIth century', *Irish Theological Quarterly*, 6 (1911), 429.
[37] Ibid., 437.
[38] Luscombe, *The School of Peter Abelard*, p. 174.
[39] Ibid., p. 181 is just one example.
[40] Beryl Smalley, 'Gilbertus Universalis, bishop of London (1128–34), and the problem of the "Glossa Ordinaria"', *Recherches de Théologie Ancienne et Médiévale*, 7 (1935), 235–62; and 8 (1936), 24–60.
[41] Smalley, 'Gilbertus' (1935), 244.
[42] Quoted ibid., 247.
[43] Ibid., 249.
[44] De Hamel, *Glossed Books*, p. 2.
[45] Contreni, *The Cathedral School*, p. 2.
[46] Ibid., p. 4.
[47] Ibid., p. 37.
[48] As is the case with the later *Glossa Ordinaria*, there is 'nothing original about Wicbod's work except his system of selection and arrangement of his materials' (Contreni, *The Cathedral School*, p. 38).
[49] Ibid., Appendix A.
[50] Ibid., p. 67.
[51] Ibid., p. 70.
[52] Ibid., p. 71.
[53] For a primer on the importance and influence of Origen, see Henri de Lubac, *History and Spirit: The Understanding of Scripture according to Origen*, trans. Anne Englund Nash (San Francisco: Ignatius Press, 2007).
[54] Contreni, *The Cathedral School*, p. 76.
[55] See Flint, 'The school of Laon', 94.
[56] Ibid., 109.
[57] Marcia L. Colish, 'Another look at the school of Laon', *Archives d'Histoire Doctrinale et Littéraire du Moyen Âge*, 53 (1986), 11.
[58] Flint, 'The school of Laon', 93.
[59] Even if we were to assess the work of Bernard of Clairvaux, we would be blessed with an excess of joys.

60 Flint, 'The school of Laon', 94.
61 Colish, 'Another look', 11.
62 Flint, 'The school of Laon', 92.
63 'Perhaps Anselm had the help of others' (my translation): Smalley, 'La Glossa Ordinaria', 365.
64 De Hamel, *Glosses Books*, p. 3.
65 Karlfried Froehlich, 'Walafrid Strabo and the Glossa Ordinaria: the making of a myth', in Elizabeth A. Livingstone (ed.), *Studia Patristica*, vol. 28 (Leuven, 1993), pp. 192–6; and Smalley, *Study of the Bible*, p. 56.
66 Froehlich, 'Walafrid Strabo', p. 193.
67 Strabo's name itself is curious, 'Strabo' being a Greek nickname meaning 'squinter', used usually for someone with an eye deformation or abnormality.
68 Quoted in Froehlich, 'Walafrid Strabo', p. 193.
69 Ibid., p. 194.
70 Quoted ibid., p. 195.
71 Ibid., p. 196.
72 Smalley, *Study of the Bible*, p. 57.
73 J. de Blic, 'L'œuvre exégétique de Walafrid Strabon et la Glossa Ordinaria', *Recherches de Théologie Ancienne et Médiévale*, 16 (1949), 5.
74 Smalley, *Study of the Bible*, p. 58.
75 De Hamel, *Glossed Books*, p. 4.
76 Ibid.
77 Gross-Diaz, *Psalms Commentary*, p. 25.
78 Ibid., p. xiv.
79 De Hamel, *Glossed Books*, p. 5.
80 Gross-Diaz, *Psalms Commentary*, p. 23.
81 See De Hamel, *Glossed Books*, pp. 14–27 *passim*.
82 Gross-Diaz, *Psalms Commentary*, p. 38.
83 Gross-Diaz notes 'among the 51 twelfth-century manuscripts of the Psalms commentary there are 19 with the *cum textu* format, and 21 without' (ibid., p. 36, n. 45).
84 Ibid., p. 37.
85 De Hamel, *Glossed Books*, p. 25.
86 Ibid., p. 27.
87 Gross-Diaz, *Psalms Commentary*, pp. 35, 36.
88 Ibid., p. 36.
89 Ibid.
90 Ibid., p. 37
91 A complete discussion of the *catena* can be found in Robert Devreesse, 'Chaines exégétiques greques', *Dictionnaire de la Bible. Supplément*, ed. Louis Pirot (Paris: Létouzey and Ané, 1928), pp. 1083–1233; see also *The Oxford Dictionary of the Christian Church*, ed. F. L. Cross and E. A. Livingstone (New York: Oxford University Press, 1997), p. 247.
92 See John O. Ward, 'From marginal gloss to catena commentary: the eleventh-century origins of a rhetorical teaching', *Parergon*, 13, 2 (January 1996), 109–20.
93 Ibid., 114.
94 See, for example, Aquinas, *Catena aurea in quattuor Evangelia*.
95 Gross-Diaz, *Psalms Commentary*, p. 36.
96 Ibid.
97 Dahan, p. 216.
98 De Hamel, *Glossed Books*, p. 18.
99 Ibid., p. 14.
100 Rather than paraphrase material already well presented, I refer the reader to ch. 2 of De Hamel, *Glossed Books*, from which I borrow liberally in this brief section.
101 Bernard Bischoff, *Latin Palaeography: Antiquity and the Middle Ages*, trans. Dáibhí Ó Cróinín and David Ganz (Cambridge: Cambridge University Press, 1990), p. 28.
102 Ibid., pp. 28–9.

103 De Hamel, *Glossed Books*, p. 18.
104 Ibid., p. 19.
105 Ibid.
106 We might expect such commentary to have been forced into the margins of the text and, in some cases, forced off the page. Michel de Certeau notes this propensity in the texts of the Renaissance in his *The Mystic Fable*.
107 Gross-Diaz, *Psalms Commentary*, p. 51.
108 Granted, the assignation of numbers to the Psalms is a much later innovation. Nevertheless, even early exegetes would have examined the Psalter in the order in which the psalms appeared in the text.
109
>I and Pangur Ban my cat,
>'Tis a like task we are at:
>Hunting mice is his delight,
>Hunting words I sit all night. (trans. Robin Flower)

110 Gross-Diaz, *Psalms Commentary*, p. 58.
111 Leclercq, *Love of Learning*, p. 77.
112 Rouse and Rouse, 'Statim invenire', p. 202.
113 *Phaedrus* 275a–b.
114 Mary Carruthers, *Book of Memory*, pp. 175ff.
115 Ibid., p. 159.
116 Ibid., p. 325, n.12.
117 Ibid., p. 159.
118 Ibid., p. 325, n.12.
119 Carruthers concurs (ibid., p. 159). This is indeed disappointing as it would illustrate, wonderfully, a particular approach to learning. However, there appears to be no extant evidence to indicate so.
120 Hugh of St Victor, 'A little book about constructing Noah's Ark', in *The Medieval Craft of Memory*, ed. Mary Carruthers and Jan M. Ziolkowski (Philadelphia: University of Pennsylvania Press, 2002), p. 45.
121 Hugh of St Victor, 'Noah's Ark,' p. 45.
122 Several texts printed in Germany in the late sixteenth century offer the gloved or bare hand as a mnemonic for recollection of the Last Things in meditation and prayer.
123 Rouse and Rouse, 'Statim invenire', p. 203.
124 Carruthers, *Medieval Craft of Memory*, pp. 35, 36.
125 Ibid., p. 43.
126 The phrase is from Haskins, *The Renaissance of the Twelfth Century*, p. 35.
127 Ibid., p. 36.
128 For more on education in the Benedictine Order, see Dom Philibert Schmitz, *Histoire de l'Ordre de Saint-Benoît* (Liège: Éditions de Maredsous, 1949), esp. pp. 55–95.
129 Haskins, *Renaissance*, p. 37.
130 *Rule of Benedict*, ch. 48, pp. 86–7.
131 See ch. 48 of Benedict's *Rule*.
132 Terrence G. Kardong, *Benedict's Rule: A Translation and Commentary* (Collegeville, MN: Liturgical Press, 1996), p. 400.
133 Leclercq, *Love of Learning*, p. 17.
134 Haskins, *Renaissance*, p. 38.
135 Ibid., p. 39; also see his *The Normans in European History* (New York: Houghton Mifflin, 1915), pp. 178–80.
136 Contreni, 'Institutionalization', pp. 1–2.
137 Ibid., p. 4.
138 Gross-Diaz, *Psalms Commentary*, p. 25.
139 Ibid., p. 26.
140 See ibid. p. 26, and De Hamel, *Glossed Books*, pp. 14–27.

[141] Carruthers, *Book of Memory*, p. 6.
[142] Ibid., p. 9.
[143] Hugh of St Victor, 'The three best memory aids for learning history', in *The Medieval Craft of Memory*, ed. Mary Carruthers and Jan M. Ziolkowski (Philadelphia: University of Pennsylvania Press, 2002), p. 39.
[144] Hugh of St Victor, 'The three best memory aids', p. 33.
[145] Hugh of St Victor, 'Noah's Ark', p. 42.
[146] Hugh of St Victor, *Didascalicon*, p. 87.
[147] Ibid., p. 94.
[148] Ibid., p. 93.
[149] Ibid., p. 91.
[150] Carruthers, 'Introduction', in *Medieval Craft of Memory*, p. 1.
[151] Hugh of St Victor, *Didascalicon*, p. 92.
[152] Ibid., p. 93.
[153] Carruthers, 'Introduction', in *Medieval Craft of Memory*, p. 2.
[154] Augustine, *Confessions* ed. J. J. O'Donnell (Oxford: Oxford University Press, 1992), 3.175.
[155] *Conf.*, p. 219 (10.8).
[156] O'Donnell, 2.177.
[157] Stock, *Augustine the Reader*, p. 209.
[158] Ibid., pp. 214–15.
[159] Plato, *Phaedrus*, in *Complete Works*, trans. Alexander Nehamas and Paul Woodruff (Indianapolis: Hackett, 1997), p. 509 (228d).
[160] Ibid., p. 551 (275a).
[161] Ibid., p. 552 (275b).
[162] Carruthers, *Book of Memory*, pp. 160ff.
[163] Ibid., p. 160.
[164] Froehlich, 'The printed gloss', p. xii.
[165] Froehlich, 'Fate', p. 19.
[166] Ibid. p. 19.
[167] Ibid., p. 21.
[168] Froehlich, 'The printed gloss', p. xiii.
[169] Johann Amerbach, *The Correspondence of Johann Amerbach: Early Printing in its Social Context*, ed. and trans. Barbara C. Halporn (Ann Arbor: University of Michigan Press, 2000).
[170] Karlfried Froehlich, 'An extraordinary achievement: the Glossa Ordinaria in print', in *The Bible as Book: The First Printed Editions*, ed. Paul Saenger and Kimberly Van Kampen (London: The British Library, 1999), p. 17.
[171] Froehlich, 'Fate', p. 21.
[172] Froehlich, 'Extraordinary achievement', p. 17.
[173] De Hamel, *Glossed* Books, p. 10.
[174] Froehlich, 'Extraordinary achievement', pp. 17–18.
[175] Ibid., p. 18.
[176] Ibid.
[177] Froehlich, 'Introduction', p. xvi.
[178] Ibid., p. xvii.
[179] Ibid.
[180] Ibid., p. xx.
[181] Ibid., p. xxi.
[182] Ibid., p. xxiii.
[183] Ibid.
[184] Ibid., Preface, p. xxv.
[185] 'A good proportion of the *Patrologie Latine* and the *Patrologie Grecque* was pirated, and the rest, with the exception of a couple of volumes, was either reproduced from other editions or reproduced along with a critical apparatus, which was in some instances also pirated and

included only minor additions or changes' (R. Howard Bloch, *God's Plagiarist: Being an Account of the Fabulous Industry and Irregular Commerce of the Abbé Migne* (Chicago: University of Chicago Press, 1994), p.65).
[186] Froehlich, 'Introduction', p. xxvi.
[187] Bloch, *God's Plagiarist*, p. 12.
[188] Quoted ibid., p. 12.
[189] Ibid., p. 60.

Chapter 3

[1] Stock, *Listening for the Text*, pp. 3–4.
[2] M. B. Parkes, 'Reading, copying and interpreting a text in the early Middle Ages', in Cavallo and Chartier, *A History of Reading in the West*, p. 90.
[3] Ibid., p. 90.
[4] Ibid.
[5] Ian Frederick Moulton, 'Introduction', in *Reading and Literacy in the Middle Ages and Renaissance* (Turnhout: Brepols, 2004), p. xii.
[6] Jesper Svenbro, 'Archaic and classical Greece: the invention of silent reading', in Cavallo and Chartier, *A History of Reading in the West*, p. 41.
[7] Dhuoda, *Handbook for William*, trans. Carol Neel (Lincoln: University of Nebraska Press, 1991), p. 83.
[8] Parkes, 'Reading', p. 91.
[9] Guglielmo Cavallo and Roger Chartier, 'Introduction', in *A History of Reading in the West*, p. 9.
[10] Caroline Walker Bynum, 'Did the twelfth century discover the individual?' *Journal of Ecclesiastical History*, 31 (1980), 4.
[11] Svenbro, 'Archaic and classical Greece', p. 42.
[12] Ibid., p. 44.
[13] Ibid., p. 45.
[14] Walter J. Ong, *Orality and Literacy: The Technologizing of the Word* (London: Routledge, 1982), p. 79.
[15] Stock, *Listening for the Text*, p. 2.
[16] M. T. Clancy, *From Memory to Written Record* (Oxford: Blackwell, 1992), p. 269.
[17] Technically, the Yiddish word for 'to pray'.
[18] Burt Kimmelman, 'The trope of reading in the fourteenth century', in *Reading and Literacy in the Middle Ages and the Renaissance*, ed. Ian Moulton (Turnhout: Brepols, 2004), p. 29.
[19] Ibid., p. 30.
[20] Eric H. Reiter, 'The reader as author of the user-produced manuscript: reading and rewriting popular Latin theology in the late Middle Ages', *Viator*, 27 (1996), 151–69.
[21] Stock, *Implications*, p.334.
[22] Ibid., p. 335.
[23] Stock, *Augustine*, p. 242.
[24] Augustine, *De Trinitate*, 1.3.38.
[25] Augustine, *Conf.*, p. 214 (10.8).
[26] Ibid., pp. 214–15 (10.8).
[27] Ibid., pp. 218–19 (10.11).
[28] Ibid., p. 30 (1.9).
[29] Ibid., p. 58 (3.4).
[30] Ibid., p. 60 (3.5).
[31] Ibid., p. 69 (3.12).
[32] Ibid., p. 108 (5.14).
[33] Ibid., p. 115 (6.4).
[34] Ibid., p. 126 (6.11).
[35] Ibid., p. 146 (7.10).

36 Ibid., p. 167 (8.6).
37 Ibid., p. 168 (8.6).
38 Ibid., p. 178 (8.12).
39 Ibid., p. 178 (8.12).
40 Ibid., p. 168 (8.6).
41 Carruthers, *Book of Memory*, p. 49.
42 Augustine, *Conf.*, p. 185 (9.4).
43 Stock, *Listening for the Text*, p. 45.
44 Ibid., p. 37.
45 Ibid., p. 37.
46 Ibid., p. 112.
47 Augustine, *Conf.*, p. 182 (9.2).
48 Augustine, *DDC*, p. 11.
49 Or in visuals as with the illustrated *Biblia Pauperum*, first printed in the fifteenth century.
50 *Rule of St Benedict*, ch. 48.
51 Ibid., ch. 48.2.
52 Terrence Kardong, 'The vocabulary of monastic lectio in RB 48', *Cistercian Studies*, 16 (1981), 171.
53 Kardong, *Benedict's Rule*, p. 400.
54 Ibid., p. 387.
55 Ibid.
56 Thomas Keating, 'The dynamics of lectio divina', *Word and Spirit*, 7 (1985), 81.
57 Eileen Sweeney, 'Hugh of St Victor: The Augustinian tradition of sacred and secular reading revised', in Edward D. English (ed.), *Reading and Wisdom: The De Doctrina Christiana of Augustine in the Middle Ages* (Notre Dame: University of Notre Dame Press, 1995), p. 62.
58 Stock, *Augustine*, p. 188, emphasis mine.
59 Ibid., p. 189.
60 Ibid., p. 196.
61 Stock, *Listening for the Text*, p. 23.
62 O'Donnell, 'A Reading of the *Confessions*', p. 1.xxxii.
63 George Lakoff and Mark Johnson, *Metaphors We Live By* (Chicago: University of Chicago Press, 1980).
64 R. A. Markus, *Gregory the Great and His World* (Cambridge: Cambridge University Press, 1997), p. 44.
65 Scholes, *Protocols of Reading*, p. 8.
66 Quoted in Markus, *Gregory the Great*, p. 47 (Mor. 28.39.60).
67 Quoted in Constant J. Mews, 'Orality, literacy and authority in the twelfth-century schools', *Exemplaria*, 2 (1990), 486.
68 Quoted in Mews, 'Orality', 487.
69 Ibid.
70 Vivien Law, *The Insular Latin Grammarians* (Woodbridge: Boydell Press, 1982), p. 3.
71 Quoted ibid., p. 14, n .3.
72 Ibid., p. 23.
73 Augustine, Cassiodorus and Isidore are three examples; see Law, *Insular Latin Grammarians*, p. 31.
74 Cassiodorus, *Introduction to Divine and Human Readings*, p. 146.
75 Sweeney, 'Hugh of St Victor', p. 62.
76 Ibid., p. 127.
77 Ibid., p. 63.
78 Ibid., p. 138.
79 Ibid., p. 140.
80 Augustine, *DDC*, p.169.
81 Ibid.

82 Ibid., pp. 169-71.
83 Ibid., p. 171.
84 Augustine, *Conf.*, p. 69 (3.12).
85 Ibid., p. 208 (10.3).
86 Ralph Flores, 'Reading and speech in Augustine's Confessiones', *Augustinian Studies*, 6 (1975), 2.
87 On the early concern with silent recitation of the Canon of the Mass, see Carolo A. Lewis, *The Silent Recitation of the Canon of the Mass* (Bay St Louis: Divine Word Missionaries, 1962).
88 Augustine, *Conf.*, p. 108 (5.14).
89 *Rule of St Benedict*, 38.5.

Chapter 4

1 I have chosen to refer to the *Glossa Ordinaria* assembler as 'the redactor' because I believe he not only assembled the text but made some vital editorial decisions. Thus his job was more than clerical.
2 Augustine, *LMG*, 1.21.
3 Ibid., 1.18.37.
4 Augustine, *LMG*, 1.1.19.
5 Carruthers, *Book of Memory*, p. 69.
6 Jerome, *Saint Jerome's Hebrew Questions on Genesis*, trans. Robert Hayward (Oxford: Clarendon Press, 1995), p. 30.
7 'Plato enim tria initia vel principia . . .'
8 Although the redactor refers us to Augustine, Isidore and Bede, it is from the so-called *Isidoriana*, i.e., work attributed to Isidore of Seville without confirmation, that we find this gloss.
9 'Petro demonstratum est in actibus apostolorum.' The redactor here refers to 1.40 of Augustine's *Two Books on Genesis against the Manichees*, where Augustine explicates the sixth day of creation and Genesis 1:24: 'Let the earth produce the living.' He continues, 'But it calls a living soul the life by which they now begin to desire eternal things.'
10 See Ambrose, *Évangile de S. Luc*, 2.11: 'Putarem in tribus mystice genus hominum conprehensum, quia ex tribus filiis Noe genus omne defluxit humanum, nisi electos cernerem.'
11 The word appears in Ambrose fifty-three times.
12 De Lubac, *Medieval Exegesis*, p. 2.129.
13 Augustine, *DDC*, p. 84.
14 Quoted in de Lubac, *Corpus Mysticum*, p. 2.156.
15 Quoted ibid., p. 2.159.
16 Augustine, *DDC*, p. 3.
17 Ibid., p. 141, 3.20.
18 Ibid., p. 143, 3.20.
19 Ibid., 3.21.
20 Michel Foucault, *The Hermeneutics of the Subject: Lectures at the Collège de France, 1981–1982*, ed. Frédéric Gros (New York: Picador, 2001), p. 359.
21 The word *auctoritas* in some form appears in the *Glossa Ordinaria* more than 250 times.
22 De Certeau, *The Practice of Everyday Life*, p. xxi.
23 Lefebvre, *The Production of Space*, p. 260.
24 Ibid., p. 266.
25 De Certeau, *The Practice of Everyday Life*, p. 115.
26 Ibid., p. 125.
27 Ibid., p. 169.
28 Ibid., p. 170.
29 Colish, *The Mirror of Language*, p. 40.
30 Augustine, *Conf.*, p. 220 (10.14).

NOTES

31 Carruthers, *Book of Memory*, p. 162.
32 Augustine, *Two Books on Genesis*, 1.3, p. 50.
33 For a survey of commentary on the Fall in Genesis, see Eric Jager, *The Tempter's Voice: Language and the Fall in Medieval Literature* (Ithaca: Cornell University Press, 1993).
34 This is, admittedly, pure speculation on my part. I have compiled no other evidence to indicate that the redactor was an Augustinian monk.
35 Augustine, *De Genesi ad Litteram*, 2.135.
36 Augustine, *Against the Manichees*, 2.14 (p. 115).
37 Augustine, *De Genesi ad Litteram*, 2.136.
38 Brenda Deen Schildgen, 'Augustine's answer to Jacques Derrida in the *De Doctrina Christiana*', *New Literary History*, 25 (1994), 384.
39 Brian Stock, *Ethics through Literature: Ascetic and Aesthetic Reading in Western Culture* (Hanover, NH: University Press of New England, 2007), p. 6.
40 Ibid., pp. 60–1.
41 Augustine, *De Genesi ad Litteram*, 2.2.135–6.
42 This is particularly noteworthy, given Priscillian's heretical background.
43 Migne inaccurately prints Augustine's prologue as the prologue to John, omitting the Monarchian prologue altogether.
44 'The Father begetting, the Son begotten, and the Holy Ghost proceeding; consubstantial and co-equal, co-omnipotent and co-eternal, the one principle of the universe, Creator of all things invisible and visible, spiritual and corporeal, who from the beginning of time and by His omnipotent power made from nothing creatures both spiritual and corporeal, angelic, namely, and mundane, and then human, as it were, common, composed of spirit and body' (Canon I).

Chapter 5

1 Roger Chartier also writes about this idea: 'The reader constructs the meaning of any article by relating it, even unconsciously, to what precedes it, accompanies it, or follows it, and from his or her perception of the editorial intent and of the intellectual or political design that governs the publication' ('Languages, Books, and Reading', *Critical Inquiry* 31, 1 (Autumn 2004), 146).
2 Theodor Holm Nelson, *Literary Machines 93.1* (Sausalito, CA: Mindful Press, 1992), p. 2/10.
3 Ibid., p. 2/9.
4 Ibid., p. 2/11.
5 Ibid., p. 0/3.
6 Ibid., p. 6.
7 R. J. Spiro and J. Jehng, 'Cognitive flexibility and hypertext: theory and technology for the non-linear and multidimensional traversal of complex subject matter', in *Cognition, Education, and Multimedia*, ed. D. Nix and R. J. Spiro (Hillsdale, NJ: Lawrence Erlbaum), p. 165.
8 Ted Nelson, 'Computers, creativity, and then ature of the written word', ACM Twentieth National Conference, 1965, p. 84.
9 Ibid.
10 P. W. Foltz, 'Comprehension, coherence, and strategies in hypertext and linear text', in *Hypertext and Cognition*, ed. J. Levonen, J. F. Rouet, A. Dillon and R. J. Spiro (Hillsdale, NJ: Lawrence Erlbaum, 1996), p. 117.
11 Roland Barthes, *S/Z*, trans. Richard Miller (New York: Hill and Wang, 1974), p. 5.
12 Chartier, 'Languages, Books, and Reading', 150.
13 George P. Landow, *Hypertext 2.0* (Baltimore: Johns Hopkins University Press, 1997), p. 4.
14 Ibid., p. 6.
15 Ibid., p. 31.
16 Anders Klitgaard, 'The difference between analogue and digital textuality: an epistemological enquiry', *Readerly/Writerly Texts*, 9 (2002), 83.
17 See Ronald Wright, *A Short History of Progress* (New York: Carroll and Graff, 2005).
18 Michel Foucault, 'Of other spaces', *Diacritics*, 16 (Spring 1986), 22–3.

[19] Admittedly, the complete *Glossa Ordinaria* was not printed until 1481, towards the end of what we would think of as the Middle Ages. Nevertheless, even if the scholar were to be using only one book of the Bible in its *Glossa Ordinaria* form, the idea I am offering follows.
[20] Jerome McGann, 'Visible and invisible books: hermetic images in n-dimensional space', *New Literary History,* 32 (Spring 2001), 284.
[21] Augustine, *DDC*, p. 124
[22] Thomas O'Loughlin, *Teachers and Code-Breakers: The Latin Genesis Tradition, 430–800* (Turnhout: Brepols, 1998), p. 53.
[23] Bolter, *Writing Space*, p. 9.
[24] Ibid., p. 11.
[25] Ibid., p. 210.

Bibliography

Abramson, Henry, *Reading the Talmud: Developing Independence in Gemara Learning* (New York: Feldheim, 2006).
Augustine, *Confessions*, ed. J. J. O'Donnell (Oxford: Oxford University Press, 1992), 3 vols.
Augustine, *Confessions*, trans. R. S. Pine-Coffin (New York: Penguin, 1961).
Augustine, *De Doctrina Christiana*, ed. and trans. R. P. H. Green (Oxford: Clarendon Press, 1995).
Augustine, *The Literal Meaning of Genesis*, trans. John Hammond Taylor (New York: Newman Press, 1982), 2 vols.
Augustine, *Two Books on Genesis against the Manichees* and *On the Literal Interpretation of Genesis: An Unfinished Book*, trans. Roland J. Teske, SJ (Washington, DC: Catholic University Press, 1991).
Ausonius, *Epigrams on Various Matters*, in *Ausonius*, with an English translation by Hugh G. Evelyn-White (Cambridge: Cambridge University Press, 1921).
Baker, Nicholson, *The Mezzanine* (New York: Vintage, 1988).
Barthes, Roland, *S/Z*, trans. Richard Miller (New York: Hill and Wang, 1974).
Baswell, Christopher, 'Talking back to the text: marginal voices in medieval secular literature', in C. Cook Morse, P. Reed Doob and M. Curry Woods (eds.), *The Uses of Manuscripts in Literary Studies* (Kalamazoo: Western Michigan University, 1992), pp. 121–60.
Benedict, Barbara, *Making the Modern Reader: Cultural Mediation in Early Modern Literary Anthologies* (Princeton: Princeton University Press, 1996).
St Benedict, *Benedict's Rule: A Translation and Commentary*, trans. Terrence Kardong (Collegeville, MN: Liturgical Press, 1996).
Berger, Samuel, *Histoire de la Vulgate: pendant les premiers siècles du Moyen Âge* (Paris: Hachette et Cie, 1893).
Berthaud, l'abbé, *Gilbert de la Porrée: évêque de Poitiers et sa philosophie (1070–1154)* (Poitiers: Oudin, 1892).
Bertola, Ermenegildo, 'La Glossa Ordinaria biblica ed i suoi problemi', *Recherches de Théologie Ancienne et Médiévale*, 45 (1978), 34–78.
Betteridge, Maurice, 'The bitter notes: the Geneva Bible and its annotations', *The Sixteenth Century Journal*, 15 (1983), 41–62.

Bischoff, Bernhard, *Latin Palaeography*, trans. Dáibhí Ó Cróinín and David Ganz (Cambridge: Cambridge University Press, 1990).
Black, Robert, *Humanism and Education in Medieval and Renaissance Italy: Tradition and Innovation in Latin Schools from the Twelfth to the Fifteenth Century* (Cambridge: Cambridge University Press, 2001).
Bolter, Jay David, *Writing Space: The Computer, Hypertext, and the History of Writing* (Hillsdale, NJ: Lawrence Erlbaum Associates, 1991).
Boyarin, Daniel, *Intertextuality and the Reading of Midrash* (Bloomington: Indiana University Press, 1994).
Bright, Pamela (ed.), *Augustine and the Bible* (Notre Dame: University of Notre Dame Press, 1986).
Bruns, Gerald, 'The originality of texts in a manuscript culture', *Comparative Literature*, 32 (1980), 113–29.
Burdon, Christopher, 'The margin is the message: commentary's displacement of canon', *Literature and Theology*, 13 (1999), 222–34.
Bush, Vannevar, 'As we may think', *Atlantic Monthly*, 176 (July 1945), 101–8.
Bynum, Caroline Walker, 'Did the twelfth century discover the individual?' *Journal of Ecclesiastical History*, 31 (1980), 1–17.
Camille, Michael, *Image on the Edge: The Margins of Medieval Art* (London: Reaktion, 1992).
Camille, Michael, 'Seeing and reading: some visual implications of medieval literacy and illiteracy', *Art History*, 8 (1985), 26–49.
Carruthers, Mary, *The Book of Memory: A Study of Memory in Medieval Culture* (Cambridge: Cambridge University Press, 1990).
Cary, Phillip, *Augustine's Invention of the Inner Self: The Legacy of a Christian Platonist* (Oxford: Oxford University Press, 2000).
Casey, Michael, *Sacred Reading: The Ancient Art of Lectio Divina* (Liguori, MO: Triumph Books, 1995).
Cassiodorus, *An Introduction to Divine and Human Readings*, trans. Leslie Webber Jones (New York: Columbia University Press, 1946).
Castells, Manuel, *The Rise of the Network Society* (Malden, MA: Blackwell, 1996).
Cavallo, Gugliemo, 'Between *volumen* and codex: reading in the Roman world', in G. Cavallo and R. Chartier (eds.), *A History of Reading in the West*, trans. Lydia G. Cochrane (Amherst: University of Massachusetts Press, 1999), pp. 64–89.
Chartier, Roger, 'Languages, books, and reading', *Critical Inquiry*, 31, 1 (Autumn 2004), 133–52.
Chenu, M. D., 'Auctor, Actor, Autor', *Bulletin Du Cange*, 3 (1927), 81–6.
Cicero, *De Inventione* in *Cicero: On Invention, The Best Kind of Orator, Topics*, trans., H. M. Hubbell (Cambridge, MA: Harvard University Press, 1949).
Cleaver, Laura, 'Grammar and her children: learning to read in the art of the twelfth century', *Marginalia*, 9 (2009), http://www.marginalia.co.uk/journal/09education/cleaver.php.
Colish, Marcia L., 'Another look at the school of Laon', *Archives d'Histoire Doctrinale et Littéraire du Moyen Âge*, 53 (1986), 7–22.
Colish, Marcia L., *Medieval Foundations of the Western Intellectual Tradition, 400–1400* (New Haven: Yale University Press, 1997).

Colish, Marcia L., *The Mirror of Language: A Study in the Medieval Theory of Knowledge* (New Haven: Yale University Press, 1986).
Colish, Marcia L., *Peter Lombard* (Leiden: E. J. Brill, 1994).
Contreni, John, 'A propos de quelques manuscrits de l'école de Laon au IXe siècle: découvertes et problèmes', *Le Moyen Âge*, 78 (1972), 5–39.
Contreni, John, *The Cathedral School of Laon from 850 to 930: Its Manuscripts and Masters* (Munich: Arbeo-Gesellschaft, 1978).
Corns, Thomas N., 'The early modern search engine: indices, title pages, marginalia and contents', in Neil Rhodes and Jonathan Sawday (eds.), *The Renaissance Computer: Knowledge Technology in the First Age of Print* (London: Routledge, 2000), pp. 95–105.
Courtenay, William J., 'The Bible in the fourteenth century: some observations', *Church History*, 54 (1985), 176–87.
Courtenay, William J., 'The institutionalization of theology', in John Van Engen (ed.), *Learning Institutionalized: Teaching in the Medieval University* (Notre Dame: University of Notre Dame Press, 2000), pp. 245–56.
Cyril of Alexandria, *Select Letters*, ed. and trans. Lionel R. Wickham (Oxford: Oxford University Press, 1983).
de Blic, J., 'L'œuvre exégétique de Walafrid Strabon et la Glossa Ordinaria', *Recherches de Théologie Ancienne et Médiévale*, 16 (1949), 5–28.
de Certeau, Michel, *The Mystic Fable*, I: *The Sixteenth and Seventeenth Centuries*, trans. Michael B. Smith (Chicago: University of Chicago Press, 1992).
de Certeau, Michel, *The Practice of Everyday Life*, trans. Steven Rendall (Berkeley: University of California Press, 1984).
De Hamel, Christopher, *The Book: A History of the Bible* (London: Phaidon, 2001).
De Hamel, Christopher, *Glossed Books of the Bible and the Paris Book Trade* (Woodbridge: D. S. Brewer, 1984).
de Lubac, Henri, *Corpus Mysticum: The Eucharist and the Church in the Early Middle Ages*, trans. Gemma Simmonds (Notre Dame: University of Notre Dame Press, 2006).
de Lubac, Henri, *Medieval Exegesis*, II: *The Four Senses of Scripture*, trans. E. M. Macierowski (Grand Rapids: W. B. Eerdmans, 2000).
Derrida, Jacques, *Margins of Philosophy*, trans. Alan Bass (Chicago: University of Chicago Press, 1982).
Dove, Mary (ed.), *Glossa Ordinaria in Canticum Canticorum: Pars 22* (Turnhout: Brepols, 1997).
Eden, Kathy, *Hermeneutics and the Rhetorical Tradition* (New Haven: Yale University Press, 1997).
Eisenstein, Elizabeth, *The Printing Press as an Agent of Change: Communications and Cultural Transformations in Early Modern Europe* (Cambridge: Cambridge University Press, 1979).
Evans, G. R., *The Language and Logic of the Bible: The Earlier Middle Ages* (Cambridge: Cambridge University Press, 1984).
Fishbane, Michael, *Biblical Interpretation in Ancient Israel* (Oxford: Oxford University Press, 1989).
Fishbane, Michael, *The Garments of Torah: Essays in Biblical Hermeneutics* (Bloomington: Indiana University Press, 1992).

Flint, Valerie I. J., 'The school of Laon: a reconsideration', *Recherches de Théologie Ancienne et Médiévale*, 43 (1976), 89–110.
Flores, Ralph, 'Reading and speech in Augustine's Confessiones', *Augustinian Studies*, 6 (1975), 1–13.
Foltz, P. W.' Comprehension, coherence, and strategies in hypertext and linear text', in J. Levonen, J. F. Rouet, A. Dillon and R. J. Spiro (eds.), *Hypertext and Cognition* (Hillsdale, NJ: Lawrence Erlbaum, 1996), pp. 109–36.
Foucault, Michel, *The Hermeneutics of the Subject: Lectures at the Collège de France, 1981–1982*, ed. Frédéric Gros (New York: Picador, 2001).
Foucault, Michel, 'Of other spaces', *Diacritics*, 16 (Spring 1986), 22–7.
Froehlich, Karlfried, 'Church history and the Bible', in Mark S. Burrows, Paul Rorem and Karlfried Froehlich (eds.), *Biblical Hermeneutics in Historical Perspective: Studies in Honor of Karlfried Froehlich on His Sixtieth Birthday* (Grand Rapids: W. B. Eerdmans, 1991), pp. 1–15
Froehlich, Karlfried, 'An extraordinary achievement: the *Glossa Ordinaria* in print', in *The Bible as Book: The First Printed Editions* (London, 1999), pp. 15–21.
Froehlich, Karlfried, 'The fate of the *Glossa Ordinaria* in the sixteenth century', in David C. Steinmetz (ed.), *Die Patristik in der Bibelexegese des 16. Jahrhunderts* (Wiesbaden, 1999), pp. 19–47.
Froehlich, Karlfried, 'Introduction', in *Biblia Latina cum Glossa Ordinaria: Facsimile Reprint of the Editio Princeps Adolph Rusch of Strassburg 1480/81* (Turnhout: Brepols, 1992), p. xii.
Froehlich, Karlfried, 'Postcript', in Mark S. Burrows, Paul Rorem and Karlfried Froehlich (eds.), *Biblical Hermeneutics in Historical Perspective: Studies in Honor of Karlfried Froehlich on His Sixtieth Birthday* (Grand Rapids: Eerdmans, 1991), pp. 339–49.
Froehlich, Karlfried, 'The printed gloss', in *Biblia Latina cum Glossa Ordinaria: Facsimile Reprint of the Editio Princeps Adolph Rusch of Strassburg 1480/81* (Turnhout: Brepols, 1992), pp. xii–xxvi.
Froehlich, Karlfried, 'Walafrid Strabo and the *Glossa Ordinaria*: the making of a myth', *Studia Patristica*, 28 (1993), 192–6.
Gamble, Harry Y., *Books and Readers in the Early Church: A History of Early Christian Texts* (New Haven: Yale University Press, 1995).
Gellrich, Jesse M., *The Idea of the Book in the Middle Ages: Language Theory, Mythology, and Fiction* (Ithaca: Cornell University Press, 1985).
Ghellinck, J., SJ, 'The Sentences of Anselm of Laon and their place in the codification of theology during the XIIth century', *Irish Theological Quarterly*, 6 (1911), 427–41.
Gibson, Margaret T., 'The continuity of learning circa 850–circa 1050', *Viator*, 6 (1975), 1–13.
Gibson, Margaret T., 'The De Doctrina Chrisiana in the school of St Victor', in *Reading and Wisdom: The De Doctrina Christiana of Augustine in the Middle Ages* (Notre Dame: University of Notre Dame Press, 1995), pp. 41–7.
Gibson, Margaret T., "The Glossed Bible", in *Biblia Latina cum Glossa Ordinaria* (Turnhout: Brepols, 1992), pp. vii–xi.
Gibson, Margaret T., 'The Latin apparatus', in Margaret T. Gibson, T. A. Heslop and Richard W. Pfaff (eds.), *The Eadwine Psalter: Text, Image, and Monastic Culture in*

Twelfth-Century Canterbury (London: Modern Humanities Research Association, 1992), pp. 108–22.

Gibson, Margaret, 'The place of the Glossa Ordinaria in medieval exegesis', in Mark D. Jordan and Kent Emery Jr (eds.), *Ad Litteram: Authoritative Texts and their Medieval Readers* (Notre Dame: University of Notre Dame Press, 1992), pp. 5–27.

Gibson, Margaret T., 'The twelfth-century glossed Bible', *Studia Patristica*, 23 (1990), 232–44.

Graff, Harvey J., 'The legacies of literacy: continuities and contradictions in Western culture and society', in Suzanne De Castell, Allan Luke and Kieran Egan (eds.), *Literacy, Society, and Schooling* (New York: Cambridge University Press, 1986), pp. 61–86.

Grafton, Anthony, *Commerce with the Classics: Ancient Books and Renaissance Readers* (Ann Arbor: University of Michigan Press, 1997).

Grafton, Anthony, *The Footnote: A Curious History* (Cambridge, MA: Harvard University Press, 1997).

Greetham, D. C. (ed.), *The Margins of the Text* (Ann Arbor: University of Michigan Press, 1997).

Gross-Diaz, Theresa, The *Psalms Commentary of Gilbert of Poitiers: From Lectio Divina to the Lecture Room* (Leiden: E. J. Brill, 1996).

Hagen, Kenneth, 'What did the term Commentarius mean to sixteenth-century theologians?' in Irena Backus and Francis Higman (eds.), *Théorie et pratique de l'exégèse* (Geneva: Librairie Droz, 1990), pp. 13–38.

Halporn, Barbara C. (ed.), *The Correspondence of Johann Amerbach: Early Printing in Its Social Context* (Ann Arbor: University of Michigan Press, 2000).

Häring, N. M., 'The case of Gilbert de la Porée, bishop of Poitiers (1142–1154)', *Mediaeval Studies*, 13 (1951), 1–40.

Häring, N. M., 'Epitaphs and necrologies on Bishop Gilbert II of Poitiers', *Archives d'Histoire Doctrinale et Littéraire du Moyen Âge*, 44 (1969), 57–87.

Haskins, Charles, 'A list of text-books from the close of the twelfth century', *Harvard Studies in Classical Philology*, 20 (1909), 75–94.

Haskins, Charles, *The Renaissance of the Twelfth Century* (Cambridge, MA: Harvard University Press, 1927).

Hill, Marylu, 'Reading without moving your lips: the role of the solitary reader in liberal education', in Kim Paffenroth and Kevin L. Hughes (eds.), *Augustine and Liberal Education* (Aldershot: Ashgate, 2000), pp. 179–97.

Hugh of St Victor, *The Didascalicon of Hugh of St. Victor: A Medieval Guide to the Arts*, trans. Jerome Taylor (New York: Columbia University Press, 1961).

Hugh of St Victor, 'A little book about constructing Noah's Ark', in Mary Carruthers and Jan M. Ziolkowski (eds.), *The Medieval Craft of Memory* (Philadelphia: University of Pennsylvania Press, 2002), pp. 41–82.

Hugh of St Victor, 'The three best memory aids for learning history', in Mary Carruthers and Jan M. Ziolkowski (eds.), *The Medieval Craft of Memory* (Philadelphia: University of Pennsylvania Press, 2002), pp. 32–40.

Hunt, Tony, 'Vernacular glosses in medieval manuscripts', *Cultura Neolatina*, 39 (1979), 9–37.

Illich, Ivan, *In the Vineyard of the Text: A Commentary to Hugh's Didascalicon* (Chicago: University of Chicago Press, 1993).

Irvine, Martin, *The Making of Textual Culture: 'Grammatica' and Literary Theory, 350–1100* (Cambridge: Cambridge University Press, 1994).
Jackson, H. J., *Marginalia: Readers Writing in Books* (New Haven: Yale University Press, 2001).
Jaeger, Stephen C., *The Envy of Angels: Cathedral Schools and Social Ideals in Medieval Europe, 950–1200* (Philadelphia: University of Pennsylvania Press, 1993).
Jager, Eric, *The Tempter's Voice: Language and the Fall in Medieval Literature* (Ithaca: Cornell University Press, 1993).
Jerome, *Saint Jerome's Hebrew Questions on Genesis*, trans. Robert Hayward (Oxford: Clarendon Press, 1995).
Kantorowicz, Hermann (ed.), *Studies in the Glossators of the Roman Law* (Cambridge: Cambridge University Press, 1938).
Kardong, Terrence, *Benedict's Rule: A Translation and Commentary* (Collegeville, MN: Liturgical Press, 1996).
Kardong, Terrence, 'The vocabulary of monastic lectio in RB 48', *Cistercian Studies*, 16 (1981): 171–81.
Keating, Thomas, 'The dynamics of lectio divina', *Word and Spirit*, 7 (1985), 80–6.
Klitgaard, Anders, 'The difference between analogue and digital textuality: an epistemological enquiry', *Readerly/Writerly Texts*, 9 (2002), 83.
Knox, Bernard M. W., 'Silent Reading in Antiquity', *Greek, Roman and Byzantine Studies*, 9, 4 (1968), 421–35.
Kordecki, Lesley, '"Let me telle yow what I mente": The *Glossa Ordinaria* and the Nun's Priest's Tale', *Exemplaria*, 4, 2 (1992), 365–85.
Lakoff, George and Mark Johnson, *Metaphors We Live By* (Chicago: University of Chicago Press, 1980).
Landow, George P., *Hypertext 2.0* (Baltimore: Johns Hopkins University Press, 1997).
Law, Vivien, *Grammar and Grammarians in the Early Middle Ages* (London: Longman, 1997).
Law, Vivien, *The Insular Latin Grammarians* (Woodbridge: Boydell Press, 1982).
Leclercq, Jean, 'Le commentaire du Cantique des cantiques attribué à Anselme de Laon', *Recherches de Théologie Ancienne et Médiévale*, 16 (1949), 29–39.
Leclercq, Jean, *The Love of Learning and the Desire for God: A Study of Monastic Culture*, trans. Catharine Misrahi (New York: Fordham University Press, 1961).
Lefebvre, Henri, *The Production of Space*, trans. Donald Nicholson-Smith (Oxford: Oxford University Press, 1991).
Lewis, Carolo A., *The Silent Recitation of the Canon of the Mass* (Bay St Louis: Divine Word Missionaries, 1962).
Light, Laura, *The Bible in the Twelfth Century: An Exhibition of Manuscripts at the Houghton Library* (Cambridge, MA: Harvard College Library, 1998).
Lindsay, W. M., 'The Laon of AZ-Type', *Revue des Bibliothèques*, 24 (1914), 15–27.
Lipking, Lawrence, 'The marginal gloss', *Critical Inquiry*, 3 (1977), 609–55.
Lobrichon, G., 'Conserver, réformer, transformer le monde? Les manipulations de l'Apocalypse au Moyen Âge central', in Peter Ganz (ed.),*The Role of the Book in Medieval Culture: Proceedings of the Oxford International Symposium 26 September–1 October 1982* (Turnhout: Brepols, 1986), IV, pp. 75–94.
Lobrichon, Guy, 'Une nouveauté: les gloses de la Bible', in Pierre Riché and Guy Lobrichon (eds.), *Le Moyen Âge et la Bible* (Paris: Beauchesne, 1984), pp. 95–114.

Lottin, D. O., 'Aux origines de l'école théologique d'Anselme de Laon', *Recherches de Théologie Ancienne et Médiévale*, 10 (1938), 101–22.

Luscombe, D. E., *The School of Peter Abelard: The Influence of Abelard's Thought in the Early Scholastic Period* (Cambridge: Cambridge University Press, 1970).

Macrobius, *The Saturnalia*, trans. Percival Vaughan Davies (New York: Columbia University Press, 1969).

Markus, R. A., *Gregory the Great and His World* (Cambridge: Cambridge University Press, 1997).

Markus, R. A., *Signs and Meanings: Word and Text in Ancient Christianity* (Liverpool: Liverpool University Press, 1996).

Martin, Thomas F., 'Augustine's *Confessions* as pedagogy: exercises in transformation', in Kim Paffenroth and Kevin L. Hughes (eds.), *Augustine and Liberal Education* (Aldershot: Ashgate, 2000), pp. 25–51.

Matter, E. Ann, 'The Church Fathers and the *Glossa Ordinaria*', in Irena Backus (ed.), *The Reception of the Church Fathers in the West: From the Carolingians to the Maurists* (Leiden: E. J. Brill, 1997), pp. 82–111.

Matter, E. Ann, 'Gregory the Great in the twelfth century: the *Glossa Ordinaria*', in John C. Cavadini (ed.), *Gregory the Great: A Symposium* (Notre Dame: University of Notre Dame Press, 1995), pp. 216 26.

McGann, Jerome, 'Visible and invisible books: hermetic images in n-dimensional space', *New Literary History,* 32 (Spring 2001), 283–300.

McKitterick, Rosamond, *The Carolingians and the Written Word* (Cambridge: Cambridge University Press, 1989).

Mews, Constant J., 'Orality, literacy and authority in the twelfth-century schools', *Exemplaria*, 2 (1990), 475–500.

Minnis, A. J. *Medieval Theory of Authorship: Scholastic Literary Attitudes in the Later Middle Ages*, second edn (Philadelphia: University of Pennsylvania Press, 1988).

Moss, Ann, *Printed Commonplace-Books and the Structure of Renaissance Thought* (Oxford: Clarendon Press, 1996).

Mundo, Anscari, '"Bibliotheca". Bible et lecture du Carême d'après saint Benoît', *Revue Bénédictine*, 60 (1950), 65–92.

Nelson, Ted, 'Computers, creativity, and the nature of the written word', ACM Twentieth National Conference, 1965.

Nelson, Theodor Holm, *Literary Machines 93.1* (Sausalito, CA: Mindful Press, 1992).

Nielsen, Lauge Olaf, *Theology and Philosophy in the Twelfth Century: A Study of Gilbert Porreta's Thinking and Theological Expositions of the Doctrine of the Incarnation during the Period 1130–1180* (Leiden: E. J. Brill, 1982).

Norris, Christopher, 'Justified margins', *Southern Humanities Review*, 18 (1984), 289–98.

O'Donnell, J. J., ed., *Augustine Confessions* (Oxford: Oxford University Press, 1992), 3 volumes.

O'Donnell, J. J., 'A Reading of the *Confessions*' in his *Augustine Confessions* (Oxford: Oxford University Press, 1992), 1.xxxii–xli.

O'Loughlin, Thomas, *Teachers and Code-Breakers: The Latin Genesis Tradition, 430–800* (Turnhout: Brepols, 1998).

Ong, Walter, *Orality and Literacy: Technologizing the Word* (London: Methuen, 1982).

Parkes, M. B., 'The influence of the concepts of ordinatio and compilatio on the development of the book", in J. J. G. Alexander and M. T. Gibson (eds.), *Medieval Learning and Literature: Essays Presented to Richard William Hunt* (Oxford: Clarendon Press, 1976), pp. 115–41.

Parkes, M. B., 'Introduction', in Peter Ganz (ed.), *The Role of the Book in Medieval Culture: Proceedings of the Oxford International Symposium, 26 September–1 October 1982* (Turnhout: Brepols, 1986), III, pp. 11–16.

Parkes, M. B., 'Reading, copying and interpreting a text in the early Middle Ages', in G.Cavallo and R. Chartier (eds.), *A History of Reading in the West*, trans. Lydia G. Cochrane (Amherst: University of Massachusetts Press, 1999), pp. 90–102.

Pelster, Franz, SJ, 'Gilbert de la Porrée, Gilbertus Porretanus oder Gilbertus Porreta?' *Scholastik*, 24 (1949), 401–3.

Piazzoni, Ambrogio M., 'Exegesis as a theological methodology between the eleventh and twelfth centuries', *Studi Medievali*, 35 (1994), 835–51.

Pollard, Alfred W., 'Margins', *The Printing Art*, 10, 1 (1907), 17–24.

Quain, Edwin, A., SJ, 'The medieval accessus ad auctores', *Traditio*, 3 (1945), 215–64.

Quasten, Johannes, *Patrology*, III: *The Golden Age of Greek Patristic Literature from the Council of Nicaea to the Council of Chalcedon* (Westminster, MD: Newman Press, 1960).

Reiter, Eric H., 'The reader as author of the user-produced manuscript: reading and rewriting popular Latin theology in the late Middle Ages', *Viator*, 27 (1996), 151–69.

Reynolds, Suzanne, '"Let him read Satires of Horace": reading, literacy and grammar in the twelfth century', in James Raven, Helen Small and Naomi Tadmor (eds.), *The Practice and Representation of Reading in England* (Cambridge: Cambridge University Press, 1996), pp. 22–40.

Reynolds, Suzanne, *Medieval Reading: Grammar, Rhetoric and the Classical Text* (New York: Cambridge University Press, 1996).

Ricœur, Paul, *Hermeneutics and Human Sciences: Essays on Language, Action and Interpretation* (Cambridge: Cambridge University Press, 1981).

Ricœur, Paul, *Memory, History, Forgetting*, trans. Kathleen Blamey and David Pellauer (Chicago: University of Chicago Press, 2004).

Robinson, Peter 'The history, discoveries, and aims of the Canterbury Tales Project', *The Chaucer Review*, 38, 2 (2003), 126–39.

Roose, Pieter, 'Lectio divina among the monks', *Communio*, 13, 4 (Winter 1986), 368–77.

Rouse, M. A. and R. H. Rouse, *Authentic Witnesses: Approaches to Medieval Texts and Manuscripts* (Notre Dame: University of Notre Dame Press, 1991).

Rouse, M. A. and R. H. Rouse, 'Florilegia of patristic texts', in *Les genres littéraires dans les sources théologiques et philosophiques médiévales* (Louvain-la-Neuve: Université Catholique de Louvain, 1982), pp. 165–80.

Rouse, M. A. and R. H. Rouse, 'Statim invenire: schools, preachers, and new attitudes to the page', in Robert L. Benson and Giles Constable (eds.), with Carol D. Lanham, *Renaissance and Renewal in the Twelfth Century* (Cambridge, MA: Harvard University Press, 1991), pp. 201–25.

Rouse, M. A. and R. H. Rouse, 'The verbal concordance to the Scriptures', *Archivum Fratrum Praedicatorum*, 44 (1974), 5–30.

Rouse, R. H., and M. A. Rouse, *Preachers, Florilegia and Sermons: Studies on the Manipulus Florum of Thomas of Ireland* (Toronto: Pontifical Institute of Medieval Studies, 1979).

Saenger, Paul, *Space between Words: The Origins of Silent Reading* (Stanford: Stanford University Press, 1997).

Salomon, Richard, *Opicinus de Canistris; Weltbild und Bekentnisse eines avignonesischen Klerikers des 14. Jahrhunderts von R. G. Salomon mit beiträgen von A. Heimann und R. Krautheimer* (London: Warburg Institute, 1936).

Scalise, Charles J., 'The "sensus literalis": a hermeneutical key to biblical exegesis', *Scottish Journal of Theology*, 42 (1989), 45–65.

Schildgen, Brenda Deen, 'Augustine's answer to Jacques Derrida in the *De Doctrina Christiana*', *New Literary History*, 25 (1994), 383–97.

Scholes, Robert, *Protocols of Reading* (New Haven: Yale University Press, 1989).

Silvain, René, 'La tradition des Sentences d'Anselme de Laon', *Archives d'Histoire Doctrinale et Littéraire du Moyen Âge*, 16 (1940), 1–52.

Slights, William W. E., *Managing Readers: Printed Marginalia in English Renaissance Books* (Ann Arbor: University of Michigan Press, 2001).

Slights, William W. E., '"Marginall notes that spoile the text": scriptural annotation in the English Renaissance', *The Huntington Library Quarterly*, 55 (1992), 255–78.

Smalley, Beryl, 'A collection of Paris lectures of the later twelfth century in the Ms. Pembroke College, Cambridge 7', *Cambridge Historical Journal*, 6 (1938), 110–13.

Smalley, Beryl, 'Les commentaires bibliques de l'époque romaine: glose ordinaire et gloses périmées' *Cahiers de Civilisation Médiévale. Xe–XIIe siecles*, 4 (1961), 11–71.

Smalley, Beryl, 'Gilbertus Universalis, bishop of London (1128–34), and the problem of the Glossa Ordinaria', *Recherches de Théologie Ancienne et Médiévale*, 7–8, (1935–6): 7, 235–62; 8, 24–60.

Smalley, Beryl, 'La Glossa Ordinaria: quelques prédécesseurs d'Anselme de Laon", *Recherches de Théologie Ancienne et Médiévale*, 9 (1937), 365–400.

Smalley, Beryl, *The Study of the Bible in the Middle Ages* (Notre Dame: University of Notre Dame Press, 1964).

Spence, Jonathan, *The Memory Palace of Matteo Ricci* (New York: Penguin, 1984).

Spence, Sarah, *Texts and the Self in the Twelfth Century* (Cambridge: Cambridge University Press, 1996).

Spiro, R. J. and J. Jehng, 'Cognitive flexibility and hypertext: theory and technology for the non-linear and multidimensional traversal of complex subject matter', in D. Nix and R. J. Spiro (eds.), *Cognition, Education, and Multimedia* (Hillsdale, NJ: Lawrence Erlbaum), pp. 163–205.

Stahl, William Harris, *Martianus Capella and the Seven Liberal Arts* (New York: Columbia University Press, 1971).

Stallybrass, Peter, 'Books and scrolls: navigating the Bible', in Jennifer Andersen and Elizabeth Sauer (eds.), *Books and Readers in Early Modern England: Material Studies* (Philadelphia: University of Pennsylvania Press, 2002), pp. 42–79.

Stanley, David, SJ, 'A suggested approach to lectio divina', *American Benedictine Review*, 23 (1972), 439–55.

Stirnemann, Patricia, 'Où ont été fabriqués les livres de la Glose Ordinaire dans la première moitié du XIIe siècle', in *Le XIe siècle: mutations et renouveau en France dans la première moitié du XIIe siècle* (Paris, 1994), pp. 257–301.

Stock, Brian, *After Augustine: The Meditative Reader and the Text* (Philadelphia: University of Pennsylvania Press, 2001).

Stock, Brian, *Augustine the Reader: Meditation, Self-Knowledge and the Ethics Self of Interpretation* (Cambridge, MA: Harvard University Press, 1996).

Stock, Brian, *Ethics through Literature: Ascetic and Aesthetic Reading in Western Culture* (Hanover: University Press of New England, 2007).

Stock, Brian, *Listening for the Text: On the Uses of the Past* (Baltimore: Johns Hopkins University Press, 1990).

Stock, Brian, *The Implications of Literacy: Written Language and Models of Interpretation in the Eleventh and Twelfth Centuries* (Princeton: Princeton University Press, 1983).

Stuehrenberg, Paul F., 'The medieval commentary tradition: the Glossa Ordinaria, Hugh of St. Cher and Nicholas of Lyra and the study of the Bible in the Middle Ages', *Journal of Religious and Theological Information*, 1 (1993), 91–101.

Sturges, Robert S., *Medieval Interpretation: Models of Reading in Literary Narrative, 1100–1500* (Carbondale: Southern Illinois University Press, 1991).

Svenbro, Jesper, *Phrasikleia: An Anthropology of Reading in Ancient Greece*, trans. Janet Lloyd (Ithaca: Cornell University Press, 1993).

Sweeney, Eileen C., 'Hugh of St. Victor: the Augustinian tradition of sacred and secular reading revised', in Edward D. English (ed.), *Reading and Wisdom: The De Doctrina Christiana of Augustine in the Middle Ages* (Notre Dame: University of Notre Dame Press, 1995), pp. 61–83.

Taylor, John Hammond, SJ, 'St. Augustine and the *Hortensius* of Cicero', *Studies in Philology*, 60 (1963), 487–98.

Ward, J. O., 'From antiquity to the Renaissance: glosses and commentaries on Cicero's *Rhetorica*', in James J. Murphy (ed.), *Medieval Eloquence: Studies in the Theory and Practice of Medieval Rhetoric* (Berkeley: University of California Press, 1978), pp. 25–67.

Ward, J. O., 'From marginal gloss to catena commentary: the eleventh-century origins of a rhetorical teaching', *Parergon*, 13, 2 (January 1996), 109–20.

Ward, John O., 'Rhetoric, truth, and literacy in the Renaissance of the twelfth century', in R. L. Enos (ed.), *Oral and Written Communication: Historical Approaches* (Newbury Park, CA: Sage Publications, 1990), pp. 126–57.

Wasselynck, René, 'L'influence de l'exégèse de saint Grégoire le Grand', *Recherches de Théologie Ancienne et Médiévale*, 32 (1965), 157–204.

Wathen, Ambrose, 'Monastic lectio: some clues from terminology', *Monastic Studies*, 12 (1976), 207–15.

Wieland, Gernot R., 'The glossed manuscript: classbook or library book?' *Anglo-Saxon England*, 14 (1985), 153–73.

Wielockx, R., 'Autour de la "Glossa Ordinaria"', *Recherches de Théologie Ancienne et Médiévale*, 49 (1982), 222–8.

Wilmart, A., "Les livres légués par Célestin II à Città-di-Castello", *Revue Bénédictine*, 35 (1923), 98–102

Wilmart, A., 'Un commentaire des Psaumes restitué à Anselme de Laon', *Recherches de Théologie Ancienne et Médiévale*, 8 (1936), 325–44.

Wright, David F., 'Augustine: his exegesis and hermeneutics', in Magne Sæbo (ed.), *Hebrew Bible/Old Testament: The History of Its Interpretation*, I: *From the Beginnings to the Middle Ages (Until 1300)* (Göttingen: Vandenhoeck & Ruprecht, 1996), pp. 701–30.

Wright, Ronald, *A Short History of Progress* (New York: Carroll and Graff, 2005).

Zier, Mark A., 'The manuscript tradition of the Glossa Ordinaria for Daniel, and hints at a method for a critical edition", *Scriptorium*, 47, 1 (1993), 3–25.

Zier, Mark A., 'Peter Lombard and the Glossa Ordinaria on the Bible'*, A Distinct Voice: Medieval Studies in Honor of Leonard E. Boyle, O. P.* (Notre Dame: University of Notre Dame Press, 1997), pp. 629–41.

Zimmerman, Odo John, OSB, trans., *Saint Gregory the Great: Dialogues* (New York, 1959).

Zinn, Grover A., Jr, 'Exegesis and spirituality in the writings of Gregory the Great', in *Gregory the Great: A Symposium* (Notre Dame: University of Notre Dame Press, 1995), pp. 168–80.

Zinn, Grover A., Jr, 'Hugh of Saint Victor and the Art of Memory', *Viator*, 5 (1974), 211–34.

Zinn, Grover A., Jr, 'The influence of Augustine's De Doctrina Christiana, upon the writings of Hugh of St. Victor', in *Reading and Wisdom: The De Doctrina Christiana of Augustine in the Middle Ages* (Notre Dame: University of Notre Dame Press, 1995), pp. 48–60.

Index

bold type refers to illustration

Abelard, Peter 37, 39
Alighieri, Dante 95
Ambrose, St 24, 71, 84
Amerbach, Johann 58, 59
Anselm of Laon 33, 34, 36–7, 39–40, 53
annotation, textual 8
Aquinas, Thomas 45, 47
Aristotle 84
auctor 15–16, 87
auctoritas 15–16, 17, 20, 84, 87
Augustine, St 10, 20, 23, 55–6, 63, 67, 69–73, 77, 84, 89, 91, 99
    conversion 71, 72
    Confessiones 17, 24, 56, 64, 70–1, 78, 81, 88–9
    De Doctrina Christiana 16, 19, 24, 25, 29, 56, 74, 78, 80–1, 85, 90
    De Genesi ad Litteram 18, 25, 82, 89, 90
Ausonius 7
authorship 2

Babylonian Talmud 24, 28, **42**, 43
Baker, Nicholson 26–7
Barthes, Roland 94
Bec Abbey 53
Benedict, St 20–1, 53, 74, 75–7, 81, 90
Bernard of Clairvaux 85
Bible
    Douai Old Testament 46
    Geneva 46, 87
    Latin Vulgate 1, 10, 12, 59
    Rheims New Testament 46
    Septuagint (LXX) 18
Boethius 31, 77
Bolter, Jay David 98
boundaries 12
Bush, Vannevar 70, 97

canon law 11
Chaucer, Geoffrey 13, 25, 31
Cicero 16, 25, 26, 31, 71, 82
cogitare 70–1
cognitive flexibility 93, 96
commonplace book 30–1, 57
contemplation 12
corpus mysticum 68, 73
Council of Trent 2
cum textu (text format) 6, 14, 41, 42, 43, **44**, 46, 48–50
Cyril of Alexandria 14
de Certeau, Michel 9, 12, 85, 88

Derrida, Jacques 27, 97
Descent to Hell 14
Dhouda 65
distinctiones 23
Donatus 79

electronic book 28

figural reading 75
florilegium 31
footnote 10, 26
Foucault, Michel 97
Fourth Lateran council 92

Gilbert of Poitiers 6, 17, 23, 37, 41–2, 43, **44**, 46, 48–50, 54
Gilbert the Universal 37
'gloss' 7–8, 30
Glossa Ordinaria
    editio princeps 4, 13, 31
    facsimile edition 13, 57, 62
    illustration **86**
    prefaces 17, 18, 82
    prologues 17–18, 19

glossaries 29–31, 38
Gospel of Nicodemus 14–15
Gregory the Great 78–9
Grosseteste, Robert 50

Hildegard of Bingen 72
Hofstadter, Douglas 98
Hugh of St Cher 16
Hugh of St Victor 20, 52, 54, 56, 76
　Didascilicon 16, 23, 29, 55, 80
hypertext 2, 93ff

illumination 10
imitatio 17
index 50–2
intertextuality 3, 12, 25, 28
Isidore of Seville 21, 30, 79

Jerome 17, 18, 79, 83, 91
John of Salisbury 80
Joyce, Michael 57

Landow, George P. 95
Laon 34, 37, 42
Laon A-Z type 36
Laon, Cathedral School at 12, 28, 34–6, 37, 38, 39
Latin grammar 35, 63–4, 66, 79–80
lectio 5, 20, 21, 22, 55, 64–5, 77–8
lectio divina 20, 64, 68, 75–6, 90
Lefebvre, Henri 97
legere 5, 20–1, 22, 55, 64–5, 77–8

Macrobius 30
margins
　of society 9
　of text 8, 10, 12, 27, 97
memory 11, 23, 35, 51, 54–7, 69, 72, 73, 96
metaphor of space 78
Migne, J.-P. 4, 40–1, 60, 62
monastic reading 20

Monte Cassino 52–3
mystice 84–5
mysticism 9, 25

Nelson, Ted 69, 93, 94, 98
Nicholas of Lyra 59, **61**
node 94, 97, 97

ordinary gloss 7
Origen 16, 25, 38, 85

'Pangur Ban' 50
Paradise Lost 11, 95
Peter Lombard 43, 91
Peter the Chanter 36
Petrarch 23
Plato 51, 56, 84
Priscillian 91
Priscian 35, 79

Quintillian 82

Ricci, Matteo 70
Robert of Melun 79
ruminatio 78, 90
Rusch, Adolph 13–14, 18, 31–2, 58

Salomon, Richard 17
self, development of 67, 71, 98
Seneca 87
sententia 30, 79
signs (marks) 26, 59, 60
signs (semiotics) 12
silent reading 24, 64, 67, 28, 81
Strabo, Walafrid 33–4, 40–1, 60, 91

textual boundaries 88
textual communities 11, 77, 90
translation theory 83
Trithemius, Johannes 40

Wicbod 38